PRAISE FOR *SLOW TRAINS AROUND BRITAIN*

"Easy-going, discursive and digressive, even those to whom trains are a closed timetable will find this a charming travelogue"

Stuart Maconie, author of *The Full English: A Journey in Search of a Country and Its People*

"What a pleasure to share this railway odyssey with Tom Chesshyre, whose intrepid wanderings and wry observations present an engaging portrait of Britain in 143 trains"

Simon Bradley, rail historian and author of *Bradley's Railway Guide*

"This is a book to inspire even the most sluggish of armchair travellers. Not only a paeon to the many deep pleasures of train travel, it is full of practical details, hearty enthusiasm and quirky observations. In his 143 circular train visits all over Britain, Tom Chesshyre meets passengers, railway workers, bureaucrats and trainspotters, and listens to their stories of eccentric hobbies as well as their struggles with red-tape and timetabling and making things work. And although he conveys beautifully the romance of the golden age of steam travel, he never wallows in nostalgia, taking an infectious delight, for example, in the many Wetherspoons pubs he finds in railway stations all over the country"

Lucy Lethbridge, author of *Tourists: How the British Went Abroad to Find Themselves*

"Seasoned traveller that he is, Chesshyre still manages to give a fresh perspective to every new discovery on his journey round the nooks and crannies of the British rail network"

Christian Wolmar, author of *Blood, Iron & Gold: How the Railways Transformed the World*

"Tom Chesshyre has a gift for transforming the seemingly mundane world of trains into a thrilling ride. Slow Trains Around Britain left me itching to grab a ticket and set off on my own cross-country rail adventure"

George Mahood, author of *Free Country: A Penniless Adventure the Length of Britain*

"A splendid reminder that all (rail) roads lead to Darlington and that, as with food, so with trains: speed can be greatly overrated. Two hundred years on from the dawn of the railway, Tom Chesshyre brilliantly captures the enduring appeal of George Stephenson's world-changing creation. A must-read bicentennial tribute from a self-confessed railway 'nut' who is, mercifully, neither nerd nor trainspotter"

Robert Hardman, author of *Charles III: New King. New Court. The Inside Story.*

PRAISE FOR *TICKET TO RIDE*

"*Trains, dry wit, evocative descriptions, fascinating people and more trains – what's not to like?*"

Christian Wolmar

"*This is an engaging, enjoyable and warm-hearted book that will appeal as much to general readers as to lovers of trains*"

Simon Bradley

"*Like mini-odysseys, Chesshyre's railway journeys are by turns gentle and awesome, and full of surprises*"

John Gimlette, author of *Elephant Complex: Travels in Sri Lanka*

"*Funny and illuminating from Crewe to Korea,* Ticket to Ride *is a hugely entertaining account of the author's travels on the rails the world over – chance encounters fly like sparks*"

Sara Wheeler, author of *The Magnetic North*

PRAISE FOR *SLOW TRAINS TO ISTANBUL*

"*Chesshyre's sharp wit, journalistic eye and knack for finding colourful characters make for cracking travel writing*"

Ben Clatworthy, *The Times*

PRAISE FOR *TALES FROM THE FAST TRAINS*

"*Compulsory reading…*"

Mark Smith, *The Man in Seat 61*

"*If you've 'done' Paris and Bruges and are wondering, 'Where next?', then this may be a quiet revolution*"

Andrew Marr

"*Splendid 21st-century railway adventure. At last this IS the age of train*"

Simon Calder, *The Independent*

PRAISE FOR *SLOW TRAINS TO VENICE*

"*He casually, and beautifully, bats away the earnestness of travel literature*"

Caroline Eden, *The Times Literary Supplement*

"*There is something nostalgic about the clatter of wheels and sleeper trains… by the end, the reader will struggle to resist the urge to follow his lead*"

The Economist

"*A work of brilliant geekery*"

National Geographic

"*Entertaining and enjoyable*"

Christian Wolmar

"*A diverting and thought-provoking read*"

Simon Bradley

"*Tom Chesshyre pays homage to a Europe that we are leaving behind and perhaps never understood.* Che bella corsa! *He is the master of slow locomotion*"

Roger Boyes, *The Times*

"Tom Chesshyre is a kind of railway flâneur, drifting across Europe... Hugely enjoyable"

Andrew Martin, author of *Night Trains*

"Tom Chesshyre... makes you want to experience all his adventures and mishaps for yourself"

Christian Wolmar

"Combining a train geek's delight with a keen eye for history"

Andrew Eames, author of *The 8.55 to Baghdad*

"Wry, funny and perceptive, very little escapes Tom Chesshyre's piercing eye on this entertaining odyssey... I loved this book"

Michael Williams, author of *On the Slow Train*

PRAISE FOR *SLOW TRAINS AROUND SPAIN*

"A lovely book"

Michael Portillo

"Chesshyre takes us on a wondrously hypnotic meander across Spain... a highly relaxing and subtly addictive read"

Glen Mutel, *National Geographic Traveller*

"If you ever need convincing that it's better to take the train than to fly, this is the book that makes a persuasive case... a fine read"

Nicky Gardner, *hidden europe*

"By turns humorous and sharply insightful, he affectionately paints a vivid portrait of a deeply divided and contrasting country, bringing to life its characters and landscapes like few other travel writers can. Always curious, witty and intelligent, his writing style and subject matter are deeply rewarding"

Francisca Kellett, travel writer

PRAISE FOR *LOST IN THE LAKES*

"*A carnival of characters*"
Christopher Somerville, author of *Britain's Best Walks*

"*A charming book… uplifting at every turn*"
Rebecca Lowe, author of *The Slow Road to Tehran*

"*Part travelogue, part social commentary, this gem of a book succeeds in being both politically engaged and uproariously entertaining – a rare feat in travel writing and a welcome new direction for the genre*"
Oliver Balch, author of *Under the Tump*

"*Chesshyre has a journalist's ability to intersperse descriptions of dazzling scenery with brisk historical facts… this book makes you yearn to go there*"
Kate Green, *Country Life*

"*Chesshyre [has] an eye for the lives of ordinary folk, the sweat and smoke behind the idyll*"
Brian Morton, *Times Literary Supplement*

PRAISE FOR *FROM SOURCE TO SEA*

"*A portrait of England and the English in our time, it is peppered with fascinating historical and literary markers*"
Christina Hardyment, author of *Writing the Thames*

"*An enjoyable refuge from everyday life*"
Clive Aslet, *The Times*

"*A highly readable and entertaining saunter along England's iconic river*"
Christopher Somerville

"*I found myself quickly falling into step beside Tom Chesshyre, charmed by his amiable meanderings, pointed observations and meetings with strangers*"
Fergus Collins, *BBC Countryfile Magazine*

"Readers should perhaps prepare themselves for a whole new wave of *Whither England?* type books in the months and years ahead, and Chesshyre's is a not unwelcome early attempt to answer that seemingly urgent question"

Ian Sansom, *Times Literary Supplement*

PRAISE FOR *TO HULL AND BACK*

"Tom Chesshyre celebrates the UK… discovering pleasure in the unregarded wonders of the 'unfashionable underbelly' of Britain. The moral, of course, is that heaven is where you find it"

Frank Barrett, *The Mail on Sunday*

"You warm to Chesshyre, whose cultural references intelligently inform his postcards from locations less travelled"

Iain Finlayson, *The Times*

PRAISE FOR *HOW LOW CAN YOU GO?*

"Highly readable Bill Bryson-esque travel writing"

Clover Stroud, *The Sunday Telegraph*

"A hilarious record of a low-cost odyssey around the least salubrious corners of Europe"

Celia Brayfield, *The Times*

PRAISE FOR *A TOURIST IN THE ARAB SPRING*

"A charming travel companion, entertaining and engaging"

Times Literary Supplement

PRAISE FOR *GATECRASHING PARADISE*

"Revealing aspects of a surprising little tropical nation wholly unknown to holidaymakers, *Gatecrashing Paradise* compares honorably with Arthur Grimble's A Pattern of Islands"

Alexander Frater, author of *Chasing the Monsoon*

TOM CHESSHYRE
SLOW TRAINS AROUND BRITAIN

Notes from a 4,088-Mile Adventure on 143 Rides

SLOW TRAINS AROUND BRITAIN

Copyright © Tom Chesshyre, 2025

All rights reserved.

No part of this book may be reproduced by any means, nor transmitted, nor translated into a machine language, without the written permission of the publishers.

Tom Chesshyre has asserted their right to be identified as the author of this work in accordance with sections 77 and 78 of the Copyright, Designs and Patents Act 1988.

Condition of Sale
This book is sold subject to the condition that it shall not, by way of trade or otherwise, be lent, resold, hired out or otherwise circulated in any form of binding or cover other than that in which it is published and without a similar condition including this condition being imposed on the subsequent purchaser.

An Hachette UK Company
www.hachette.co.uk

Summersdale Publishers
Part of Octopus Publishing Group Limited
Carmelite House
50 Victoria Embankment
LONDON
EC4Y 0DZ
UK

This FSC® label means that materials and other controlled sources used for the product have been responsibly sourced

www.summersdale.com

The authorized representative in the EEA is Hachette Ireland, 8 Castlecourt Centre, Dublin 15, D15 XTP3, Ireland (email: info@hbgi.ie)

Printed and bound by Clays Ltd, Suffolk, NR35 1ED

ISBN: 978-1-83799-527-1
eISBN: 978-1-83799-528-8

Substantial discounts on bulk quantities of Summersdale books are available to corporations, professional associations and other organizations. For details contact general enquiries: telephone: +44 (0) 1243 771107 or email: enquiries@summersdale.com.

For Robert and Christine

ALSO BY TOM CHESSHYRE

How Low Can You Go?
To Hull and Back
Tales from the Fast Trains
A Tourist in the Arab Spring
Gatecrashing Paradise
Ticket to Ride
From Source to Sea
Slow Trains to Venice
Slow Trains Around Spain
Park Life
Lost in the Lakes
Slow Trains to Istanbul

ABOUT THE AUTHOR

Tom Chesshyre is the author of 13 travel books. He attended a state school and studied politics at Bristol University and newspaper journalism at City University. He worked on the travel desk of *The Times* for 21 years and is now a freelance writer, contributing to the *Daily Mail*, *The Mail on Sunday* and *The New European*. He lives in Mortlake in London.

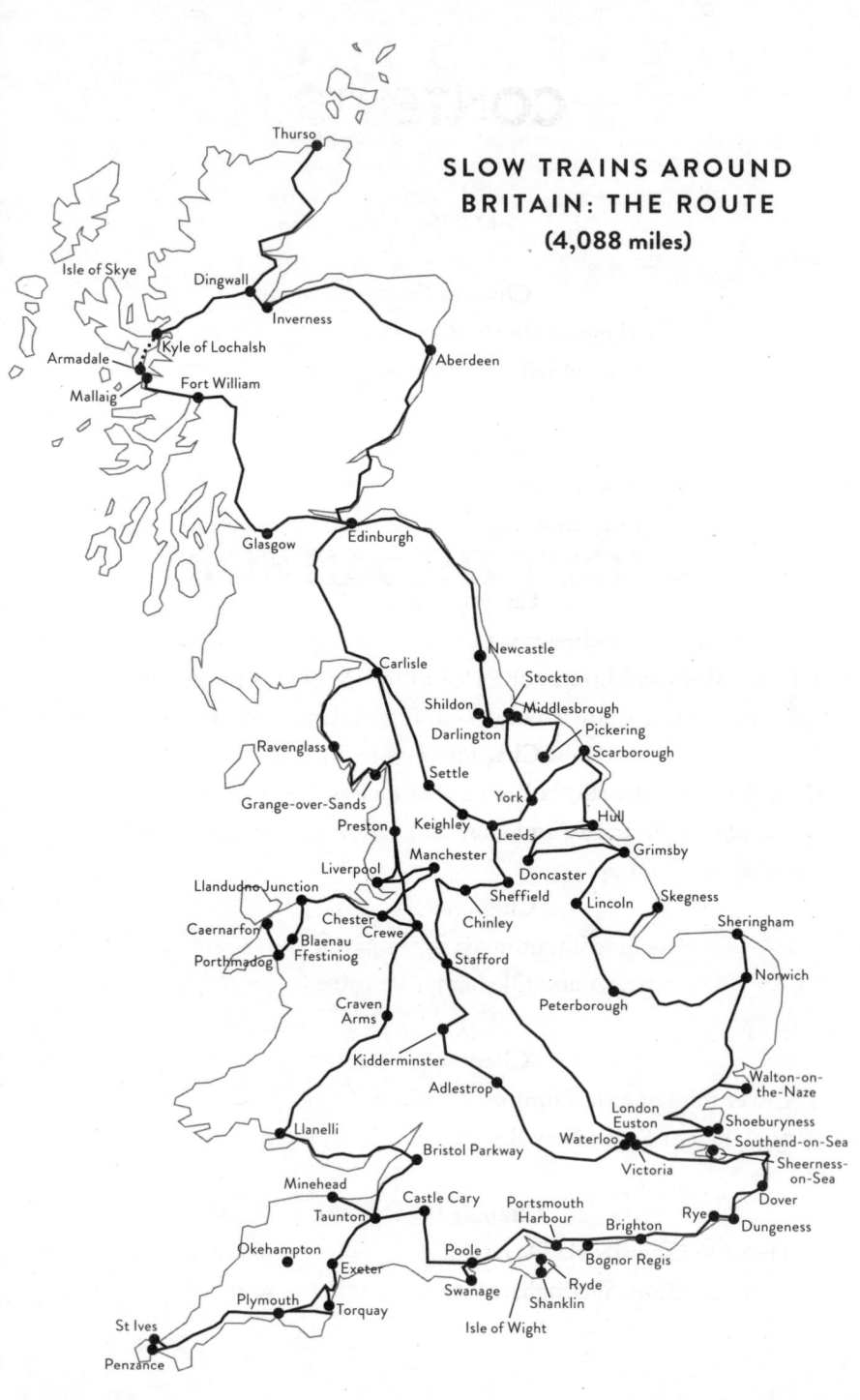

CONTENTS

Preface | 17

Chapter One | 19
Darlington via Shildon, back to Darlington:
"A small railway that changed the world"

Chapter Two | 41
Darlington to Settle via Middlesbrough, Grosmont,
Pickering, York, Leeds and Keighley: Lost in locos

Chapter Three | 73
Settle to Manchester via Carlisle, Ravenglass, Grange-over-
Sands and Liverpool: "Disrupting the established order"

Chapter Four | 111
Manchester to Llanelli via Blaenau Ffestiniog, Porthmadog, Caernarfon,
Prestatyn, Crewe and Craven Arms: Voices from the tracks

Chapter Five | 147
Llanelli to Taunton via Penzance, St Ives, Torquay,
Exeter and Okehampton: Brunel's Britain

Chapter Six | 185
Exeter to Hythe via Taunton, Minehead, Poole, Swanage, the Isle of
Wight, Bognor Regis, New Romney and Dungeness: Steamy in the south

Chapter Seven | 221
Hythe to Grimsby via Dover, Sheerness-on-Sea, Southend, Walton-
on-the-Naze, Sheringham and Skegness: Dreaming up the east

Chapter Eight | 253
Grimsby to London Euston via Doncaster, Hull, Scarborough,
Chinley, Stafford and Adlestrop: Snakes and ladders

Chapter Nine | 285
London Euston to Darlington via Aberdeen, Thurso, Kyle of Lochalsh,
Mallaig, Glasgow, Dalmeny and Edinburgh: Back to the beginning

Afterword | 315

Acknowledgements | 325

Trains Taken | 326

Index | 331

"An engine on a public railroad would be a perpetual nuisance"
George Overton, original surveyor for the
Stockton and Darlington Railway, 1825

*"I am never sure of time or place upon a Railroad…
I can only dream… I know nothing about myself —
for anything I know, I may be coming from the Moon"*
Charles Dickens

*"You go away for a long time and return a different person —
you never come all the way back"*
Paul Theroux

In some instances, names of those encountered during the train journeys for this book have been altered.

PREFACE

In a small market town in the north-east of England 200 years ago (in 1825), something momentous happened: ticket-bearing human beings began moving along wrought-iron tracks on a contraption with wheels powered by an engine.

This contraption was called a "train". The name came from a French word around since the Middle Ages – *traîne* (to be in tow, tugged behind) – first used to describe parts of gowns trailing after the wearer. Over the years, the word morphed to refer to those following VIPs in a procession, a line of people/animals, and eventually to carriages clattering down tracks.

However, what happened in Darlington along a 26-mile line to Stockton, chosen as it connected collieries, was groundbreaking.

Horse-tugged trains had been around for years, yet this was quite different. A machine known as a "locomotive" was now up front: a combination of two Latin words, *loco* ("from a place") and *motivus* ("causing motion"), welded in French in the seventeenth century to form *locomotif*, meaning "pertaining to movement".

Over time this had morphed too, becoming *locomotive* in early nineteenth-century Britain, and referring to an engine travelling along rails under its own power.

By the mid-2020s, 1.3 million miles of railway lines criss-crossed the planet.

The invention seemed to have proved quite popular.

And I was about to find out why.

On a whole bunch of trains round Britain.

CHAPTER ONE

DARLINGTON VIA SHILDON, BACK TO DARLINGTON

"A SMALL RAILWAY THAT CHANGED THE WORLD"

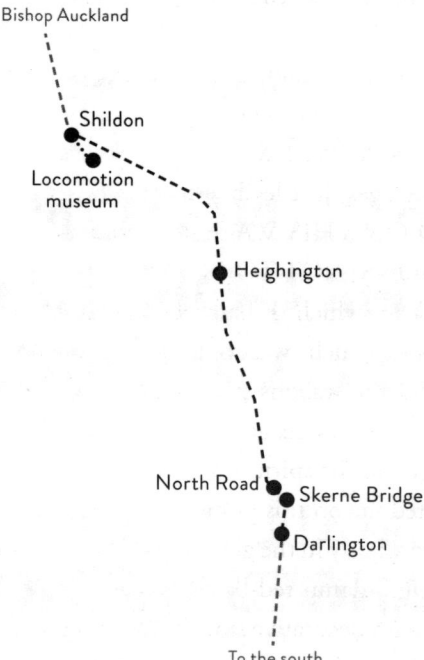

Not much was going on, but then again, quite a lot was really.

On platform two of Darlington station, on a cold February morning in North-East England, a rumble and hum emanated from a yellow and orange train with "COLAS RAIL FREIGHT" written on it.

A man nearby was observing this unusual yellow and orange two-tone train. This man, Dave, had a beard and glasses and wore a woolly hat. He held a small camera, which he occasionally raised as though struck by some inner impulse. His general demeanour was, perhaps, best described as *transfixed*.

"Ballast wagons," he said, affectionately, glancing at some rusty old wagons connected to the yellow and orange train. These wagons were, frankly, filthy, with "NETWORK RAIL" written on them. Additional mysterious messages, just legible beneath a veneer of grime, said, "DO NOT WELD ON THIS WAGON, CALL REPAIRS ADVICE FOR INSTRUCTIONS. NOT TO BE LOOSE/HUMP SHUNTED."

The "train" to which I had been referring was more accurately a "locomotive", which was pulling the wagons. The entirety, the locomotive and the wagons put together, constituted a "train". When I had arrived at Dave's side, gestured at the yellow and orange locomotive and commented in the spirit of railway camaraderie "nice train", he had swiftly corrected me on this point.

We stood wordlessly in the gloomy, echoey hall. Darlington station had surprisingly high, damp red-brick walls. Fluted wrought-iron columns rose all about with decorative shields depicting trains, crosses and castles, while a fine old clock from when the station was built in 1887 curled out above the platform, connected to a red and gold fitting; redolent of the age when folk used to set their watches by such station necessities.

In between the two platforms, on a wide island-like space, was a cramped WHSmith selling a great number of magazines and books about trains, with names such as *Today's Railways*, *Trackside*, *Classic Locomotives of the UK* and *Railway Track Diagrams, Book 5: Southern & TfL*. Beside this was a spacious Pumpkin Café offering expensive coffees. Inside, old horseshoe-shaped leather armchairs were scattered at one end beside dingy walls, a bar area with spirits on mirrored shelves and a restlessly flashing Beat the Banker fruit machine.

Dave's eyes remained fixed on the yellow and orange "COLAS RAIL FREIGHT" locomotive. "It's come from Doncaster," he said, though how he knew this I did not know. "I started watching these when they first came out in the late 1970s. It's a Class 56 loco. I've seen it quite a few times."

Dave, who was aged 58, he told me, wore a dreamy expression. "It's from when trains used to be trains. Nowadays, at almost any rural station there's a couple of platforms and a car park. There used to be goods traffic and sidings [at those stations]. There used to be an open ticket office." Dave used the word "open" pointedly. Many ticket offices in the UK had recently been threatened with closure as part of a cost-cutting exercise, although an outraged-public backlash had caused a political U-turn, and they were no longer shutting down (for the time being).

He returned his gaze to the "COLAS RAIL FREIGHT" loco. "That was when they were horrible polluting things," he said, referring to "when trains used to be trains". He did not say this in a censorious manner as though horrible polluting things were bad things. Quite the opposite. A stench of diesel was emanating from the loco, hanging in the atmosphere of the big, damp hall. "COLAS RAIL FREIGHT" was one of his *horrible polluting things*: a somehow lovely, *horrible polluting thing*.

"They're hardly ever made like that any more. Heritage lines, that's just about the only place you'll see them. Most of the ones [the locomotives] I remember from when I was a boy [were diesels]. Trainspotting they used to call it."

We stood in silence for a while, trainspotting ourselves, you might say. There was a train. We had spotted it. No further words were required. Trains used to be good. Now they were not so good. But there were still a few that were quite good. This was just life.

From the opposite platform, I boarded the 09:55 from Darlington to Shildon, about nine miles to the north-west; the final destination was

DARLINGTON VIA SHILDON, BACK TO DARLINGTON

Bishop Auckland, said a digital display, not much further down the line. The train, a Northern service, was fitted with worn, blue-spotted seats (with USB sockets). Dirt streaked the windows. Hardly anyone was on board, just a few stragglers, and it had begun to pour. Rain swept across the rooftops of Darlington as though a gale had rolled in from the sea. Perhaps it had; we were 20 miles from the coast. The train puttered onwards alongside terraced houses and across a bridge above a swirling river, after which some muddy plots lay to one side of North Road station as though construction work was in the offing. We passed the Builder's Arms, a cluster of old warehouses and a gathering of bedraggled horses in a sodden field. Then the 09:55 drew to a halt at Heighington station, where it paused for some time and we listened to the patter of rain on the carriage roof. No announcement was made, though passengers seemed neither bothered nor especially surprised by the hold-up.

I regarded Heighington station. It had a downbeat air and was tiny, little more than a narrow platform beside a derelict, boarded-up building and an empty lot, home to a jungle of weeds and strewn with debris (old railway-crossing barriers and pavement slates dumped in a heap). No one got off at Heighington, no one got on either. Nobody did anything, except stare out, thinking whatever thoughts they might have been thinking, such as *I'm glad I'm not out there right now*. The 09:55 purred contentedly. Then a whistle blew, the doors creaked shut, the 09:55 made a grinding sound and proceeded, gathering speed beyond a small mountain of discarded washing machines in a yard, a business park, an electrical-products firm and a pair of plastic-fabrication companies. This stretch of County Durham with its depots streaked with rain and works units with billowing steam was unlikely, perhaps, to attract a tourist stampede anytime soon, though there was interest to be had if you were not just seeking "pretty sights".

The 09:55 passed onwards into more boggy fields, these ones demarcated by leafless hedgerows. No creatures dwelled in these fields. Rain descended in curtains, swirling across the landscape. Through the grimy Northern windows, all looked bleak, bleak, bleak. It was late winter, coming on early spring. It was chilly and extremely damp in County Durham, up in the north-east of England.

Why? You may rightly ask. Why? Get a grip! Book a holiday to Barbados! This was not, however, as you may have already gathered, the point. I was on a mission. This mission involved trains. More specifically, British trains. Having had the great fortune to have travelled on many exciting railways to many exciting places elsewhere in the world, from the wide-open plains of America to the tea plantations of India, the ancient cities of Iran, the Australian Outback and the badlands of North Korea (and written about them too), I was about to set forth by means of the mode of transport that rattled down the end of my very own street in south-west London. From my home, a first-floor maisonette, I could hear these trains – ordinary British trains – rumble by at night. Sometimes, when freight wagons passed, my building even shook lightly, making me worry that roof tiles might (eventually, one day) come loose. British trains were not exotic trains like Peruvian trains or Japanese trains or trains in Cambodia or Sri Lanka. They were just regular British trains: ones that clattered by 30 metres or so from my front door, transporting me and squadrons of commuters to workplaces in the city. Sometimes late. Often overcrowded. Regular British trains, in other words.

Yet I still wanted to take quite a few of these regular, ordinary British trains – as well as some quite irregular ones too – on quite a long journey along quite a few regular, ordinary British railways.

Was I nuts? Was I losing it? Quite possibly, you might conclude. Why was I not embarking on an island-hopping jaunt in the South Pacific, or following some long, mighty river in Asia or Africa, or ascending remote slopes in the Himalayas: doing something somewhere just a little more adventurous before returning and putting pen to paper to capture far-flung tales of derring-do? Instead, my journey was starting – in effect – on tracks that rumbled by my home, or at least which were ultimately linked to them via a connection or two. Where was my Indiana Jones spirit? David Livingstone and Henry Morton Stanley in Africa – had I not heard of them and their exploits in search of the source of the

Nile? Sir Richard Burton had dressed up in Bedouin robes and gone undercover, risking life and limb, all the way to Mecca. Why was I not dressing up in Bedouin clothes, breaking frontiers, setting forth to Antarctica in a canoe or across Amazonian jungles in search of lost cities? Somewhere a little more "out there" than on a train from Darlington on a rainy February day.

Yet the answer to "why" was straightforward, as contrary as this may sound to some: I wanted to *celebrate* British railways. To travel along a roughly imagined route around the country that invented trains, as we know them, back in 1825 while taking stock of the current "train situation" and nosing about with a positive frame of mind and general spirit of train appreciation.

Had not the British, 200 years earlier, created the "iron horses" that were to go on to conquer the planet? Was this not a great British success story? A reason to take pride and bang some British train drums? Something about which to be effusive, exuberant and even, on occasion, positively gung-ho? Or at least try one's best to be, the realities of British train travel permitting. Delays, high ticket prices, overcrowding and strikes had been much in the news.

Maybe such a "celebration", given all of that (and more, when you began to consider Britain's national *rail strategy*), would be pushing it. Would the rides ahead turn out to be a long, tricky slog along lines that were in a poorly organized mess? Or a joyous journey to parts of the country you might not otherwise have visited? A hidden world unfurling along the tracks? Whichever, I would report what I saw, with the big anniversary – the bicentenary jamboree – framing the journey ahead. No more, no less. No PR job.

Hence my arrival in the town of Darlington (population 107,800). Hence my continuation to Shildon (population 9,976). I was travelling to commemorate the invention of trains – to *big up* British railways in this historic context – and glory in their many intricacies, old stories, oddities and the places you could take them on a mission to acknowledge a great British achievement. An act of patriotism, you might say. A journey in honour of king and country! And queen and country, thinking back to Queen Victoria in the good old early train days. Maybe I should have picked up a Union Jack hat and a flag or two, like a Brexiteer "taking back control", and really gone for it. *Rule Britannia, Britannia rules the rails…* that kind of stuff. Or maybe, on reflection, better not to go down that line.

This was just the beginning. The start of what might best, in all honesty, be described as a long mooch around Britain on its trains. A long, indulgent mooch with no greater purpose than that – and *general train appreciation*, of course. A wallow in British trains. A happy wallow of gentle affirmation, assessment and "train thoughts", in the company and with the insights, I hoped, of fellow train travellers, such as Dave, encountered along the way.

Those seeking more – solutions to great mysteries of the human condition, perhaps, or the future of the planet – might find such musings few and far between. They might choose instead to consult weightier tomes published on those matters and find themselves more enlightened. I was embarking on a wallowing mooch *on a whole bunch of trains*. No more. No less. Just some thoughts from some trains.

I looked with quiet pleasure along the rows of worn, blue-spotted seats on the 09:55 Northern service from Darlington to Shildon, with their bright-yellow handles for keeping your balance, as dim light filtered through the grimy windows, illuminating a grubby grey floor, mustering as much train-style *joie de vivre* as happened at that moment to be pulsing through my veins.

I will not deny the truth of what I saw: things could be better.

But this was not the point. Not the point at all. And it was no time to grumble.

This was never going to be a journey on fancy *Orient Express* carriages with staff in bow ties dishing out caviar canapés and flutes of chilled champagne. It was, as I have said, to be a rail adventure on regular British trains. Such trains did not usually, in my experience, come with staff in bow ties delivering caviar and bubbly. Such trains were slightly different to that. Mostly, or at least, very often, they had worn seats and grimy windows and grubby grey floors. No point in setting expectations too high early on.

Anyway, I was not after "luxury". Luxury was so overrated (and expensive). I was, as the train juddered onwards past a row of old terraced houses, quietly rather enjoying myself already. There was a certain pleasure – a certain almost illicit sense of freedom – of heading off on trains, I was finding, a *whole bunch of trains*, with no other purpose than to salute the invention of wheels powered by engines taking you down a track. Deep within, a simple "train zeal" was bubbling.

For some time, I let this rail-induced zest quietly effervesce while watching a housing estate and some more soggy fields slide by.

Yet it was hardly surprising that this "train zeal" was rising. For it was not by accident that I was heading for Shildon.

Back on 27 September 1825, the first public passenger train pulled by a steam locomotive set forth on a 26-mile journey from Shildon, via Darlington, to the town of Stockton (population 84,815) on the river Tees.

This locomotive was called *Locomotion No 1*, and the line upon which it huffed and puffed was built by the prolific early railway engineer, self-educated and self-made man, George Stephenson. A solitary coach for bigwigs on the inaugural ride, a bulky wooden carriage appropriately called *Experiment*, was attached to this legendary loco. Behind it, a large number of coal wagons had also been connected; the tracks had been created principally to link collieries around Shildon to Stockton, from where coal could be shipped. On the special first journey, however, many of these working wagons had been fitted with temporary wooden benches for more ordinary passengers.

As many as 600 people were crammed on board as the train trundled along, attaining a top speed of 15 mph for a brief spell on its way to Darlington, crossing Skerne Bridge near North Road station and entering the market town, where 40,000 spectators waited, cheering on the extraordinary contraption. One onlooker, as quoted in Frank

Ferneyhough's *The History of Railways in Britain*, commented, "The welkin [sky] rang with loud huzzas [cheers], while the happy faces of some, the vacant stares of others and the alarm depicted on the countenances of not a few, gave variety to the picture." Meanwhile, a wonderful painting by the artist John Dobbin also captured the moment. Dobbin, a local, who was ten years old at the time and who had witnessed *Locomotion No 1* come by, recreated the scene 50 years later (so it may not have been quite the same on the actual day), though it was nice to imagine the fellows in bowler hats and the elegant women in flowing frocks and bonnets gathered as horse-drawn carriages waited by the banks and Stephenson's loco steamed along.

In short, the Stockton and Darlington Railway, from its very first day, had been a resounding success.

So much so the line was soon lengthened to Middlesbrough, then to a tiny settlement of 25 people beyond Stockton, where the water was deeper for shipping coal, and a whole new city soon sprang up (population currently more than 148,000). The railway was rapidly, quite dramatically altering the local landscape. Middlesbrough, little more than a handful of abodes back in 1825, was to overtake Darlington and Stockton, spawning ironworks, steelworks, shipbuilding yards and, later, a university and (sometimes) top-tier football team.

Buoyed by how well *Locomotion No 1* had fared, five years after that inaugural run, Stephenson completed what some consider to be the first *proper* public passenger line between the important industrial hubs of Manchester and Liverpool. I use "proper" because it was built with both freight and paying passengers in mind, whereas the Stockton and Darlington Railway ran occasional passenger carriages, often pulled by horses, not steam engines, and was quite a higgledy-piggledy, ad hoc arrangement as opposed to a regular steam-powered service with several daily passenger trains. This first inter-city connection was an international sensation. After the Liverpool and Manchester Railway opened in 1830, covering 31 miles at speeds of up to 35 mph, pulled by *Rocket* (designed by Stephenson's talented son, Robert, just as *Locomotion No 1* had been, along with his father), news spread far and wide, with great interest in starting up copycat railways across Britain and in many other countries.

In Britain alone, a mere thirteen years later in 1843, 1,800 miles of railway were open to traffic, rising to 6,000 miles by 1854 after an incredible bout of "railway mania", and 23,440 miles by 1914 (latest figures indicate 10,072 route miles of network tracks in the UK today, a reduction from 1914 caused partly by the decommissioning of many lines in the mid-twentieth century). Beyond British shores, railways spread quickly too, with Stephenson's advice being sought on key lines in Europe. Meanwhile in America, the symbolic Golden Spike was hammered into the tracks at Promontory Summit in Utah as soon as 10 May 1869, connecting the United States from the Atlantic to the Pacific oceans. The economic benefits of transporting goods by rail, combined with the convenience and logic of getting about without the discomfort and expense of stagecoaches, were simply impossible to ignore.

Two hundred years later, railways were, of course, just about everywhere save the most mountainous and remote regions, with trains whizzing about as fast as 268 mph, the eye-watering speed attained on the Shanghai maglev electromagnetic line.

Yet it all really started, whatever champions of the Liverpool and Manchester Railway might like to argue to the contrary, on the Stockton and Darlington Railway, where George Stephenson had cut his teeth.

Where the very first journey began in Shildon.

Which was where the 09:55 from Darlington had just pulled in.

Two other passengers were on board: Paul and David from Sheffield. We disembarked and fell into step, heading in the rain down a path along the line in the direction of the Locomotion railway museum, a big warehouse-like hulk of a building a couple of hundred yards away. This museum was opened in 2004 by the then local MP and Prime Minister Tony Blair to commemorate the Stockton and Darlington Railway and to highlight the importance of railways for north-east collieries as well as for providing local jobs. And its big attraction was

Locomotion No 1, which had previously been on display at Darlington station.

"I'm a driver," said Paul as we shivered and shuffled along.

What kind of driver?

"A train driver," he replied.

"I'm a driver too," said David, cutting in.

A train driver?

"No, no. A tram driver," he replied, as though I really ought to have known this and that there was an important distinction.

They were old friends on a few days of "train holiday" during which they intended to take railways to visit Wetherspoons pubs.

"Wherever we go, we go to Wetherspoons. We've got seventy-five to go. Seven hundred and thirty so far. They're cheap and cheerful, aren't they?" said Paul. The highly popular Wetherspoons pub chain had 805 pubs across the UK (when we met).

They were wearing sensible winter jackets with hoods and were middle-aged (like Dave back at Darlington station). They looked very happy. They were coming to the museum as a diversion, to pay homage to *Locomotion No 1* and because they had "time to kill" before travelling on to Bishop Auckland.

I asked Paul, the taller of the two, with a calm, thoughtful manner, what he liked about trains, other than driving them.

"That I'm travelling along the same rails as my parents, just the traction is different. Same as my parents in the 1930s. I like that," he replied.

I asked David the same question.

"They are what they are," he answered, as though meaning *what you see is what you get*. He paused and added, "I've just always been interested in railways. Sitting on bridges and watching what goes by."

David, like Dave back in Darlington, said he preferred trains from the 1980s and 1990s: "Old locos had more character."

He was coming to the right place. Shortly afterwards, we arrived at a siding by the museum on which a collection of carriages and locomotives had been "parked" for inspection by visitors.

"That's a Class 43 HST," said Paul, a fond look spreading over his face. HST stood for High-Speed Train, he said.

We stood there in silence for a few moments, regarding this 43 HST.

Then, I asked him what he thought of trains in Britain today.

He pulled a face as though this was a subject that pained him.

"We're pricing people off the railways and we should be getting people on them," he replied. Ticket prices were, he believed, far too high. He said no more.

Was he sad about this, I asked.

"Yes," he replied, and said no more once again. He did seem pretty glum about it.

With that, we entered the Locomotion museum (admission free) and went our separate ways.

The interior of the Locomotion museum was like an airport terminal, with a high curved roof with skylights, except that, instead of check-in desks and security gates, you had trains. Lots of trains. Lots of lovely old, shiny trains. I made a beeline for *Locomotion No 1* and stood for a moment or two admiring its studs of rivets, its confusion of lacquered black pistons and its heavy iron wheels set around a varnished wooden barrel that was presumably the water tank. At the front, a distinctive chimney curved upwards in a backwards "J", while a polished, gold-coloured "LOCOMOTION" nameplate was attached to the wooden barrel. To one side, a sign said that this loco was an "international celebrity" built by Robert Stephenson at the Forth Street Works in Newcastle in early 1825, and it had altered somewhat over the years due to repairs and additions. The initial ride had hauled a train of 90 tonnes and the locomotive had continued in use until 1841.

On the bicentenary of the Stockton and Darlington Railway, I was paying homage to what some considered to be the first proper steam locomotive to pull passengers along a train line. I tapped a wheel for good luck.

You were, frankly, spoilt for trains at Locomotion. For a while it was a pleasure simply to wander up and down corridors of parallel tracks chock-a-block with gleaming carriages and locos, as though you had entered some kind of heavenly maze of trains smelling of oil and diesel, varnish and polish, upholstery and dust, cinder and soot: a strangely heady concoction, even without the star attractions. No wonder off-duty train and tram drivers, between visiting 805 Wetherspoons pubs, made detours to visit.

A short stroll from *Locomotion No 1*, you promptly came to *Rocket*, another "international celebrity", looking slightly sleeker than *Locomotion No 1* and with a straighter chimney but without wood panels: a veritable legend of a train just resting in a corner, minding its own business, with no one else about. Tempting as it may have been, I did not, however, hang around: there was too much else to ogle. For that was what you could not help but do at the Locomotion museum: *ogle old trains*.

Close by were the smart navy-blue-and-gold Southern Railway and Compagnie Internationale des Wagons-Lits "Night Ferry" carriages used before the Channel Tunnel opened in 1994, when these sleepers rattled down to Dover to be rolled onto specially designed ships with passengers staying on board all the way to Paris.

I ogled this early cross-Channel train.

Not far from it was a shiny black loco named *Hardwicke*, which had reached record speeds in the 1890s, you learn, travelling at over 90 mph and frightening the life out of many passengers at the time.

I ogled *Hardwicke* for a while, too.

Then you had blue-and-white APT-E "tilting trains" from 1972, designed to better handle the curves of Britain's West Coast Main Line.

More ogling… it was a good one.

Then there was *Sans Pareil*, an 1829 locomotive rival to *Rocket*, built by the superintendent of the Stockton and Darlington Railway, Timothy Hackworth, but which was not chosen for the Liverpool and Manchester Railway (so *Sans Pareil* and Hackworth never hit the historical-train big time).

Then there were battered old mining wagons from the 1960s; creaky-looking trolleys used to transport workers for repairs from the 1930s; director saloon carriages from the 1870s, with fancy seats for the chief of the North London Railway; and third-class East Coast Joint Stock carriages from 1898.

Ogle, ogle, ogle, ogle, ogle.

There were a great many trains: an abundance of wonderful, well-maintained, groundbreaking, important British trains.

At the café by the entrance, I sat at some old grey-and-yellow Eurostar seats and promptly met some important British train people.

The first was Sarah Price, head of Locomotion, in charge of the museum. I had not made an appointment, but she found time to talk. She was wearing an orange hi-vis jacket, Buddy Holly–style glasses and a stripy jumper. She was full of enthusiasm about trains (as I suppose it helped to be in her job). I was about to receive a pre-trip briefing.

"If you don't understand the importance of Shildon in railway history, as soon as you start to understand it, you start to understand about trains in Britain," she said. "We want to tell the story of how a small railway changed the world quietly, unassumingly and modestly. It had a global impact. Within five years of opening, there were trains in other parts of Britain, Russia, North America. It was a nascent industry. It was the knowledge economy. There was a generosity. A different way of working. People came here to see the future."

By this she meant that people travelled to Shildon, where there was a major train-building works, from far and wide to learn the tricks of the trade of running a railway, and that there was a feeling of everyone being in it together. Robert Stephenson and Timothy Hackworth, for example, while rivals, had also been close friends. That was the spirit of it all back then.

We talked about trains in Britain now, 200 years after the glory of *Locomotion No 1*.

"I think people are still understanding the critical role they play," Sarah replied, picking her words carefully. "Not just carrying passengers. It's also about freight. To me, railways are still the future. There are hiccups in every journey."

She was referring here to a recent British government decision to cancel a part of HS2, the high-speed line that was being planned between

Birmingham and Manchester. Instead of continuing – once the section from London to Birmingham was finished – onwards to the north, the part between Birmingham and Manchester, plus another branch from Birmingham to Leeds, had been controversially scrapped.

"We must not lose faith. If we want to have a sustainability about future travel, we can't give up hope," said Sarah. "It's always disappointing when things like that happen. HS2 was a large opportunity to revolutionize freight. Taking freight off the road. Taking lorries off the road. Cheaper transport. It was not just about passengers. Railways have always been the backbone of the transport system."

Sarah believed that by transferring freight to trains on north–south routes, motorways would be cleared of traffic jams, and trains on the east and west coast main lines would be less busy. She spoke passionately about the subject.

She returned to what Shildon and the Stockton and Darlington Railway meant to Britain: "Two hundred years ago, people came here to see the future. Well, that's important because actually the north-east wants to be a powerhouse again." She paused. She was speaking even more fervently; she believed that the successes of the Stephenson days could somehow rub off on, or at least provide an example to, modern times. "What you have here," she said, "is the past and present and future of railways."

All wrapped up in one museum. As if to confirm this point, a train whirred by between Darlington and Bishop Auckland – the tracks ran adjacent to the museum.

"You see, we're down by the line, it's right there," said Sarah, highlighting how the "present" was still alive at the museum.

What a charming, inspiring head of Locomotion.

She seemed to get what it was all about.

Sarah left and Clive Goult arrived.

I had not made an appointment with Clive either. Clive's job was "workshop and traction manager" for Locomotion, and he had previously been a "locomotive engineer" and fireman on the *Flying Scotsman* – the famous, sleek steam locomotive built in 1923 by the renowned train engineer Nigel Gresley and now a heritage service – as well as "shed master" at the North Yorkshire Moors Railway, a heritage line, in charge of fifteen staff and more than a hundred volunteers. A train man through and through.

He also wore an orange hi-vis jacket, although his, unlike Sarah's (which had been pristine), was covered in grime and oil. He was in his late fifties and had a shock of grey hair, a rosy complexion, a couple of days' stubble, a whimsical sense of humour and a can-do attitude (that was about to do me a lot of favours).

As we drank coffees, we talked about this and that. He had a laid-back, devilish manner.

"King Charles III…" he said, pausing and waiting for me to respond. I had been asking him about his days on the *Flying Scotsman*.

What about him, I enquired.

"I collected him on the *Scotsman* from York and took him to Pickering," Clive said, in the manner of a taxi driver discussing a famous passenger they have had *in the back of my cab*.

As I had with Paul and David, I asked Clive what he liked so much about trains, which he had been involved in since childhood, when his father had volunteered on a heritage railway.

"What's so special about trains?" he replied. "I don't know. Why do people wave at trains? They don't wave at planes. Why do people wave at trains?"

It was a rhetorical question, though I could not think of the answer why, other than *to be friendly*. That was why I imagined people waved at trains (and boats, for that matter), not that I could remember waving at any trains myself. It was simply about making a connection, saying an old-fashioned "hello". Maybe boats came into that; people had no doubt waved at passing vessels from riverbanks and coastlines for centuries gone by, ever since folk dug out tree trunks to make canoes: a primeval urge, of sorts. I realized I was not particularly breaking new ground with these observations, but I relayed them to Clive nevertheless.

"Everyone's got their own reason," said Clive, on hearing this. "But I bet no one can quite tell you *exactly why*."

He gave me a canny look as though to suggest trains had some almost mystical essence and it was no good banging on about being companionable through the ages. There was a secret to the attraction of trains, his steady gaze seemed to be saying. To understand this mystery was beyond the ken of ordinary folk such as Clive and myself.

I asked Clive how important the Stockton and Darlington Railway really was – just to establish I was not about to set off all the way round Britain, celebrating something that really did not matter all that much.

Clive looked at me as though I ought to know better… and then he explained: "Pre-1829 you could travel as far as a horse would take you or as far as you could walk. The furthest many people ever went was the next village or town really. Suddenly, you could go thirty miles an hour between Liverpool and Manchester. Suddenly, the whole world…" Clive used his hands to indicate *shrinking*. "… It went from walking and horses to thirty miles an hour in forty years." And that had all begun, he said, ahead of the Liverpool and Manchester Railway, right by the tracks where we were talking.

"Then in the 1870s it was sixty miles an hour," said Clive. "Then the first official one hundred miles an hour was 1928–29. Within one hundred years that had been achieved. From thirty miles an hour to one hundred miles an hour. Before then we'd had millions of years of hardly moving… apart from ships. It began here in 1825 at ten miles an hour. It was up to thirty miles an hour in 1829. The development in those four years…" Clive made a whistling sound. "From ten miles an hour to thirty miles an hour. At the beginning, a man would walk in front of the first loco with a red flag [warning people ahead]."

He discussed William Huskisson, the unfortunate MP who had tragically died after ignoring safety instructions and taking a stroll from his carriage on the inaugural day of the Liverpool and Manchester

Railway, back on 15 September 1830, being struck and crushed by *Rocket*, with Robert Stephenson himself driving.

"We should never have changed that tradition – don't vote 'em out, run 'em over," was Clive's take on this sad moment in railway history (though he didn't, obviously, really mean it).

His comment prompted a change in subject. "HS2? My view is that we made a mistake being the first developing railways," he said. "If we'd waited forty years, we wouldn't have built so many windy railways and tunnels and bridges and gone winding around every town. We'd have had straight railways. Because we were first, and railways were improving, we had too many restrictions [such as landowners blocking the way]. And if we'd been devastated by the Second World War, like the rest of poor Europe was, we'd have had brand-new railways. Somebody would have said *let's rebuild the tracks from a blank piece of paper and improve*. What we've been doing ever since is using sticking plaster and *let's do it on the cheap*. Sadly, Tom, we can't afford it. Or we think we can't afford it. It's the British problem. We don't look at the benefits against the direct costs."

The failure to build HS2 was the burning issue in British trains 200 years after the first public passenger train line had begun between Shildon, Darlington and Stockton. Really, it should have been called the Shildon, Stockton and Darlington Railway, but Shildon was such a small place, with a population of a few hundred back then, so it could not call the shots with the name.

The irony that the nation that invented the railways was so poorly organized in running them was, of course, not lost on anyone when discussing the matter.

HS2 loomed large, and would continue to loom large, on this journey round Britain on trains.

So began my induction into British railway matters, two centuries after British railway matters started.

Clive very kindly showed me the best route, with exact times, to the North Yorkshire Moors Railway and onwards for two days ahead. I had asked whether he thought it was possible to get there on a Sunday from Stockton, where I would be staying the next night (after a night in Darlington), and not expected such assistance. I would be travelling by train from Stockton to nearby Thornaby, changing and taking another service to a small station named Grosmont. At Grosmont, you joined the North Yorkshire Moors Railway, which ran southwards for eighteen miles to Pickering through scenery that was said to be "very pretty". I would then return to Grosmont, catch a train to Middlesbrough and another to York, where I would be staying the following night.

Simple. A lot of movement. All of it by train.

Clive had, like a train Jeeves, worked it all out for me. (Even though I had a rough idea where I wanted to go, I was winging it and needed the help.) I thanked him profusely and returned to Shildon station, where the 14:32 back to Darlington was on time.

On board, schoolkids were saying to each other "I'm going to grab your phone and smash it" and "I hate this f***in' phone" and generally larking about. At Darlington station, rain was dripping into buckets placed here and there to deal with leaks in the roof. Signs said that £100 million was about to be invested in the station (which seemed like a good idea).

I walked past a "First Step to Fitness – Ladies Only Gym", a "Nail Lab", "The Bathroom World: The World's Most Exotic Bathrooms" (only available in Darlington), "HOT PLATE" pizzas, "MOJO" pizzas, "PIZZA TOWN" and an Indian restaurant, before arriving at the Dalesman pub/hotel. This had a "no drugs" sign on the door and Kempton Park races on the television. Some elderly men were playing dominoes in a corner, and a pair of Staffordshire bull terriers was scampering about, paying particular attention as I ate a roast beef and mustard sandwich by the bar.

I walked across Market Square, passing the distinguished old hall and clock tower, to see North Road station, where yet another railway museum, named Hopetown Darlington, was closed and in the middle of renovations, gearing up for the bicentenary. This was close to Skerne

Bridge, site of John Dobbin's evocative old painting. So there it was, "the £5 note bridge", as locals called it due to Skerne Bridge – with *Locomotion No 1* puffing across the top alongside a portrait of George Stephenson – featuring on the back of the old £5 note (in circulation from 1990 to 2002): recognition by the Bank of England, no less, of its key historical importance.

No fellows in bowler hats or elegant women in flowing frocks and bonnets were lining the banks, admiring passing trains on my visit. Instead, a solitary man on a phone was leaning against a fence close to an extremely weather-worn and badly vandalized public information panel about the importance of Skerne Bridge in railway history. This bridge was, some considered, the world's first proper railway bridge. The sign told you this, just about, beneath scratches and spray-paint additions; it must have been Britain's most attacked public information panel, or at least pretty high up in the rankings.

As I read about the world's first proper railway bridge, the solitary man on his phone began a disturbing discussion: "She cheated on me... she was there with X... that's absolutely not f***ing on... she wanted weed from me... she can do what she wants... I do not trust her... I do not want her... she can hang around with X and the new coke-heads on the block... 'social' can deal with that."

He was in a terrible state, half-screaming at whoever it was down the line; no way could you miss his conversation, which was a far cry from John Dobbin's quaint old picture of the assembled "society" figures as the world's first public steam-powered passenger train chugged by on that momentous, rousing day back on 27 September 1825.

I might have said something by way of consolation had the solitary man finished his call: "You alright, mate?" Or whatever.

Except, before I could, the person he was talking to turned up on a bike and they wandered off together under the world's first railway bridge in the direction of Darlington's town centre. I followed soon after and dropped by Darlington Hippodrome, a fine Edwardian, red-brick building where the *Strictly Come Dancing* star Giovanni Pernice was performing that night and a queue of women dressed to the nines snaked out of the front door, saying things like, "He's so gorgeous, ain't he, Liz? Oh, when he gets his shirt off, Vicky! Blimmin' 'ell, that torso, Pam! Just get it off! And all 'em lovely dancers too!"

One middle-aged woman was saying to her mother, "It's a hundred and thirty quid for meet and greet, Mum. You get a picture with him and have a hug. Next time, eh?"

Mother, in her eighties, responding to daughter: "Oh, yeah!"

Then a group in the queue began chanting "Gio! Gio! Gio!"

I went across the street and ate very good curry at a very nice Thai restaurant opposite the Hippodrome, watching "Gio" fans arriving for the big torso reveal. Then I got an early night at the Dalesman in a small, perfectly comfortable room, listening to a faint thud of music rising from below.

It had been an unusual day.

Many trains awaited down the line.

I was on my way, ready to celebrate all things British train, while pottering about on quite a few of them – to wave a flag for the Stockton and Darlington Railway and George and Robert Stephenson and all the other pioneers and what they'd created. A great British achievement! A lasting source of national honour! Green too! So ahead of its time!

All of that stuff (and rightly so).

All invented up in the north-east of England 200 years ago.

CHAPTER TWO

DARLINGTON TO SETTLE VIA MIDDLESBROUGH, GROSMONT, PICKERING, YORK, LEEDS AND KEIGHLEY

LOST IN LOCOS

Embarking on a long trip around Britain's railways took some planning but not a huge amount – which was all part of the pleasure of the endeavour, although you did soon find yourself deep within the labyrinthine world of British trains.

There were two principal considerations.

First, where did the trains go? To help with this, I had consulted the website of National Rail, a body that promoted railways in Britain and was half funded by the country's mainly privately owned train operators and by Network Rail, a public body connected to the Department for Transport, which was responsible for the infrastructure (20,000 miles of tracks, 6,000 level crossings, 30,000 bridges and viaducts, and 2,500 stations). Some people confused National Rail with Network Rail. This was a big no-no in the "train world".

National Rail was there to sell tickets and be helpful by providing a "journey planner" on its website (nationalrail.co.uk) and a National Rail enquiries phone number. Its brand symbol was the distinctive red double-arrow logo that you saw at train stations in Britain. This, just to make things more complicated, was previously the symbol of British Rail, a state-owned company that took control of the "Big Four" railways (Great Western Railway; London, Midland and Scottish Railway; Southern Railway; and London and North Eastern Railway) and some smaller railways, from nationalization in 1948, under the pioneering Labour government of Clement Attlee, up until 1997. Britain's railways were then privatized during Conservative government rule, a process begun by the Conservative Party's leader Margaret Thatcher and completed by John Major. So in a way, what had happened – and continued to happen (as politics, of course, never stopped) – to railways in Britain might be said to represent wider matters connected to the general state of national affairs. A thought I considered possible that I might return to from time to time.

Anyway, labyrinthine matters aside, National Rail's website had an extremely useful "route diagram" map that showed where all the trains went.

Different colours and sizes of line indicated whether they were "principal", "regional", "local", "limited service", "high-speed" or "HS2 under construction". The latter was coloured light orange, while the completed, high-speed railway from where the Channel Tunnel emerged at Folkestone was a darker orange and had "EUROSTAR" written on it. The principal, regional, local and limited-service lines were all blue in varying thicknesses, the widest being for the principal routes.

It was interesting to look at this map and think *right, that's where you can go*. Britain had been reduced, if you like, to its railway bones. There were the tracks. There were your possibilities, rather limited way up in Scotland and out west in Wales and south-west in Cornwall. It was as though you were looking at the country afresh, before motor vehicles and roads had made their entrance, making just about anywhere accessible. As you gazed at this map, drawn by a graphic artist named Andrew Smithers, who went by the handle @MrMappy on the social media site X, the country appeared to shrink. It felt as though you had stepped back in time, perhaps to the late nineteenth century: your only real way ahead was on "iron horses", if not by actual horses. Nowhere else was possible. There was something refreshingly limiting about this nineteenth-century reduction of Britain. You knew where you stood.

The second consideration was which route to take.

So, using the National Rail map, I sketched a vague plan that went something like this. 1) Pootle about in the north of England, after Darlington, crossing from the north-east to the north-west, definitely – if I could – taking in a famous line between Settle and Carlisle that many people raved about for its general scenic wonderfulness (and viaducts) before skirting round the Lake District on the Cumbrian Coast Line and heading to Liverpool and Manchester to pay homage to the 1830 heroics and groundbreaking developments of the Liverpool and Manchester Railway. How could any self-respecting railway lover not do that?

2) Intriguingly, it then appeared possible to skirt into the mountains of North Wales, taking little heritage lines for a while, and afterwards weave through the heart of Wales on a thin "local" or perhaps "limited

service" line (it was tricky to tell the difference, not that it mattered much, on the National Rail map).

3) Move into the south-west by crossing to Bristol and swooshing down to Penzance in the far south-west of England to enjoy a few days in Cornwall, and then, as there was no other railway, retrace the tracks, perhaps investigating Somerset and Devon before dropping down to the English Channel near Poole in Dorset.

4) That seemed a sensible starting point for a sweep across the south coast of England. This would, ideally, begin with a visit to the Isle of Wight (in possession of a tiny railway, the map showed), after which it looked logical to traverse the shoreline, stopping at seaside towns, and continue in a curve round Kent.

5) Next, after ignoring London, as I did not want to get bogged down there, it appeared logical to skate along the east of England, tackling East Anglia and cutting up through Lincolnshire towards Grimsby and snaking onwards via Hull to the seaside town of Scarborough in North Yorkshire.

6) That, I realized, would bring me close to Darlington once again, where it would seem common sense to return to the beginning – back to the scene of the 1825 railway heroics – with a circular journey complete. But that would have left out Scotland. And I wanted to go to Scotland, and to take the famous *Caledonian Sleeper* night train to get there – and you normally caught that from London Euston. So I would let the tracks transport me southwards through the Midlands via the Peak District and the Cotswolds and on to London, whereupon, in a great whoosh of wheels along the tracks, I would catch the renowned sleeper service north, all the way to Aberdeen on the north-east coast of Scotland. At least, I hoped so: I had no ticket – and they were often sold out.

7) On arrival in Aberdeen, you could circle Scotland on the limited lines available, going to Thurso in the very north as well as the Kyle of Lochalsh in the west, followed by Glasgow and Edinburgh – at least it looked possible on the map.

8) Finally, it would then be time to return to Darlington on the East Coast Main Line, completing what would have been – when I looked

at it – a rather unusual journey round Britain that was shaped a bit like a messy musical treble clef: or, you might say, a load of squiggles that somehow linked.

There you had it: the route, open to last-minute alterations, extremely flexible, at the mercy of sudden whims, little more than a back-of-a-fag-packet plan really, even if it might sound quite detailed. It was surprisingly simple to look at the National Rail route diagram and sketch out a rough way ahead; though whether it would make the most of Britain's glorious railways 200 years on, only time would tell. Anyway, you couldn't go everywhere, and it could change. There were, as previously stated, 10,072 route miles of tracks in Britain – a lot. Too much for one journey (and utter madness to try).

No point in attempting to be comprehensive – or especially systematic or *organized*. No spreadsheets. No timetable-crunching in advance. I didn't want that. Too much bother (frankly). Sometimes it's best just to see what happens. Go with the flow. Besides, a true "escape", as I saw it, required a hunt for the unknown – and what is unknown could not be planned. You escaped to visit other places, usually, because something inside you simply said "go!" I would be doing just that. It was time to *go on some trains*. I had two months to spare to do so and some (modest) savings to blow. I would let the real world swirl round me – events, whatever they may be, in the news, at work, at home, anything, everything, the whole lot, all of it – and enter an alternative train existence, footloose and fancy free, a parallel universe of railways one step removed from the "normal", peering through carriage windows on a journey that would not be across the wilds of Siberia, the Sahara or South America. More like the wilds of Crewe, Bognor Regis, Clapham Junction, Staines, Doncaster, Dumbarton and *wherever the lines would lead* on a lot of British trains.

What I realized I was seeking was to enter a train zone, like a drifter hopping on freight wagons in America, except I would not be dodging fares. It would just be me and the timetables, the guards, my fellow passengers and the lines stretching ahead: a fantasy land of steel tracks, tinny announcements, out-of-the-way spots and plenty of well-known ones too. Just go for it, no need to fight it. Let it be. Let trains lead the way, wherever that might be. There was a sense of simplicity, of happy abandonment in that. Relief. Release.

Goodbye, responsibilities. Hello to a long, winding journey down the lines.

To add a little extra railway sparkle, if you like – some icing on the cake of train – occasional detours would be made to some of Britain's impressive assortment of heritage lines. The nation was in possession of more than 170 of these railways, it was staggering to discover. If there was one nearby, why not go there to soak up some more of the "pioneering train spirit" of the country that invented railways, as I would at the North Yorkshire Moors Railway?

Using this modus operandi, by the end of my journey I hoped to be imbued with the essence of British trains. To have smelt the diesel of "COLAS RAIL FREIGHT" and the soot and cinder of steam locomotives up and down the nation. To have listened to the echo of announcements on many a lonely or lively platform. To have felt the clatter, bump and sway of the carriage from north, south, east and west. To have immersed myself in British trains. To have swum in the Ganges of British trains, if you like. To have understood and appreciated fully, with due respect and reverence, British trains. To have let British trains permeate my soul. To become, you might say, a fully fledged British Train Nut. I had no problem with that.

To the Tees and on
Darlington to Grosmont via Stockton

"Brevity is the soul of wit," as Shakespeare wrote in *Hamlet*. With these words in mind, I intended to get on with it. Which would be the nature of this story of a journey on Britain's trains. No time for dilly-dallying: many miles lay ahead. As I rattled along, so would this tale from the tracks.

From Darlington I aimed to catch the 13:55 to Thornaby, where I would change to catch the 14:27 to Stockton, a six-minute journey. Both Northern trains.

I boarded the 13.55 to Thornaby, expecting a quiet Saturday afternoon ride.

Though it did not quite work out like that.

To start with it was peaceful enough as we pulled away past terraced houses, entering countryside with some puddly fields: relaxing, simply gliding away from Darlington to Stockton, via a change at Thornaby, along the line created in 1825, mulling over train matters from 200 years earlier.

And then there was almost a fight.

Noises were coming from the adjoining carriage. Raised voices.

"Get off!" said a voice. It was the conductor.

"You get off the train, you f***in' n***e!" said another voice. It was a pallid lad wearing a hoodie.

"Get off!" said the conductor. We were at Dinsdale station.

Pallid lad in hoodie: "You get off, you f***in' bastard."

Conductor: "Get off!"

Pallid lad in hoodie: "Come on then!" He was inviting the conductor to engage in a fight. The conductor would not do this but stood his ground.

Pallid lad in hoodie: "F*** off." Although he did, at this stage, do so himself of his own accord, disembarking and crossing the platform to stand on a path. In this position, he turned to the train and the conductor, who was gazing back at him by the door, and gave what was universally recognized as a very rude sign to the driver and – in effect – all the other passengers.

The pallid lad in a hoodie then kicked a metal fence railing in fury. This must have been extremely painful, though he did not show it.

The train doors shut and we moved on.

The conductor came over to check our tickets. He was about 30, wore a beard and was a little flustered, but not particularly.

I asked him about what had just happened.

"He didn't have a ticket and he didn't want to get off. They know you're on the job so you can't do anything," he replied. He meant manhandle them off the train. "So they say, *You throw the first punch*. But you can't do anything. You don't know them. They're not regulars or anything [regular troublemakers]. But they're the type – sixteen, seventeen. It's all talk. All mouth." The conductor made a mouth gesture with his hand.

Given that I had him chatting, I asked whether he otherwise enjoyed being a conductor on the world's first public passenger line to have run steam locomotives.

"To a certain extent," he replied.

He did appreciate the history, but he was not impressed by the trains. "These ones are not as modern as the ones we had with our training. Trains here are not like the ones in Leeds, where we did our training."

I had no idea what he meant by this. It seemed a pretty normal train, just like the one yesterday. Anyway, he went down the carriage and we soon arrived in Thornaby, a simple station with exposed platforms on which a group of young women was milling about, dressed for a night out in miniskirts, off-the-shoulder tops and high heels. They were going to York. It was quite cold for those outfits, and they were shivering, but pretending it did not bother them in the slightest.

The train for Stockton came; I boarded and it moved away, crossing the river Tees, passing a red-brick housing estate and arriving at a small station that was little more than a platform with a couple of shelters. The old station house had been converted into apartments. There was not much, frankly, to detain the 1825 railway-appreciating visitor.

I walked on past the Station pub and Moores Snooker Bar. Beyond was a wide-open square, the art deco facade of the Globe theatre and a small market that seemed to be selling a great number of batteries, disposable vapes and handbags. This was next to the Stockton Visitor Information Centre, which had black-and-white pictures of the Beatles in its front window, taken when the band had played at the Globe on

22 November 1963, the day President John Kennedy was assassinated, said a display.

I went inside to ask about the attractions of Stockton.

A woman wearing a white blouse, pink dress and glasses, the tourist information officer, proceeded to answer my enquiries.

"Did you see the plinth?" she asked, pointing to a plinth outside on the square.

"Yes," I replied.

"That is an attraction." She said this in a dry, deadpan manner, as though inviting further questions.

"What's so special about it?" I asked, taking the verbal bait while regarding the empty plinth.

"Every day at 1 p.m. a mechanical locomotive arises from that plinth. It's brilliant," she said, completely deadpan again. This plinth, it turned out, was a special, somewhat bizarre plinth that acted as a tribute to the Stockton and Darlington Railway. It was known as the *Stockton Flyer*, a kinetic sculpture dating from 2016: a strange tangle of metal in the shape of *Locomotive No 1* rising mysteriously from below, emitting whistles and smoke, at precisely one o'clock in the afternoon each day. It was by the sculptor and inventor Rob Higgs, who billed it as a "whimsical creation".

"It's only at 1 p.m.," said the tourist information officer. "Anyone who comes in here, we always do say to them *See the plinth, it's brilliant*." She paused. "But unfortunately, you've missed it." She paused again. "Normally we also say, *Go to the town hall*, because it's brilliant too." Apparently, it was an architecturally interesting nineteenth-century town hall. "But, unfortunately, it's covered in scaffolding right now as it's full of bots."

I asked her to repeat this.

"Bots, bots," she said, before I realized she was saying *bats*. "It *was* full of bots," she continued, correcting herself. "Six months ago, there were bots. But now they've gone. They've cleared them out. It was closed because of the bots. But it's being refurbished and they're going to reopen it."

Elsewhere in Stockton there was a place called Preston Hall. "But, unfortunately, it's a forty-five-minute walk, too far for today, and it'll close soon," she said. "Then there's the Globe." She paused again and looked at me. "But, unfortunately, there's nothing on tonight."

She smiled pleasantly. She was a friendly tourist information officer.

I thanked her and found my digs, which were above The Hoptimist pub, not far from a pawnbroker, the Twisted Nostalgia Tattoo Studio, the Munch King pizzeria and several other rival pizzerias. On arrival the receptionist/barmaid asked, "Do you mind loud music?"

"That depends," I replied cautiously.

"It's Saturday night. It's karaoke. It'll be noisy until 11.30 p.m."

I said this was fine and went out to eat an excellent chicken kebab at Shawarma City, take a look at the river and go for a pint at Moores Snooker Bar, where I fell into conversation with a red-faced man with a gold earring, crumpled overcoat and piercing blue eyes. He was drinking lager and was in an expansive mood.

"I've been all round the world, me," he told me. "All the cities. I was in construction. I can construct anything. Anything! Anything except..." He paused and leaned closer. "The Sistine Chapel." He could not construct the Sistine Chapel, he said, looking up at the ceiling of the Moores Snooker Bar as though remembering the ceiling of the Sistine Chapel from a visit he had once made. "How did they do that all that time ago? Different class."

I asked how he had got to travel round the world. His reply was unspecific and slightly affronted.

"Because I'm educated," he said. "Educated... Architecture, sport, literature, music, they all interest me." We sipped our pints and said no more. Moores Snooker Bar, with its wine-red carpet and pictures of sporting heroes on the walls – Bobby Moore, Muhammad Ali – was like that. Little bursts of conversation and fellows of a certain age, when I went at least, seeming to mull over matters in a philosophical frame of mind.

Onwards! On a miserable, damp, overcast morning, I joined the 09:57 to Middlesbrough, yet another Northern service with blue-spotted seats.

My ticket was invalid on the train because I was early. It would be quite a long wait for the next one, when the ticket would be valid, and it was wet, windy and awful at Stockton station. Being a law-abiding, British, long-distance train traveller, however, when the 09:57 arrived I asked the conductor for permission to travel and he said, "That's OK. At Middlesbrough there's a nice waiting room. It's a more comfortable seat in Middlesbrough." He paused and asked, "You were in Stockton overnight?"

I told him I had been.

"Did you have a tin hat on?" he asked.

What did he mean by that, I replied. Was he implying Stockton was "rough"?

"Oh no. I say that about anywhere south of Newcastle." He was from Newcastle, a Geordie. "You've got to be in Tynemouth, it's thriving in Tynemouth. I prefer it in Tynemouth." Newcastle was, of course, on the river Tyne and Tynemouth was an area on its northern banks, where it entered the North Sea.

The conductor nodded as though putting a full-stop after his thoughts on the superiority of Tynemouth over Teesside, the name of the area we were rolling along by the river Tees, and moved on.

Shortly after, the 09:57 arrived at Middlesbrough.

Rain was pelting on the awnings of the platforms at Middlesbrough. This station had a Gothic style. Tall, arched windows rose, casting gloomy light in a ticket office featuring wooden ceiling beams and pointed doorways that looked as though they belonged in a medieval banqueting hall. A blue plaque said the station was designed in 1877 by William Peachey. At that time, Middlesbrough, little more than a scattering of abodes half a century earlier, was one of the heroes of industrialization, considered by the then soon-to-be Prime Minister William Gladstone as an "infant Hercules" in 1862.

This was what trains could do to places back then: turn them into mythical heroes known for their legendary strength.

Gladstone had gushed, "This remarkable place, the youngest child of England's enterprise, is an infant, but if an infant, an infant Hercules." All thanks to newfangled contraptions attached to wheels, puffing steam and rolling along metal tracks.

I returned to the platform and made a friend.

This turned out to be the driver of my next train to Grosmont.

Her name was Katy, from Darlington. She was standing near a fine old, tiled map of the North Eastern Railway routes (a rail operator that existed from 1854 to 1922), listening to the rain on the awnings – which had an almost therapeutic quality as it began to hammer down. We were the only two people on the platform.

Katy was open and chatty. We got talking, as she was admiring the old map too, and she was soon telling me that she had started at Northern five years previously after working in sales jobs and call centres for planes and banks.

I asked Katy if there were many female train drivers.

"Oh, there's loads of us," she replied. "My older sister works on Lumo." Lumo was another train company, operating between London and Edinburgh.

Why did she become a train driver?

"It appealed to me. I've always been trying to find something I enjoy and get paid for," she said. "And I do enjoy it and I fit in. I'm proud to work on the trains. It's a privilege and you get out and about. Lots of people are locked in offices. Here you see the sunrise, you see the sun going up and down. On a cold morning, when the windows are frosty, it's lovely. Beautiful. It's not like a job. I do feel proud to say that I'm a train driver."

Katy was starting a shift, waiting for the 10:50 to arrive, which would be travelling along the Esk Valley Railway. She told me that this railway was a single-track line with an old-fashioned brass-token system further along. "It's a Victorian thing," she said and promised to show me when we got to Battersby.

The 10:50 was 10 minutes late; not Katy's fault, the service had been held up on the way to Middlesbrough.

It rolled off past Riverside Stadium (home of Middlesbrough Football Club), a tangle of pipes of a refinery and some semi-detached houses, entering a sedate landscape of streams, sheep farms and low hills covered in coppery bracken.

At Battersby station, the rain still pouring, Katy waved me over to the front of the train where there was a booth with two red boxes inside. Into one of these boxes, she inserted a brass "key token" she had been carrying and twisted it. Then she phoned to ask the signaller to grant her permission to continue along the single-track line ahead. The signaller did so. Without this physical act, followed by the safety call, the train could not continue.

Then Katy let me peer into the driver's cab of the 10:50, which was a Class 156 DMU; this stood for "diesel multiple unit", she said, with engines throughout the train rather than one at the front. I was learning "train things".

"I'd show you the driver's seat, but I'm not allowed," she said. The driver's seat was in a cramped space behind the open door. Then she looked out at the misty, rolling countryside ahead and sighed. "It's still bonnie, it's all bonnie round here." Even on a rainswept day.

Katy said it might be possible to "make a bit of time" before Grosmont, as she knew it was a close call to catch my Grosmont to Pickering train, although she was not that worried. "You've got five minutes?" To cross the platform to join a steam train on the North Yorkshire Moors Railway. "Five minutes! Oh, in *train time* that's nothing to worry about."

Soot, steam and serendipity
North Yorkshire Moors Railway

She was right, as it happened. Plenty of time. This was mainly due to a scrum of steam train lovers taking pictures of our ride.

There it was in all its glory: a steam train.

This journey of train appreciation had an actual proper steam train to appreciate, one that was actually properly steaming, panting, hissing and gleaming in burgundy and gold (the carriages) and olive green (the locomotive). It was a splendid sight in North-East England on a dreary day, attracting a commotion of attention among passengers who were taking endless snaps.

I joined them. The locomotive was named *Royal Scot* and was built in 1927 by the London, Midland and Scottish Railway, one of the aforementioned "Big Four" that was amalgamated to form British Railways in 1948. A gold plaque said that it had been transported in 1933 to an exhibition in Chicago entitled "The Century of Progress International Exposition", during which it huffed and puffed precisely 11,194 miles on a North American tour and was "inspected" by precisely 3,021,601 people.

This was a famous locomotive. Steam oozed from beneath the wheels. With the other assorted Train Nuts, I stood there for a while. Speechless. Then the Train Nuts and I boarded the train, which duly rolled away, entering a tunnel, turning the carriage pitch-black and steaming the windows, before juddering forth into rugged hills following boulder-strewn streams.

Some men in blue overalls were at a table across the aisle, talking trains. They were workers for the North Yorkshire Moors Railway. I eavesdropped for a while.

"Cos it sheared off, it were bouncing off each other," said one.

"It were right hammering. It s*** me up proper," said another.

"All the bars were pushed out eight millimetres," said a third.

"All the stud poles were at an odd angle – bent," said a fourth.

This conversation meandered onwards, like the tracks. I did not understand a word of it.

A couple was opposite me. They were of retirement age, huddled together on the cornflower-blue seats, which were set in pale wood fittings. He wore a turban and had a bushy grey beard. She wore a woolly hat and gold earrings. Their expressions were fixed with enormous grins. They were enjoying the ride.

"It brings back childhood memories of India," said Nirmal. "In those days there were open windows and iron bars and sparks used to come in. Sometimes they hurt the skin and damaged clothes. For us it was very exciting."

The couple was from India and had moved to England in the 1970s.

"I came for her," Nirmal said. His wife-to-be, Daljit, had moved to England in 1976. "I came in 1978. I followed her. We met in India, in Punjab, through the family."

They were Sikh and lived in Preston. Nirmal used to work in "strategic management" for social services and had become a chaplain for six businesses and been awarded an MBE for previous work for the prison service.

Daljit said, "In our childhood, means of travel was either bus or train. I used to like to go on night trains. I always wanted to go on the Delhi to Punjab train. There were lights on the train and it was nice going to sleep."

Nirmal: "The excitement of it."

Daljit: "What I used to like, at one station they would make tea in small terracotta pots and sell medicines and books."

Nirmal: "Wherever we go, if there's a steam train we'll take it. Scotland and Wales, Snowdonia – we like it."

Daljit: "Sometimes we take our grandchildren."

Nirmal: "When you close your eyes later [after going on a train], you can see the journey… reminisce." He looked out of the window as though capturing the scenery to remember later, then he said, "Only, on this ride – no greenery. The trees are thinking *sometime later, we give people shade*. This is the naked truth of their lives."

On this profundity, we fell into silence for a while – he and Daljit grinning from ear to ear, watching North Yorkshire go by.

After a while, Nirmal broke the spell: "My grandfather, he took a contract from the British military." His grandfather had supplied uniforms for officers of the Raj, who were based in Shimla in the northern Indian state of Himachal Pradesh.

I mentioned I had once travelled to Shimla on the narrow-gauge "Toy Train".

"I worked in Shimla for a year when I was twenty-three," said Nirmal. "That train, many times. One hundred and three tunnels. I remember. I was a scientist and entomologist, looking at the effects of insects on crops. *Butterflies*, I used to say, if anyone asked. *Butterflies*. Sounds better."

We fell into silence for a while again. Rain was hammering down, forming rivulets on the window.

"It is rainy," said Nirmal.

He had that right.

"We can't do anything else," said Daljit.

Apart from take a steam train across North Yorkshire.

They were simply happy *being on a train*.

And I was simply happy *being on a train*, too.

"Passionate people are usually weird," said Nirmal, out of the blue. "We are passionate. And this is the truth… passionate people are usually weird."

With that, the train pulled into Pickering, eighteen miles down the line from Grosmont, and we said goodbye.

The platforms at Pickering were a mad buzz of photography and chatter. Steam hung in a mist in the station shed. On one platform was an old-fashioned newspaper kiosk (shut) with faded newspaper advertising boards from the local *Gazette & Herald*: "PICKERING MAN WEDS", and "HINDENBURG EXPLODES, MORE THAN 30 DEAD", from the *Daily Mirror*. Nearby was the original ticket office with a spiky metal grille and scuffed wooden counter. Beyond, on the streets of Pickering, was a Cantonese restaurant, Yorkshire Quality Books, the Station Hotel and a Costa Coffee.

Staying in the station, I read up about the North Yorkshire Moors Railway.

It was easy to do so; there were information panels everywhere – and one burning topic quickly became apparent.

This railway, like many others across Britain, suffered a great indignity in the 1960s. Like the others, it was shut down by the government during the infamous "Beeching cuts", a period in British train history that seems to cast a shadow over everything that has happened since.

During these infamous cuts – almost always seemingly referred to as "infamous" – around 4,000 miles of railway were closed following the controversial 1963 publication of a report entitled *The Reshaping of British Railways* by Dr Richard Beeching, the chair of the British Railways Board. Prior to this report, after nationalization in 1948, 3,000 miles of British railways had already been slashed on the grounds they were running at great losses, but Beeching's pronouncements hugely accelerated the scaling back. At the time, the first motorways were being built (the M1 from London to Leeds via Birmingham opened in 1959), and cars and lorries looked as though they would replace trains for many journeys.

Beeching's report was a bombshell, calling on vast swathes of railways to go. The truth was that there were too many lines, partly due to the railway manias of the nineteenth century that had seen so many railways spring up. But his suggested cutbacks were drastic, with many jobs on the line – in the event more than 60,000 were to go. Remote communities previously connected to the "mainstream" by railways would also be cut off, as they were when Grosmont to Pickering closed in 1965.

How then had we just taken the train along the old line?

Well, this is where heritage railways, such as the North Yorkshire Moors Railway, came in. The passion for trains, especially steam locomotives (which were also being phased out in favour of diesel locomotives in the 1960s), led to dozens of organizations springing up, including the key Railway Preservation Association, formed in 1962. This was a forerunner of the Heritage Railway Association (1998), which had grown to include more than 300 members and had, in its own words "achieved what many thought impossible… [rebuilding] routes that had vanished almost entirely".

The North Yorkshire Moors Railway was one of these – originally called the Whitby and Pickering Railway and planned in 1831 by George Stephenson, no less, to open up trade to the port of Whitby. It had been saved by the North Yorkshire Moors Railway Trust and reopened in 1973, attracting around 350,000 passengers a year at the time of my visit.

There you had it: the infamous Beeching cuts, with which you soon become very familiar on a long series of trains rides around Britain.

There you also had it: the Beeching backlash in the form of heritage lines maintaining old trains and traditions, and generally saving the day.

It was time to return. With a piercing whistle, the 14:00 Pickering to Grosmont left on the dot.

Steam billowed into silver birch woodland beside the track, hanging in the branches and disturbing the odd squirrel. I sat alone, listening to the steady rattle and click of the wheels as we passed tea-coloured streams and tumbling hills. A large tawny owl sat on a fence, expressionlessly regarding the monstrosity passing before its deep-set eyes, the 14:00 from Pickering, its head twitching slightly. The colours of the countryside, the mauves and deeper purples and streaks of gold and green, were rich and somehow comforting, the smoke from the train casting a haze over all and infusing the carriages with the smell of sulphur.

It was not long before we arrived at Grosmont station.

And not long after that, I was standing on the footplate of the *Royal Scot* locomotive.

Clive from the Locomotion museum had somehow arranged this. While the locomotive was moving from one end of the train to the other for the return to Pickering, I could stand on the "footplate": the name given to the driver's cab area.

This was quite an experience. You immediately got the blast of heat from the furnace, which was burning bright orange, producing a more intense coal smell than ever, plus a good close-up look at various brass handles, pipes and pressure-gauge displays.

The driver was named Danny and wore spectacles and a blue blazer over blue overalls. Danny, an engineer by training, had an inscrutable yet seemingly deeply content demeanour and was in his thirties. He had been involved in heritage trains for 20 years, his father having also been a volunteer. The *Royal Scot* went at a top speed of 25 mph along the Grosmont–Pickering line, the maximum speed allowed on heritage railways, but could reach 75 mph on a main line. The carriages I had travelled in were "BR Mark 1 circa 1960s", Danny said.

He let me shovel some coal into the furnace: a strangely satisfying thing to do. Then he told me about the *Royal Scot*.

"They're basically worth scrap metal until they're restored," he said. The *Royal Scot* was one of the last of its type, owned by a company called Locomotive Services Ltd run by a multimillionaire rail enthusiast. "They're fantastic machines. It's an honour and a privilege to get to go on a machine like this."

Danny told me that the *Royal Scot*'s water tank had a 4,000-gallon capacity of which 2,000 gallons had been used up. He looked in the furnace and said, although it still looked orange, "The temperature is white hot."

Then he told me that the Grosmont to Pickering line traversed a 1:49 gradient, making it a "very steep railway" as a 1:70 gradient was more usual.

I was learning yet more "train things".

I thanked Danny.

Then I caught the 14:08 to Middlesbrough.

Then I hopped on the 18:14 to York.

I was buying tickets as I went along. It really was quite easy mooching about on trains like this, I was rapidly finding. Easy and relaxing, too. You could go where you wanted. Do what you wanted. No rules. No *official* way. No *right* way.

Just head off wherever you fancied, anywhere at all… anywhere down the line.

On this occasion on the 18:14 from Middlesbrough to York.

This one was a TransPennine Express, with white carriages and a purple star-shaped logo. Like Northern, TransPennine Express was government-owned: a former private franchise that had been taken over due to the poor performances of previous owners. Privatization of the railway companies in the 1990s had not fared well in many instances – perhaps because it had resulted in mini-monopolies across the country with little real competition. Such was the structural failure, the entire project seemed likely to be reversed by a new, yet-to-be-elected Labour government, when I went.

Two hundred years after trains were the talking point of industrialization, debated at length (and often with rancour) in parliament, the future of railways had become a hot political topic once again, along with whether the HS2 line from Birmingham to Manchester and Leeds should have been cancelled or not, of course.

The 18:14 to York sped through the darkness, whining and humming along; the train didn't mind if it was privatized or not.

Adverts flashed up on monitors, advertising jobs on the TransPennine Express – "TRAIN FOR THE FUTURE" – and taxi services at each stop. These were on a loop, along with a repeated advert for Andy's Man Club, a "talking group for men to HELP YOU through these storms".

Thornaby, Yarm, Northallerton and Thirsk came and went.

The TransPennine Express pulled into York at 7.11 p.m.

I went to find the hotel I had booked earlier in the day. I was doing this as I went along too, using a popular online booking website; all pretty easy, just like buying the train tickets. Slipping into the parallel world of railways – and zigzagging about Britain on them – was coming quite naturally. You soon, I was quickly discovering, became immersed in it all and felt pleasantly removed from regular life. You had decided to let the trains lead the way for a while. You belonged, all of a sudden, to nowhere in particular; to a "train life". The tracks had taken over. This could happen. This had happened. It was delicious and cathartic in equal measure.

Just letting go.

Just letting trains run the show.
Nothing wrong with that.

Old trains, more old trains and Brontës (on trains)
York to Settle via Leeds and Keighley

Impressions were all you could really offer on such a train journey around quite a large country – the briefest of impressions, not even "snapshots", more like "fleeting glimpses". Brevity, brevity, brevity – you had to remember brevity. And trains, trains, trains, too.

For it was the trains that mattered: train matters. Not great treatises on early twenty-first-century Britain. Nor descriptive tracts capturing the "essence" of stops along the way. Nor elegies on this. Nor eulogies on that. Nor gushing accounts of nature seen from the carriage window.

My hotel in York was basic but cheap and cheerful, with a cramped single bed. I woke to a crisp morning beneath a pale-blue sky. A walk along the battlements of the old city wall afforded fine views of both the minster, with its grand facade, as well as the more mundane exterior of the station, where renovations were on their way according to the signs: "YORK STATION GATEWAY IS COMING SOON: THE FRONT OF YORK STATION IS BEING TRANSFORMED BY WEST YORKSHIRE COMBINED AUTHORITY, CITY OF YORK COUNCIL, NETWORK RAIL AND LNER." LNER stood for London North Eastern Railway, and like Northern and TransPennine Express had been taken into government hands.

Near the station was a must-visit for any rail enthusiast: York's National Railway Museum, a sister museum to Locomotion.

Of course, I went over to have a look.

Renovations were ongoing there too; a "master plan" was in place to redo the whole site, said a sign by the entry. Everywhere you went work seemed to be underway: Darlington was in the middle of an upheaval, Middlesbrough too, plus York station and the museum as well. I entered a passageway with various further explanations of the "master plan" and, after a short stroll, came to a wall with a large, ornate, gold-and-glossy-black wrought-iron gate that was once part of a giant, mock-classical, arched entrance to London Euston station. Most of the visitors to the National Railway Museum walked straight by, attracted by the shiny locos. With a couple of others, I dilly-dallied by this gate. Something about it seemed to draw you to it.

The gate, which I had not known until reading its information panel, was built in 1837 and installed at Euston. One of the purposes of such ostentation, you learned, was to impress passengers as well as investors in the early London and Birmingham Railway. However, in 1961, this striking structure was demolished to make way for a modernist, more futuristic-looking and efficient station when Dr Beeching was at the height of his "improvements".

His actions had invoked a massive outcry, as the arch was beloved by those who appreciated a subtle beauty in the sometimes heavy-looking style of Victorian architecture. A campaign to save it, led by the prominent poet John Betjeman, had failed, although the efforts were not in vain. It was soon recognized that the destruction at Euston had been a hasty, ham-handed mistake, and Betjeman and others used its example to protect other stations that were threatened, including St Pancras.

This gleaming gate had been kept and positioned in this place of prominence as a reminder and symbol of the "infamous" Beeching cuts and Dr Beeching's generally tough, often brutal approach.

Beside it was a large and fine portrait of the railway impresario Isambard Kingdom Brunel (1806–1859) by the renowned artist John Callcott Horsley. His left hand rested on a set of plans on a tabletop, and he was, for once, depicted without his trademark stovepipe hat, looking younger and more dashing than in usual pictures. Brunel represented the next generation of British railway engineers after the Stephensons. His legacy, much of it in the West Country, awaited down the line.

Beyond the old gate and Brunel, however, you came to the National Railway Museum's real *raison d'être*: a giant hall full of locomotives, carriages, wagons and all sorts connected to railways.

In short, you might say, this was a Train Nut's dream.

There they were: from 1927, a gleaming *Atlantic Coast Express* locomotive, saved from a scrapyard in 1974; from 1846, the *Old Coppernob* locomotive, shiny and red with a copper water tank; from 1830, two replica carriages from the original Liverpool and Manchester Railway that *Rocket* had pulled; from 1937, a funny little United Dairies milk tank; from 1938, the *Duchess of Hamilton* locomotive, sleek and red with golden streaks; and, best of all, perhaps, the even sleeker royal-blue-and-glossy-black *Mallard*, the world's fastest steam train ever (126 mph in 1938).

Plenty to ogle.

Another brilliant train museum.

But I had a train to catch: the 12:20 to Leeds.

Before rushing on, though, I had saved a little time to appreciate York station.

You could not, if you were slowly immersing yourself in the history of British trains, just rush through York station.

What a place York station was, with its enormous, curved roof held aloft by classical columns and decorated with cut-outs, high in the rafters, shaped like little white roses, the symbol of Yorkshire, and giving the effect of a constellation of twinkling stars. This airy space above was made airier still down below by a station policy that allowed platforms to be open to the general public, not just those with tickets. Anyone could walk straight through from the ticket hall, without barriers blocking the way, and, even if you did possess a ticket, this added to the sense of spaciousness and general freedom of the station. York was the largest station in Britain to permit such access to platforms without barriers.

An inviting-looking pub with a circular bar and more classical columns, the York Tap, lay in a courtyard on one side. This was close to the entrance to the Milner York hotel, an ornate grand dame connected to the station and built at the same time, in 1877, by William Peachey of Middlesbrough station fame, featuring hallways so long jockeys used to jog up and down to lose a few pounds to make their weight for races at the local racecourse. From the front, the hotel looked like a mansion on a country estate.

The sheer scale of York station spoke of a time when trains really mattered, and the best place to think about all of this was bang in the middle, in a former signalman's box with a lovely, old gold-faced clock poking out on one side. Inside was a cosy little Costa Coffee with splendid views across the concourse and to the departures board. Surely one of the best spots for a cappuccino at any British station.

Refreshed, I boarded the 12:20 to Leeds, another TransPennine Express.

This was precisely the same as the one the day before, with yet more adverts for Andy's Man Club and "TRAIN FOR THE FUTURE" job opportunities. The ride was especially smooth, almost floating, as the carriages swept by suburbs, allotments and flat-green countryside before arriving at Leeds via a series of yards piled with rubbish, cranes hanging over building sites, and new apartment blocks.

We crept into Leeds station, which was cramped and busy (and not a touch on the grandeur of York station), though there was little time to hang around. The 12:56 to Keighley soon sped onwards, a Northern train this time, passing a series of old red-brick buildings on the left and the river Aire on the right.

This journey was notable for two young men sitting a row behind.

They were talking about fare-dodging and how best to get away with it.

"If you got on at Shipley, they don't know," said one. By "they" he was referring to conductors. Their "dodge" seemed to be to declare that they had embarked at the most recent station and pay a fare from there rather than where they had really alighted, such as Shipley.

Taking this in, not that I intended to fare-dodge, I watched as high, yellow-brick cooling towers, terraced houses and football fields passed by, and the train stopped at Saltaire station, where a sign said its Victorian model village, a former textile centre, was a World Heritage Site.

At the station, the young men who were discussing fare dodging took an anxious glance around – perhaps for ticket inspectors – and disembarked. We had yet to have our tickets checked. Maybe (probably maybe, judging by their shiftiness) they had got away with it.

Though they would have found themselves in a whole lot of bother if they had continued to Keighley.

At the end of the platform a team of half a dozen inspectors was waiting, blocking the way and looking like a line of players in rugby league (a popular sport up north, as I, a southerner, understood it).

In other words – like they meant business. They carefully inspected my ticket, seemingly hoping I had made some slip and adopting a manner that appeared to suggest that, even though I did have the right ticket, it was a very close call and I might not be so lucky avoiding any fines and whatever penalties they wished to dish out next time. A game of cat and mouse was clearly afoot around the Leeds and Keighley train vicinity. This time, though, the mice had won the day (and got off at Saltaire).

The ticket inspectors let me through… and I turned my mind to my new West Yorkshire destination.

I was visiting Keighley on a double mission based on trains and books.

From another part of Keighley station you could join the short Keighley & Worth Valley Railway, another heritage line, which included a call at Haworth, where you could disembark and visit the quaint village of Haworth and the Brontë Parsonage Museum, where the Brontë sisters – Charlotte (1816–1855), Emily (1818–1848) and Anne (1820–1849) – had lived their short lives and written most of their novels during, and just after, prime "railway mania" years.

This 5-mile line, opened in 1867, had closed in 1962 (the infamous Beeching again) before reopening in 1968, thanks to a local rail preservation society. Aside from the Brontë connection, it was famous for being the location of the popular 1970 film *The Railway Children*, starring Dinah Sheridan, Jenny Agutter and Bernard Cribbins, which was about a family sent to live in the countryside without their father, who has been falsely accused of spying. The children become infatuated by the railway, learning all about the characters at their local station and even averting a disaster after a landslide by using red petticoats to warn a train driver, thus becoming local heroes.

The Keighley & Worth Valley Railway had become a big tourist attraction, though not quite drawing in the same numbers as the North Yorkshire Moors Railway.

Which was how I found myself in Jackie's Café at Keighley station, waiting for a replacement bus to Ingrow West station, as work was being done on the heritage platforms at Keighley; Ingrow West was the next stop along the line. This corner café was not just a normal, run-of-the-mill corner café, however. It was a corner café decorated in railway paraphernalia, including framed pictures of old steam locomotives and model trains, with laminated tablecloths featuring pictures of yet more steam trains, and excellent tea served by Jackie, the proprietor, who wore a baseball cap saying "JACKIE".

Jackie was a chatterbox.

"We bought this fourteen years ago," she said, after delivering the tea. She was referring to the café.

"I've got twenty-three grandkids, you know," she said.

I said I had not known this, though I had seen a child running about by the kitchen.

"I've got one-year-old identical triplets and one set of twins too," Jackie continued. That covered five of the grandchildren. "The triplets were the first naturally conceived triplets in Bradford Royal. No IVF."

Jackie said that she had picked up her train models and the tablecloths from a car boot sale. She had plans for a moving train model circling the café on a shelf attached above head height. "Customers say, *Go on, Jackie, it's really good what you're doing here.*"

Many of these were connected to the Keighley & Worth Valley Railway Preservation Society. "Two times a year they come for train events and they call ahead. We enjoy the banter in the café." She paused and added, "We do SPAM sandwiches here, a proper SPAM sandwich. All home food here."

The preservation society members were apparently partial to SPAM sandwiches (though I did not order one myself).

My favourite station café so far. There was a camaraderie in train love, I was rapidly discovering. Jackie, with all her train bits and bobs, seemed to share it. People who liked old trains tended to be, usually, *very nice people*: gentle, chatty, no particular axes to grind, just getting on with things, happy to indulge in laminated tablecloths depicting old steam locomotives, dreaming of model trains circling on shelves and so forth. Who cared what anyone else thought? There was a refreshing honesty to that.

Not long after, I was on another steam train.

This one chugged along from Ingrow West to Oxenhope, pulled by a maroon locomotive built in 1949 in Crewe. That was as much as I could discern about the loco, other than a number attached to the front: 41241. It did not appear to have a name.

The brief journey covered a hilly landscape with leafless trees and drystone walls. I showed my ticket to a hulking figure of a guard with a large number of locomotive-shaped pins on the lapel of his blazer, a large number of pens sticking out of the pocket of this blazer, a red Keighley & Worth Valley Railway tie and a whistle attached to a ribbon hanging round his neck. This was Paul, who also ran the train's excellent little kiosk-bar, which offered pale ales themed to the railway, produced by Dark Horse Brewery, and bitters made by Timothy Taylor, whose brewery we had passed near Ingrow West.

Paul was a volunteer. He was retired, barrel-chested, gap-toothed, no nonsense, and I was unsure whether to refer to him as a "conductor" or a "guard". Then I noticed one of his pins said "GUARD".

"This is the only train bar in Britain with draft beer," Paul said, before quickly adding, "Well, maybe there may be two others."

He told me the carriages on the train were "1950s, all Mark 1 Corridor Coaches" and that at the railway he acted as "guard, fireman, barman, steward, and I do the Father Christmas each year".

He had been volunteering seven years: "I've always been a train buff. Always steam. After I retired, I needed something to do, so I came here."

He said that the Duke of Kent, the line's patron, regularly came for rides, and that one of the problems he sometimes faced in his job was people taking pictures out of the windows and dropping their phones: "We have to ring the nearest station and they have to retrieve them."

Yet another very nice Train Person.

The journey was not long, nineteen minutes, and we were soon drawing to a halt in Oxenhope station, notable for a proper coal fire burning in its old ticket office, as well as quite a few signs informing that it was 660 feet above sea level.

While the steam locomotive moved from one end of the train to the other for the journey back, I looked around, thinking, *cute little station*. Then we returned to Haworth, where you disembarked and hiked up a hill along a narrow, cobbled lane, with cute little souvenir shops, tearooms, vintage clothes shops, vinyl record shops and inviting-looking pubs, to the Brontë Parsonage Museum, which was in a gaunt, Victorian, stone building beside windswept fields.

Railways, undoubtedly, had a big impact on the lives of the authors of *Jane Eyre*, *Wuthering Heights* and *Agnes Grey*. And how the trio of sisters interacted with the new "iron horses" shed some light on the early days of British trains.

Charlotte, the oldest, was nine when the Stockton and Darlington Railway began and fourteen when the Liverpool and Manchester Railway started. During these impressionable years trains were the "big new thing", and the sisters were soon to hit the tracks themselves. Charlotte took a trip with a friend on the Leeds and Selby Railway in 1837 on a visit to Bridlington, near Hull – travelling through Richmond Hill Tunnel on the way into Leeds, the world's first train tunnel designed to accommodate steam locomotives – while Emily and Anne were to visit York by rail from Leeds on an early tourist excursion to see York Minster.

Not long after, in 1842, the sisters' dissolute brother Branwell, a sometime poet, was to land a job as a clerk at Sowerby Bridge station on the Manchester and Leeds Railway, rising to chief clerk, where he was later dismissed for a discrepancy in the ticketing accounts. No doubt the sisters had heard all sorts of train tales from him, as Branwell, who was possibly, or perhaps not, just unlucky with the accounting error (there was zero tolerance for such mistakes), knew prominent railway engineers and was in the thick of it all.

Meanwhile, in 1842, Charlotte and Emily travelled to Brussels to attend school, taking a train to London from Leeds, then a ship to Belgium, departing along the Thames, followed by a stagecoach. Trains, by then, were opening up continental getaways, with Thomas Cook, the Baptist minister from Leicester – having taken temperance campaigners on an 11-mile day trip from Leicester to Loughborough in 1841 – beginning to branch out into Europe, with trips to the International Exposition in Paris in 1855.

The three literary sisters were also getting involved in railways in another fashion: by acquiring train company shares during the "railway mania" of the 1840s and suffering subsequent losses when the railway investment bubble burst in 1846, with Charlotte writing in a letter to a former teacher "The business is certainly very bad – worse than I thought, and much worse than my father has any idea of. In fact, the little railway property I possessed... scarcely any portion of it can with security be calculated on. When I look at my own case and compare it with that of thousands besides – I scarcely see room for a murmur. Many – very many are – by the late strange Railway System deprived almost of their daily bread."

Almost staggering to think that just 21 years after the Stockton and Darlington Railway's first locomotive transporting eager passengers piled in coal wagons, trains had spread so far and wide so quickly that they had managed to both "boom" and "bust".

Of the three sisters, Charlotte's life was, perhaps, most closely entwined with railways.

She had picked up the name "Eyre" on a train trip to visit a friend in Hathersage, Derbyshire, in 1845; Eyre was a local family in the Peak District. She was later to send the package containing her *Jane Eyre* manuscript – which she had written secretly and not told her father about – by train from Keighley station to a publisher in London in August 1847; it was accepted and printed by October.

Then, almost a year later, in July 1848, she set off on foot in pouring rain with Anne for the four-mile walk to Keighley station to catch a train to Leeds and then another, a night train, from Leeds to London. Arriving at 8 a.m., without having slept, they made their way to her publisher's office to surprise staff that their new star author was female, not male (her book had been published under the androgynous name Currer Bell). She had gone to settle a confusion over her pseudonym and wanted to confront her publisher, George Smith, about it.

This is Charlotte's account of the encounter:

"Is it Mr. Smith?" I said, looking up through my spectacles at a tall young man.
"It is."
I then put his own letter into his hand directed to Currer Bell. He looked at it and then at me again.
"Where did you get this?" he said.
I laughed at his perplexity [and] a recognition took place. I gave my real name: Miss Brontë.

All made possible thanks to (newly invented) trains.

With this story raising a smile 170 years on, I caught the 16:06 for the short ride back to Ingrow West.

The train for this journey was, according to a man with a hat and a whistle at Haworth station, "A DMU Class 144 Pacer from the 1980s. They're railway carriages designed like buses, and they go bump, bump, bump, bump. They stole the design from buses." Apparently, they were bumpy because the carriages were quite rigid, if I had that right, and these DMU Class 144 Pacers were considered "classics", once a regular feature on the railways of West Yorkshire – though, if I were pushed for an opinion, I would have to admit the "41241" was more to my growing taste for all these old trains. I was not shaping up to be a "diesel-head", as some rail enthusiasts are known.

You were either a "diesel-head" or "not a diesel-head", it appeared. You could not force the matter.

Then I took a bus to Keighley station and its skylit ticket hall, which Charlotte Brontë would have known so well – she visited the 1851 Great Exhibition in London by train no fewer than five times. The Great Exhibition had played a key role in bringing railways to the mass public with cut-price fares, many offered by Thomas Cook, and there was fierce competition among rail operators to entice people to the much-heralded show about the wonders of the world (and the Victorian conquest of much of it). Charlotte did not live to see the line that opened to Haworth in 1867, created after a passing Brontë enthusiast, who happened to be a railway engineer with an eye for an opportunity, visited Haworth.

Even back then, the cult of the Brontës was attracting hordes of tourists. Charlotte was to pass away four years after the Great Exhibition, believed to have died of hyperemesis gravidarum, a severe form of morning sickness.

The great writer – and early train user – was aged 38.

Plenty to ponder on the 17:13 from Keighley to Settle.

This was yet another Northern service, with yet more blue-spotted seats.

It left on time and looming landscapes soon rose in fading light beneath leaden skies. Puddles gleamed in the gloom. Shadowy sheep stood motionless in patchwork fields with drystone walls. Darker and darker, and darker still, hills slid by into Settle and one of Britain's best-loved railways.

My immersion in all things train was winding north-west: almost-fights (between passengers and guards), strange locomotive plinths, steam trains across moors, Dr Beeching, old station gates loved by old poets, fare-dodgers, more steam trains, literary connections, railway mania, rattling lines down darkening dales… I could feel the world of trains engulfing me.

It was a pleasant sensation. Just letting it happen. Just sitting back and enjoying the ride.

CHAPTER THREE

SETTLE TO MANCHESTER VIA CARLISLE, RAVENGLASS, GRANGE-OVER-SANDS AND LIVERPOOL

"DISRUPTING THE ESTABLISHED ORDER"

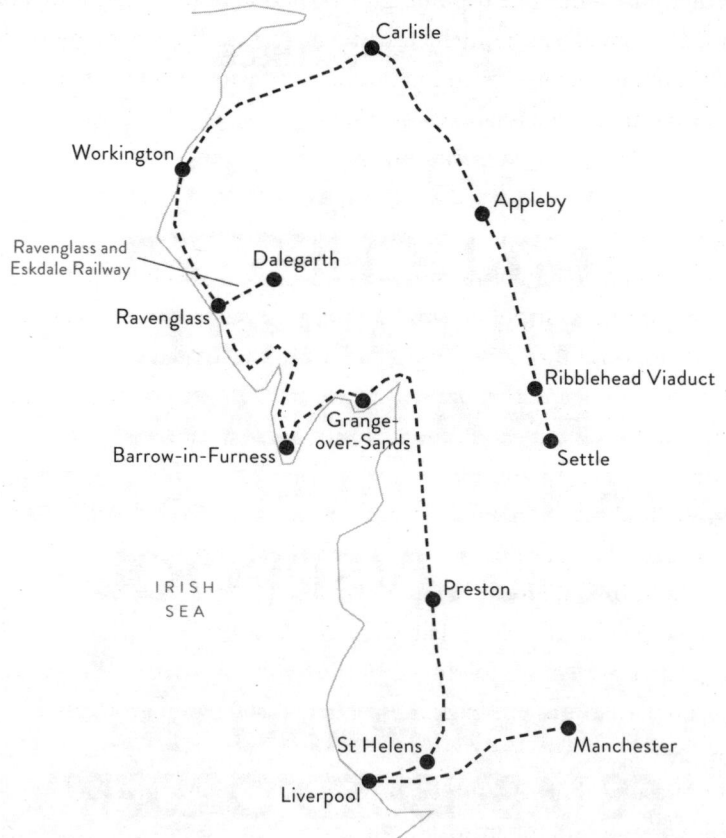

When the Brontës lost out after the bubble burst on railway mania back in 1846, you might have thought that was that as far as fevered speculation in the early days of trains was concerned. But it was not to be.

Another period of railway-building madness was to follow, and another bust – this one beginning in 1866 due to the collapse of a bank named Overend Gurney, which had lent cash to finance many projects in Britain and further afield in Canada and Spain, where borrowers had subsequently proved unable to maintain payments. The result was a scare in the City and a crash of Britain's financial system. Trains had brought the country to its knees, and another prominent nineteenth-century writer, Charles Dickens, damningly pointed his finger at "a muddle of railways in all directions possible and impossible, with no general public scheme, no general public supervision, enormous waste of money, no fixable responsibility".

The economy and the main rail companies were to bounce back soon enough. However, it was in the middle of this devastating fallout, during which many went bankrupt, that those behind the proposed Settle and Carlisle Railway wondered if they had made the wisest of decisions. The costly 73-mile line across rugged moorland had been given the green light in Parliament before the crash. The project, which had been championed by the financially buoyant Midland Railway Company, would cost a fortune. Its directors approached Parliament once more, this time attempting to back out, but politicians refused to allow them to do so.

The result, after six and a half years and the employment of 6,000 hard-working, often hard-drinking navvies (or "navigators", many from Ireland), was a new railway linking England with Scotland to rival the West Coast and East Coast Main Lines. It opened to passengers in 1876. The cost? A phenomenal £3.6 million – the equivalent of £530 million today and double the original budget, covering the cost of 14 tunnels and 22 viaducts, including the much-photographed, 24-arch Ribblehead Viaduct.

Thank goodness the politicians back in the 1860s stuck to their guns. Thank goodness also that when it was deemed an uneconomical line by Dr Beeching (him again) in 1963, a rearguard action began and – although many stops along the remote line across some of England's wildest terrain serving a series of pleasant small towns and villages were cut, and British Rail, in the early 1980s, announced that it would drop the line altogether – campaigners stopped the rot on the back of a wave of public support. The closed stations were reopened and, in 1989, the railway was officially declared saved.

Viaducts, navvies and Michael Portillo
Settle to Carlisle

So it was with high expectations of the journey ahead the next day that I checked into a pub named the Royal Oak, by a fine, old market square, having strolled down a hill from the station in Settle.

The Royal Oak was just about deserted: a couple of regulars at a long bar in a big, otherwise empty lounge with a pool table and colourful old railway posters on the walls. These were great and one near the stairs caught my eye. It depicted clouds hanging above moorland and farmland, casting long shadows, while a farmer on a red tractor nattered to someone in a lane by a barn. The message below said, "YORKSHIRE. SEE BRITAIN BY TRAIN." It had been issued by British Railways, so it must have been sometime after British Railways came into being as a nationalized body on 1 January 1948, but before its name was shortened to British Rail in early 1965 for corporate brand marketing purposes (when the double-arrow logo was adopted). There was no date on the poster, but the artist was Gyrth Russell, and a later check revealed it was from 1954 and a painting of Upper Wharfedale in the Yorkshire Dales. The poster stood out among the many others on the old wood-panel walls for its honesty; although sunny in the foreground, where geese gathered in a paddock near the farmer, clouds up above suggested it might bucket down at any moment. Come to Yorkshire and see Britain by train… but you might get wet.

The Royal Oak was an unusual place. I asked the barmaid/receptionist when check-out was, and she replied, "Twelve or it could be three. I'm not sure."

I asked if any food was being served.

"Not here. You could try the Talbot," she said, with an air of *what would be the point of offering food here when there's no one here?*

So I went to the Talbot Arms on the other side of the square, ate a chicken curry near a blazing fire and got chatting to a secondary school PE teacher from Manchester, who was on a two-day getaway in his campervan with his springer spaniel: a regular outing for him. He had blond hair and was in his late twenties, from Halifax.

"It would be interesting to know what it would be like here without trains," he said, assuming a teacherly manner. "Trains powered the industrial revolution. At Ribblehead you can still see remnants of the houses of the workers [the navvies]. The trains here connected to Halifax and Bradford. West Yorkshire cloth got its wool from here."

He asked me about my trip. Then he told me about his career plans. He was thinking of becoming a landlord: "I want to get into property, Airbnb and all that. A terraced cottage is £180,000, or it's £400,000 to £500,000 for a three-bed detached. So it's not cheap."

"Why the switch?"

Work as teacher was not easy, he replied.

"In what way?"

"Behaviour," he replied. "It's all down to parenting. I think in society, marriage rates are declining and divorce rates are going up, and kids' behaviour is getting worse because of that. I spend more time trying to sort out issues at home… neglect, a lot of issues that kids are not ready to talk about. Men up here, it's just control-alt-delete." Lads at his school would not easily open up. "When I speak to colleagues who've been working there twenty years, they've taught the parents of these kids. It's cyclical behaviour – mental health issues, substance abuse." His school was in north Manchester. "I think it's in the bottom five per cent of the country. But ideas of 'success' in those rankings are considerably different to ours. Where we are, it's to get a job, to work in a factory, not to live on benefits."

He told me he was considering writing a book entitled *What's Happened to Our Kids?* "If something happens on social media, we have to deal with it… bullying and sexual exploitation. It's hard to police. We don't really know what's going on; nor do the parents."

We shook hands. He told me he was going for a long walk the next day and that what drew him to the Dales was its isolation. I said that it seemed pleasantly more relaxed in Settle than back home in London and he replied, "London is so busy, everyone's in a rush, a hurry." He paused, looking a little horrified by the thought of London. "I can't stand it," he said – and looked like he really meant it. I never did get his name.

Breakfast was not on offer at the Royal Oak. Nothing was on offer – not even someone to take the key. The big bar with the wood panels and the railway posters was completely empty, so I let myself out, traversed the square and stopped for breakfast at the Golden Lion, where a map of the route of the Settle and Carlisle Railway (known by many as the "S&C") hung above the bar, and I had another chat, this time with Joan, a local.

She was at the next table, in her early eighties and had time to talk. One of the joys of the S&C, without even taking a train, was clearly the small, close-knit communities along the way (the population of Settle was 2,700).

"I'm a farmer's daughter and wife," she said. "And my son's farming sixty acres and does odd jobs… shed building."

She wanted to tell me about milk production. "We'll be importing a lot of milk before too long," she said. "A pint of milk costs the same as a pint of beer. It's absolute madness. When you think what's gone into making that. The price of milk is far too low. We got rid of the Milk Marketing Board. Everything was standardized then and we thought it was excellent. But then some politicians thought there was no competition." Adding competition, she said, had caused havoc with milk production.

Joan also wanted to tell me all about government tree-planting initiatives. "I just think we're going too far with tree planting," she said. "Really good farming land is being used. We're gonna run out of food eventually. All this farmland is going to environmental concerns. People think that if land is just left it will be lovely, but it won't be. It will be a mess. It will be awful. I saw it after foot and mouth [the 2001 outbreak of the livestock disease]. I saw what it was like. A farmer maintains the countryside, keeps it in order."

Her family had owned land around Settle since 1938. "After the war, farmers were pushed to be as intense as possible, intense farming. Now it's the opposite."

I thanked Joan for this insider briefing on the landscape through which the S&C would be heading and strolled to the station.

Settle station comprised quaint-looking, little, grey-stone structures with gables on platforms facing two dead-straight tracks. The doorways and the windows by the ticket hall and the shop were painted maroon. The shop sold an enormous number of old books about the S&C, including *Over the Summit: How Britain's Railways Crossed the High Hills* by Christopher Awdry, *Settle & Carlisle Revival: The Line That Refused to Die* by Brian Sharpe and *Settle to Carlisle: A Pictorial Guide to the Most Dramatic Train Journey in England* by Anthony Lambert. Each was second-hand and the titles alone offered a flavour of what was to come, as well as of a seeming train cult surrounding the legendary S&C.

An assistant at the shop, which was run by the Friends of the Settle–Carlisle Line, a charity that maintains stations, said, "In here, the wife says to her husband, 'Don't buy any,' and then he'll get three. That's the enthusiast. They can't resist."

The 10:21 Northern train arrived and the crowd milling on the platform boarded. Through the carriage window you watched as rolling countryside spread out into the distance, with the odd patch of snow on the hills. Rows of long stone walls lined fields, looking like fences at a

National Hunt race. Solitary, low, leaden clouds hurtled below a canopy of higher milky-grey clouds. The countryside had an emerald gloom, with streaks of copper and lilac. It was both beautiful and bleak.

After a quarter of an hour, the train pulled into Ribblehead, where a handful of S&C enthusiasts shuffled onto Blea Moor Common to inspect the Ribblehead Viaduct from an angle where you could take pictures of its two dozen arches, which soared 32 metres above the damp mud-and-clay moor. Piers for the viaduct were sunk eight metres into this impractical turf. All the guides told you this. They also advised you to look out for the few stone remains of the old navvies' abodes, as the PE teacher at the Talbot Arms had mentioned. These were to the east of the line. This seemed a suitable spot to pause for a moment to pay homage to these workers, many of whom died during the construction of the line, some from disease spreading in their makeshift camps. There was no official death toll, but the many unmarked graves at local parish churches suggested the figure was high; perhaps more than three deaths per mile of track. Maybe many more. A hundred died building the viaduct alone. This had been one of the most difficult railways to construct in Britain and hardly surprising that the Midland Railway Company had attempted to back out once they had surveyed the hostile land and realized what they had got themselves into.

A train rattled above on the way to Leeds, the sound echoing across the almost eerily empty landscape.

Yet, as desolate as the setting was, and despite the torrid history, this was, quite frankly, wonderful to watch. How could anyone not enjoy the sight? The carriages slipping across the arches steadily and sublimely defying the landscape. *Humankind conquering nature... the triumph of progress... good old Victorian grit* – you might be thinking. Or simply, *isn't that quite a strange and marvellous thing.*

Afterwards, I ventured into the Station Inn. Inside, Elton John and Beatles songs were playing, and a huge fire roared in a corner; the type of fireplace you dream of in a pub in the British winter. "It's beautiful. It's absolutely beautiful," some Americans, whom I had spotted on the train earlier, were saying to one another, almost transfixed as they gazed out of a window across the scenery. They had got that right. The S&C and the Yorkshire Dales had cast its spell, just as it had, already, with me.

Ribblehead station was delightfully isolated and in the same architectural style as the one at Settle. I boarded the 12:07 and it rolled away across the viaduct, with a conductor explaining that the whale-shaped mountain to the left was Ingleborough and behind us to the right, though we could not see much of it, was Pen-y-ghent, two famous peaks. Never mind the bicentenary of British trains, it was the twentieth anniversary of the installation of trolley services on the S&C, the conductor said over a public announcement. She also explained we were about to begin "what is known as the Long Drag, 600 feet up to Dent, the highest main-line working station in England at 1,150 feet".

The commentary stopped and the conductor, Sue, who used to work as a representative for Thomas Cook and who lived in Langwathby further down the line, paused for a while as she served tea. Her father had worked as a signalman on the railway, and both he and Sue were full of praise for Michael Portillo, the railway broadcaster famous for his colourful clashing trousers and blazers, his easy manner and his previous political roles as the country's former Chief Secretary to the Treasury, Secretary of State for Employment and Secretary of State for Defence – all during governments run by the Conservative Party, where he was at one time a serious contender for leader and, potentially, the top job of all: PM.

A through-and-through Train Nut might well have run Britain.

This had been a tantalizing almost-moment in the recent history of British trains: a fellow wearing pink and lime-green blazers, with a copy of one of George Bradshaw's nineteenth-century railway guides tucked in his ministerial box, calling all the shots.

The ramifications, looking back, were mind-boggling.

Anyway, from lesser political heights, Portillo had campaigned to support the S&C railway during its touch-and-go days. "Michael Portillo

– it was his campaign that saved it in the 1980s," Sue said. "Michael Portillo saved my dad's job. He loves Michael Portillo. We wish he'd come back."

Then Sue told me that she did miss some of the perks of her former Thomas Cook job, which had taken her to the Maldives, Greece and Switzerland, but she liked it "just as much on the train. It's special to me". I commented that it was a peaceful ride and she replied, "Today, yes. Not on a Saturday when supporters are going to watch Leeds and Carlisle. It's not peaceful then."

The train entered a long tunnel.

Afterwards, the line continued steadily upwards. Streaks of snow marked the slopes above, looking like spilled milk on the hills. Enclosures of land were divided by drystone walls, and long, rocky, grey ridges emerged along with damp-ruined stone buildings, streams with reeds, and occasional cliffs at the end of ridges, giving the terrain a sharp geometrical aspect. Sunlight broke through, issuing precise beams, illuminating little patches of momentarily "blessed" terrain. From time to time, gorges appeared with narrow chutes of waterfalls and tumbling scree. What splendid, dramatic landscape Britain's trains could take you to quite quickly, if you let them. Awe-inspiring, even.

The train stopped at Dent, another quaint little station, this one distinguished by its altitude (England's highest main-line station at 350 metres), followed by Appleby, where I got off and went down the hill to inspect the squat pink-and-grey-stone St Lawrence's Parish Church, a couple of antique shops and the gently trickling river Eden from its stone bridge. Appleby was famous for its annual horse fair in June, when thousands of Romani people descend with horse trading, music and traditional storytelling. That would be later in the year. There was no hint of those wild days to come; it was sleepy, verging on fast asleep. I entered the Crown and Cushion pub, next door to St Lawrence's, where I drank a pint of lime and soda (£2.10) at a window table, with hardly any other customers about, and read a railway-related article in *The Cumberland News* about Aspatria station in Cumbria and how Northern trains were pronouncing it incorrectly in their recorded onboard announcements, saying, "As-spat-tria" instead of "As-spay-tria". This was a disgrace, said locals, and "after criticism from passengers for the errors, the operator had attempted to correct the mispronunciations of place names across the region, yet it is unclear how many changes have been implemented as of yet".

The controversy, apparently, rumbled on.

I made my way back up the hill to the station, where there was a little station shop.

This was run by Janet and, like the one at Settle station, was full of many a heavyweight train tome about the S&C and elsewhere – as in, literally, heavy. Everywhere you looked, heavyweight train tomes rested on shelves, looking as though they contained a great deal of "train knowledge". There were blockbusters such as *The World's Greatest Railways* by Christopher Chant, *North East Steam 1948–1968* by Peter Tuffrey and *250 Years of Steam* by Alan Bloom (covering steam engines from even before the Stockton and Darlington Railway, it would seem, but not engines going down tracks pulling passengers, presumably). Then you had venerable titles entirely devoted to locomotives, such as *The Power of Steam, Steam for Pleasure, Classic Steam, A Passion for Steam* and – simply – *Steam*. Writing about old locos in books with "Steam" in the titles appeared to have been extremely popular over the years, though most seemed from a while back judging by the faded covers; they were all second-hand. I looked at these books, there were dozens of them, and something came over me: a combination of genuine interest, amusement (how could there be so many of them?) and a feeling of panic; *what if one of these books is the must-have train book, the book that will provide entry to the secret "world of trains" previously locked away, hidden to the outsider, just waiting in black-and-white and available for a couple of pounds* (none of them was particularly expensive)? What if I did not buy this book? Would the secret world be forever lost to me within the dusty jackets of a large hardback from 1973 in the Appleby station shop?

What was I to do? The answer was, perhaps, inevitable. I bought several heavy railway tomes from Janet, who had been watching me and – I sensed – waiting for this "breaking moment" in the full knowledge of what was about to happen. I took them to the platform in a second-hand plastic bag, planning to squeeze them into my backpack on the train.

One of my new acquisitions was *The Complete Great British Railway Journeys*, an offshoot of the BBC television series by Michael Portillo. It was a good one, based on nine journeys that had formed the framework for his TV shows. On the platform I opened the pages and read the introduction in which the S&C's saviour commented that the speed of societal change after the early Stephenson railways of 1825 and 1830 was "difficult even for us to grasp, because although the mobile phone and computer have led to a revolution over the past 20 years [he was writing in 2010], modern-day Britain doesn't undergo physical change as fast as Victorian Britain did". By 1850 there were 6,000 miles of tracks in Britain "reaching all but the remotest parts of the country" (including the Yorkshire Dales). "We would have to visit modern Shanghai, perhaps, to gain any understanding of the speed of change and the scale of the undertaking [of the Victorians]."

In no place do you feel this more strongly than on the S&C, where communities would have been cut off without the railway.

The 15:16 swept across the flatter countryside of the Eden Valley and onwards, entering an urban zone with warehouses protected by fences topped with curls of barbed wire. This was Carlisle. The train arrived at 3.58 p.m. in a long, rectangular Gothic station, or Carlisle Citadel station as it was known when it was constructed in 1847 by another renowned Victorian architect, Sir William Tite, who aped the style of the Tudor citadel next to the tracks and laid claim that he was "the first man who attempted to make a Gothic railway station".

From this Gothic station I found my place for the night, the County Hotel, opposite a bar/club called the House of Vodka, asking at reception whether it had a pool and being told in a dry, seemingly amused manner by the receptionist, "Er... no, sir."

I had not really expected it would... but no harm in asking.

My room was extremely warm, verging on a sauna. I left my heavily weighed-down rucksack – bulging with newly acquired, dusty, old train books – in this extremely warm room and went to have a look at Carlisle's imposing, old red-stone castle, which was closed. Outside the castle, on its steps, I listened to and watched a succession of police cars tear by as though some major crime was afoot. And then I ate dinner at a large Wetherspoons pub named The William Rufus after the son of William the Conqueror, who had entered Carlisle through a nearby city gate and restored the city to the English in 1092, a long time before railways.

The border with Scotland was eight miles to the north, and I wondered whether Paul and David from the Locomotion museum had been to this Wetherspoons. Probably. It was, I had to concede, excellent value with a promo curry night, fast service and decent katsu chicken and rice. You couldn't knock it, whatever your preconceptions may have been of a mass-market pub chain nicknamed "Spoons".

Amid gallivanting Carlislians ordering small green drinks, lagers and large glasses of white wine, I read *John Betjeman on Trains* by Jonathan Glancey, quite contentedly.

It was good to mug up on train stuff between all the train rides.

"For the cump-peny"
Carlisle to Grange-over-Sands via Ravenglass

Down by platforms one and two at Carlisle station there are two benches. On those benches sat Mike, John, Stuart and Brian. They ranged in age from 73 to 77. They were old mates. They wore flat caps or woolly hats, jeans or chinos, trainers or laced-up shoes, glasses or no glasses, sturdy jackets with or without fur hoods – looking like no-nonsense chaps who would not mind stopping for a few in The William Rufus every now and then. Their benches were beneath a sign that said "TAKE LIFE EASY: The Cumbrian Coast Line takes you to the edge of the sea through historic and scenic places." They were taking the first three words to heart, leaning back and exchanging chitter-chatter. They were trainspotters, very casual but matter-of-fact trainspotters.

When I met them, Mike was saying to Brian, Stuart and John, "That 776-775, it's a disgrace. The loco at one end was black. They can't have cleaned it for six months. Dirt. Caked in it."

I said he seemed impassioned on the subject, although I had no idea which train he was talking about (but did not let on). I was standing nearby, waiting for a ride to Ravenglass, a few stops along the Cumbrian Coast Line. I somehow sensed that they would not mind me joining their talk.

They did not.

"Well," said Mike. "All the other companies have cleaned their locos. Those GBRf locos appear to be completely caked in muck, unlike other companies."

GBRf, I had to ask them, stood for GB Railfreight.

I enquired whether they knew a lot about trains.

"We're not experts. We're not anything," said Mike. He stopped short and looked up.

Some trains were moving down the line.

"Seems to be the 66129. Or was that OM73?" asked Mike of the others, or something along those lines.

"I don't know," said John, as though he was not particularly bothered. Their interest in trains was not obsessive, more a case of watching the world pass by with some friends: habit, not hopeless addiction.

John was a retired lathe machine worker from Workington, aged 77. What did he like about trains? "Well, I've followed them all my life in Carlisle. Followed them since a boy. Since 1956 I've been coming here."

An unusual train went by. "That cleans the leaves and that off the track," he said, catching my gaze.

"Locos on each end. Rail Head Treatment Trains. RHTT for short," said Mike, who was 73, though I did not get his former occupation.

Stuart was a retired fitter, aged 77. "We come here for the cump-peny," he said: the company. "It's a day out. If not here today, I'd have gone to Nuneaton," said John. "But I do come here every Wednesday unless it's freezing or snow."

So he could meet his old friends. Trainspotting was a social pursuit, down by platforms one and two of Carlisle station.

What was his favourite type of train? "DMU," he replied, quick as a shot. I've been doing this twenty, thirty years. It's alright." He explained that Nuneaton was popular, "Cos you get a lot of freight. That's what we're interested in, the wagons. It's a main run from Felixstowe to Birmingham, Crewe, Manchester, Liverpool."

Were they trainspotters? "Oh yeah, we're trainspotters," John replied. Any harm in calling them that? "Oh no, none at all."

I asked because trainspotters, with so many "anorak" and "Norman no mates" associations often seemed to be the butt of jokes. The classic, with variations, perhaps being *How many trainspotters does it take to change a lightbulb? Three – one to change it, one to write down the serial number and one to bring the anoraks and the flask of tea.*

Some, on online forums, had expressed anger at this typecasting. One annoyed rail enthusiast – this was the less-loaded terminology (although I was finding Train Nut more to my own taste and plunging condition) – had said, "Such 'jokes' are nothing but adult bullying. They are no better than what nine-year-olds say in the playground. They reflect on the pathetic nature of the individual saying them, not the target. They are truly pathetic – they are not even original."

To which a reply had come: "Everyone can have a joke about whatever they want as far as I'm concerned."

To which the annoyed enthusiast had replied, "So council house jokes are OK?"

To which the respondent had said, "Give it ya best shot."

So ended the correspondence.

Personally, I had always wondered about all the fuss with "anoraks". I looked up the definition in my *Collins English Dictionary*, and this is what it gave: "a warm waterproof hip-length jacket usually with a hood, originally worn in polar regions, but now worn for any outdoor activity". Didn't just about everyone, by this description, wear an anorak from time to time? Didn't just about everyone drink tea of some description? And, for that matter, didn't most people, secretly at least, have a soft spot for trains? Weren't most of us, therefore, trainspotting anoraks these days? Train Nuts one and all?

Mike, John, Stuart and Brian moved on to the subject of the Royal Train.

There was such a thing, as Clive back in Shildon had mentioned. Queen Victoria, being regent during the railway boom (first taking a train ride from Slough to Paddington in 1942), had naturally started it all off. In a Royal Train Shed at Wolverton Works in Buckinghamshire, a few luxurious carriages painted "royal claret", a dark burgundy colour, were stored, with bedrooms, bathrooms (including a bathtub in one) and a dining carriage for King Charles III to use when the fancy took him.

"I've seen it many times," said Mike. "They hide the fact that it's really there. But a couple of times it's even stopped here. The curtains are drawn and you think *they're up to something*." What he thought the royals might be up to, he did not say.

Were they sure? Was Queen Elizabeth II, monarch at the time to which they were referring, really stuck on a train – albeit a royal train – at Carlisle station?

"Well, the police were here," said Brian, aged 77. It did seem unlikely that an unoccupied royal train would come by with police protection.

Brian changed tack and began to talk about some of the best places for trainspotting, which he believed were in Nuneaton in Warwickshire, Peterborough in Cambridgeshire, Doncaster in South Yorkshire, Westerfield in Suffolk, and Tamworth in Staffordshire ("if you count freight").

SETTLE TO MANCHESTER

"If you didn't go trainspotting, what would you do?" I asked the group.

Mike replied on their behalf: "Stay at home."

Which more than justified the clearly social (for them) hobby.

A spotless, gleaming Avanti West Coast train whizzed by. "Pendolino," said Mike. A Pendolino was an Italian-made, high-speed tilting train. This one, unlike the earlier 776-775, met his approval: "Pendolino going to Edinburgh. Must have been cleaned overnight."

He looked on with a nod of satisfaction as it disappeared in the direction of Scotland.

With that we said our goodbyes and I boarded the 09:02 to Ravenglass.

This Northern service rattled across countryside, passing Wigton and controversial "As-spay-tria" to Maryport on the coast. It was a wet, dreary day with heavy, grey clouds. A few information panels on the windswept platform at Maryport offered details about Roman interest in the town; in 122 CE legionnaires had established a supply fort for Hadrian's Wall, which comes to its western end 24 miles to the north-east, at Bowness-on-Solway. Remains of the fort could be visited, apparently.

No one boarded. The 09:02 moved on, coming to the Irish Sea, hugging the coastline and traversing mud-sand flats, with the sea on the horizon a slip of slate grey obscured by a murky mist. Creating an even grimmer perspective, the carriage windows were streaked with dirt. Mike would have had a few things to say about that. It seemed probable, however, that the view was wonderful on a clear day (with a clean train).

Not long after, the train stopped again at Workington, once an iron and steel hub, where railway tracks were formerly produced. Workington's Moss Bay Iron and Steel Works was a major concern and a big local employer, producing tracks, fishplates, sleepers and clips for railways from the 1870s until it closed in 2006, plunging the local area into deeper economic decline (steel had stopped being made in the area in the early 1980s and production had been moved to a plant in Teesside and elsewhere).

The reason given for the shutdown and loss of 250 jobs was, with bitter irony, that the steelworks needed to produce 108-metre tracks, which had become the industry standard, but this was nigh on impossible as the factory site was crammed between the sea and the railway along the coast. A work operations manager at the time had said, "Basically, the site is in the wrong direction. It goes from the sea to the rail tracks, and it needs to be the other way round to make one-hundred-and-eight-metre rails." At least that was what Corus officially said at the time, announcing that production would be moved to Scunthorpe in Lincolnshire. Some locals, however, believed that track manufacturing would go abroad to cheaper factories, and there was evidence this happened, at least to some degree.

The job losses led to even more local "unemployment blackspot" headlines and great sadness at the demise of a proud local industry. Tracks from the works had been considered the best in class worldwide, benefitting from cutting-edge innovations over the years, including many initially introduced by yet another prominent Victorian engineer, Henry Bessemer, who had made Workington internationally famous, with millions of his rails sent around the world. As early as the 1880s, orders were being taken from as far afield as Alabama and Texas. A statue of Bessemer lurked somewhere by the station.

Trains, it was easy to forget, were not just facilitators of industrialization; the very making of them was industrialization in itself – all part of the mind-blowing "speed of change and scale of undertaking" that took place after the first locomotive began chugging down Britain's railways to which Portillo referred.

The 09:02 rolled on, passing a New Balance trainers factory (evidence of modern local production of a difference kind: trainers not train lines) and a cluster of wind turbines. A man had staggered into the carriage at Workington, clutching a can of Stella lager, and begun muttering loudly and occasionally singing to himself. I wondered if he was a former rail-track maker but did not ask. Beachcombers were out in the dreary weather near Harrington, where you might on a much better day see the outline of the Isle of Man.

Another man, not drinking Stella lager, sitting at my table said dreamily, looking out into the mist, "I don't know anywhere else in the UK where the line goes so far along the shore for so long."

Then we came to Whitehaven. Then St Bees, Nethertown and Sellafield, where somewhere in the haze beyond curls of barbed wire was a nuclear power plant in a state of being decommissioned.

The passenger opposite me told me that he was travelling on a £1 ticket. He had, he said, downloaded apps for Northern, ScotRail and Avanti West Coast: "If you get their apps on your phone, you're automatically informed in advance of any special train offers."

He tapped his nose in a canny manner and advised never to buy tickets from a well-known, online train ticket agency as there were fees. I had been buying my tickets from this well-known, online agency, which I found extremely convenient and the fees so small I did not mind. That said, I was not travelling on a £1 ticket like my neighbour.

Further down the carriage, the man with the can of Stella had begun talking incomprehensibly to himself and laughing as though having imparted particularly funny jokes. He was only in his sixties but seemed in a terrible way. A sad sight. Something, whatever it was, had clearly gone badly wrong for him.

The Cumbrian Coast Line was an unusual stretch of railway, with the beauty of the coastline and the "unemployment blackspot" stories too.

At Ravenglass station I disembarked and walked across a car park, leaving the Cumbrian Coast Line behind and joining another Ravenglass station, this one for trains on the Ravenglass and Eskdale Railway, which ran on narrow-gauge (15-inch wide) tracks. Main-line train tracks were, of course, precisely 4 feet 8½ inches wide, the "standard gauge" chosen by George Stephenson himself and adopted in most places round the world.

Every good rail enthusiast knew that.

The effect of seeing the smaller carriages and the smaller locomotive on the smaller tracks by a smaller platform made you feel as though the whole world had suddenly shrunk, but in a nice way.

Everything was nice about the Ravenglass and Eskdale Railway.

By the platform were nice old railway company posters declaring, "FROM THE CUMBRIAN COAST TO ENGLAND'S HIGHEST HILLS... VISIT THE HIGHEST MOUNTAIN, THE DEEPEST LAKE AND ALMOST THE SMALLEST CHURCH IN ENGLAND – BY THE SMALLEST RAILWAY IN THE WORLD... A JOURNEY THROUGH THE BREATHTAKING SCENERY OF WEST CUMBRIA." I was not sure what the "almost smallest church" was all about, though I had no doubt it was a very nice one.

Nearby, a very nice indeed, if not absolutely gorgeous, little locomotive was puffing away quietly. It was named *River Mite* and painted wine-red with black stripes. Beside the platform was a nice, cosy tearoom where I had a nice cup of tea. Then I boarded a nice, comfortable carriage, and nice, wintry Cumbrian countryside soon passed by, with steam from the engine nicely falling in a silky white trail to the side of the nicely bouncing and swaying carriages before evaporating nicely in miniclouds by clumps of nice russet-coloured bracken, silver birch trees, rhododendrons and nicely tumbling granite boulders.

In my compartment was Sid Edwards, a long-time volunteer for the line, which twisted for seven miles to the tiny settlement of Dalegarth. Opened in 1875, the Ravenglass and Eskdale Railway was first used to transport iron ore to the coast before becoming a heritage line in the 1960s after enthusiasts formed the Ravenglass and Eskdale Railway Preservation Society – nothing to do with Dr Beeching that time. The line, nicknamed locally La'al Ratty, had simply ceased to be needed for transporting both iron ore and granite from a quarry for supply and demand reasons. All of this I learned from Sid, who had a neat moustache, hunched shoulders, a softly spoken military manner and was in his early seventies. Living up to the tag "rail enthusiast", he was extremely enthusiastic about La'al Ratty and talked for some time about the ins and outs of its operations.

Sid had a mischievous streak. He told me about how "we used to have boozer specials. I don't think head office knew, though the stationmaster knew." The Ravenglass and Eskdale Railway was also "the only train in Britain that ran on millennium night," he said. This had been put on for staff and friends, with Sid one of the organisers. A locomotive had been fired up for a quick return ride up to Dalegarth, with "time for two pints and some fireworks". What a way to see in the new millennium… if you were into steam trains.

A very nice chap, Sid.

Watching the scenery unfold was a treat on the Ravenglass and Eskdale Railway.

Ridges were rising on mountains, and flashes of bright-yellow gorse lit up the gloom of the day in a beautiful way that was somehow comforting and uplifting in equal measure. Brambles cascaded over old stone walls. Tall indigo reeds rose by a stream. Sheep close to the tracks hopped away. Others huddled beneath the shelter of trees, standing dead still with their heads facing downwards but not bothering to eat. They looked depressed but were probably just thinking *what a dreadful day* – or, more likely, nothing at all. Bales of hay were wrapped in black plastic sheeting near a farmhouse. A solitary heron in a field appeared to be taking a rest from fishing on the Mite river. And all the time the train rose steadily, finally coming to a halt at Dalegarth station, where on a better day you had a view of Scafell Pike, England's highest mountain at 978 metres. From Ravenglass, close to sea level, the ascent to Dalegarth was 64 metres (so still quite a way to go).

There was a nice, cosy tearoom at Dalegarth station too, where I had a nice up of tea once again and a nice chat with a nice drone-photographer who specialized in train pictures.

His name was Tim. He was wearing a peaked flat cap similar to the ones favoured by former Labour Party leader Jeremy Corbyn and had a similar grey beard, although that was where the similarities ended. Tim was not interested in establishing socialism in Britain. Tim was interested in drones and trains.

"A lot will depend on the weather," he said, referring to his ability to take drone pictures that day. "It was appalling yesterday. Rain is an absolute no-no for the drone. It will bring it down. There are very fine micro-electronics. The latest ones are incredibly sophisticated. Sub-two hundred and fifty grams, you are still bound by the drone code. Anything bigger, then you can't fly over people. Can buy them dirt cheap, one thousand one hundred pounds with spare batteries. I got mine two and a quarter years ago. Following a train can be surprisingly difficult four hundred feet above the ground. There are people in the States flying them at eleven and a half thousand feet, but if authorities find you doing that here, you really will be in trouble. They're selling very well."

Tim had opinions about food offerings at British stations. He happened to be from near Darlington. "At Darlington station, when I was a boy, you could get a freshly cooked meal round the clock, not a pre-packed sandwich during office hours only."

Standards, he said, had slipped.

Tim had opinions about the announcement to cancel HS2 between Birmingham and Manchester: "We have a long history of grand plans that never come to fruition. Look at the Channel Tunnel and how long that took."

While he sat there, we did just that, there and then – using my smartphone.

The Channel Tunnel had taken six years to construct before opening in 1994, though a Channel railway tunnel had first been mooted as far back as 1839 (a mere 14 years after the Stockton and Darlington Railway opened). Some digging on an early attempt at a tunnel, we learned, had begun in the 1880s. Meanwhile, Winston Churchill, no less, had written an article for the *Daily Mail* in 1936 beneath the headline "WHY NOT A CHANNEL TUNNEL?"

Standards in railway planning, Tim believed, had always been pretty low.

Tim had opinions on women train drivers: "They would be unthinkable when I was a boy. People would have said, *don't be silly, that's man's work.*"

Standards in this area were improving, he thought, with more equality.

Tim, unsurprisingly, also had opinions about handling drones in bad weather as well as weather reports: "If you believe in weathermen, you probably believe in Santa Claus and the tooth fairy."

So far as weathermen were concerned, Tim said, standards were abysmal and far from improving or ever being likely to improve.

Back down the line and onwards to Barrow-in-Furness from Ravenglass (after an inexplicably cancelled train and a half-hour wait) the tracks wound along the coast. We crossed hazy marshland. We slid by remote farms. We skirted dunes. Then after Barrow-in-Furness, and a tight connection onto a new Northern train, the tracks wound eastwards to Grange-over-Sands.

It was on board this train, the 16:51 (eventual destination Manchester Airport) that I met, or at least listened to, The Crisp Eater.

Crisp Eaters on trains had long been an "issue" – or pet hate, gripe, neurosis, call it what you will – with me.

It was maybe the case that I should, sometime ago, have learned to get over this; perhaps developed a "coping technique" and "moved on". However, I had not done so. I had not moved on. On trains, I was at the mercy, at any moment, of The Crisp Eater.

It began, as it always began, with the telltale rustle – the crinkly, crackly, crinkle-crackle – of the opening of a crisp packet. Soon after (I was waiting for it) emanated "crisp": the pungent, chemical tang, perhaps-bacon, perhaps-beef, perhaps-chicken, perhaps-pork, perhaps-anything, barbecued, charred, salty, herby, aromatic and sweet, mysteriously sweet. A sub-wave of tangy, salty sweetness previously enclosed within sealed plastic yet released by The Crisp Eater into the confines of the 16:51. Confines I shared. A small fury of rustles. A slow crunch. Licking sounds. Crunches. Salivating noises. A brief pause. Silence. Then again: crunch, lick, crunch, crunch, crunch, salivation, pause... crunch, lick, crunch, crunch, salivation, pause. Repeat, repeat, repeat. Slowly the packet was consumed while outside, Irish Sea and southern Cumbrian fields came and went in a green and grey, grimy-windowed gloom.

Some might regard me as being over fussy about The Crisp Eater. He was a man, possibly in his thirties, with a pasty complexion and a large mobile phone with flickering images propped on his table, who did not appear to intend misery or harm.

However, those were my feelings and thoughts on the matter and that was how the 16:51 to Grange-over-Sands went... listening to The Crisp Eater.

Intercity breakthrough
Grange-over-Sands to Manchester via Liverpool

Grange-over-Sands was a pit stop. But it was an interesting pit stop in railway terms. The tracks had been slow to come to Grange, arriving in 1857 when an embankment was built along the edge of the sands; "bathing machines" (small huts on wheels pulled by horses) were introduced, which could be rolled out to the water across the often-low tides, providing privacy for changing and Victorian discretion; and a pier was constructed for steamers, to bring visitors from Fleetwood and Morecambe. The effect was the rapid transformation of Grange into a place for rest and recreation away from the smoky cities of the north of England during its industrialization boom, as well as a place where wealthy industrialists from Manchester and Liverpool could live in large houses. Most visitors came via the Ulverstone and Lancaster Railway, which was key to transporting coke from the north-east to furnaces for iron ore in Barrow-in-Furness. The population swelled more than eightfold, from 200 to 1,700 by 1881. As with Middlesbrough, but slightly differently, Grange-over-Sands had been transformed by trains.

It was a quaint place with an ornamental garden by the station, which was balanced precariously on the embankment, facing the wide expanse of Morecambe Bay. Tearooms led to artisan bakeries, boutique fashion shops, smart little cafés, elegant bistros, the odd Turkish barber shop and the Commodore Inn, where I had an excellent room facing the train tracks and the bay. Occasionally, a filthy Northern train, looking as though it had survived a Saharan sandstorm, would rumble by, framed by the soft-pewter-coloured sea. Then silence descended, broken only by the sound of gulls. A drizzle fell. The tracks lay empty for a while. Then the next Northern service arrived, maybe half an hour later. The Commodore Inn was a trainspotter's delight, if slightly limited in the variety of trains it was possible to spot.

A busy day on the rails lay ahead.

First, the 09:22 from Grange would arrive at Preston at 10:08.

Then the 10:29 from Preston would arrive at 11:20 at Liverpool Lime Street, from where I intended to walk to the original location of Crown Street station, where the world's first intercity train – with George Stephenson orchestrating proceedings and the prime minister, the Duke of Wellington, on board – began its inaugural journey from Liverpool to Manchester on 15 September 1830.

This station was no longer a station, I had already learned; it had become a small park. From there, after investigating the surroundings, I would walk the short distance to Edge Hill station, the first proper remaining station from 1830, and return by foot to Liverpool Lime Street.

Next, I would catch the 13:54 to Manchester Victoria, arriving at 2.30 p.m.

From Manchester Victoria, I would walk to the terminus of the 1830 line at Liverpool Road station, which, unlike Crown Street station (demolished in 1836 to make way for better-located Liverpool Lime Street), had survived and, although no longer a working station, was part of Manchester's Science and Industry Museum.

Having paid homage to the Stockton and Darlington Railway of 1825, I was about to do the same to the equally revered Liverpool and Manchester Railway of 1830.

Another day, another train pilgrimage – one of the most important of all.

I walked to Grange-over-Sands station along the promenade by the tracks, with its well-maintained gardens and view across Morecambe Bay. It was a mellow, grey morning, and no one else was about.

At the ticket office, I asked about a second-hand bookshop called Over-Sands, which used to be at the station but was no more. It was considered by some to be one of the country's loveliest bookshops, located in one of the little grey-stone buildings on the platform by the sea. "Oh, that closed ages ago," said the assistant as though it belonged to the nineteenth century, though I had dropped by fifteen years earlier when passing through. Back then, I had chatted to a man named Stephen, who had been running the shop, and we had discussed the noticeable lack of sand at Grange-over-Sands. There seemed to be a lot of grass and reeds where the sand might be, leading to a muddy-looking section stretching a long way out to low, gently flopping waves. Sand seemed in short supply in the immediate vicinity of Grange-over-Sands. He had replied, "It got silted up and raised about four or five feet, then the grass came. People who came here ten years ago are amazed, they can hardly recognize the place." Some local wags back then had taken to calling the town Grange-over-Grass.

Over-Sands had been mentioned in a book by Simon Jenkins, a former editor of the *Evening Standard* and *The Times* (and a railway fan), published three years earlier and entitled *Britain's 100 Best Railway Stations*. Grange-over-Sands had made this prestigious list, praised for its "sublime" location, "impressive monkey-puzzle tree" in the forecourt (I went out to look at this; it was indeed impressive, as though it belonged in Kew Gardens) and "splendid" bookshop. It was sad the latter had gone.

With a cup of tea in hand from the station shop, and copies of *The Mail* and *The Westmorland Gazette*, I boarded the 09:22, which was packed.

It trundled away past the grey flats of Morecambe Bay, across a bridge and beyond some fields of sheep. I sat on a fold-down seat next to a woman from Lancaster who was making phone calls about purchasing buildings and then demolishing them and building new buildings where the old buildings had been while I read *The Mail* and *The Westmorland Gazette*. Aside from a teenagers assaulting a police officer, a botched attempted robbery at a Chinese takeaway and a local visit of a celebrity chef (Rick Stein), *The Mail* featured an article about a pair of holidaymakers who had been caught by an incoming tide on Morecambe Bay two days earlier and saved by the Bay Search and Rescue team, while *The Westmorland Gazette* ran a story about a walker on Scafell Pike being brought down the mountain by the Wasdale Mountain Rescue Team and helicoptered off after suffering a head injury in a fall.

Much safer to be a train tourist in these parts, it seemed.

Preston station was home to high, hoop-shaped windows and a prominent gold, black and red oval sign inscribed with "WELCOME TO LANCASHIRE". Iron railings featured a red rose motif, the symbol of Lancashire. Neoclassical columns shot upwards. There were archways here and hanging baskets there, and red-and-white-striped candy-stick-style decorations all around. It was busy and noisy, an aural and visual cacophony at the centre of which was the cavernous Beer House bar and restaurant, on a large "island" between the two main platforms. In years gone by, in a different format, this had been a hectic place where long-distance travellers would grab a bite before catching the steam train to Scotland or the south. Preston back then had been a key station in the middle of the long journey. It was still pretty busy, as though ghosts from those "glory days" hung in the atmosphere. Train announcements for Blackpool North, Glasgow Central, Ormskirk (as it happened, my mother's hometown), "Oxenholme Lake District", Manchester Airport and London Euston echoed across the crowded platforms. Preston clearly remained a pivotal junction.

The 10:29 slid onwards through a drizzle, beyond warehouses and red-brick terraces.

My neighbour on board was tapping out multiple texts with her black-and-white piano-patterned nails. After a blur of black and white, she would pause and stare out of the window as though resting her eyes from her phone screen. Then a ping would break her reveries and she would be off again: piano fingers performing another symphony of messages ending in a series of red hearts – a love concerto, perhaps.

The scenery was not exactly tourist-brochure stuff. Litter cascaded down banks. Industrial depots slid by with corrugated roofs and connecting pipes and chutes, yards with vans, lifting machines and piles of this and that. Cooling towers poked up. Steam emanated urgently before settling in a layer below the clouds, seeming to decide enough was enough.

After Wigan North Western station, we crossed the Leeds and Liverpool Canal, and I thought for a moment: *poor old canals they never stood a chance against the trains.* Then, as we negotiated the M6, the sun broke through for a while in magnesium streaks, illuminating heavy traffic running in a stream below: lorries loaded with freight that might have been transferred to the tracks had HS2 happened properly, perhaps (as Sarah Price had said back at the Locomotion museum). Then we drew into St Helens Central station, where a lot more passengers embarked, and pulled away past the cooling towers of the Pilkington glass factory.

The texter departed and a man with a bushy moustache sat down next to me at St Helens. He was not sending little red hearts to anyone on his phone. He had folded his arms and was regarding the carriage. After a while, noticing me peering at the glass factory, he commented, "Been taken over by a foreign company now, so it's no longer Pilkington's as it was. Ten to fifteen years ago, like everything else."

In 2006 a Japanese company named Nippon Sheet Glass had assumed control of the famous old glassmaker founded in 1826, just a year after the Stockton and Darlington Railway. The new owners had closed the main Watson Street glassworks and moved production to another pre-existing site within the town. "For a time, they kept the jobs [in the former glassworks]. Then it slowly wound down. Pilkington has done a lot for St Helens though. There was the Pilkington sports centre, there was a separate Pilkington hospital once."

I asked him if he had ever had anything to do with Pilkington, but he shook his head. His name was John and he was aged 74. He had a calm, wise manner, wore a green jumper and had a shiny, gold signet ring. He said he was retired from a customer survey job at Merseytravel, the Liverpool-area public transport authority.

"I would ask people 'What tickets are you using and what's the purpose of your travel?' on trains and buses. Sometimes they just told you impolitely to go away or you got their whole life story. One time, a young lady said, when I asked her purpose of travel, 'To go to town to get drunk.' She did invite me to join her, but I had to say that my boss wouldn't be happy, so I declined."

It was quite a job to have held down for many years, as John had. Were people ever aggressive when asked questions? "If someone came across as rude or aggressive we didn't have to persist in getting answers," he said quietly and matter-of-factly. He did not mind me asking questions at all; we were, after all, kindred spirits of a kind.

He was from St Helens, though born in Liverpool and a supporter of Liverpool FC, he said. For a while we gazed out of the carriage window, watching north-west England going by, before John, looking left, piped up once more: "Over there, when they did the Rainhill Trials, that was one end of it. Rainhill village was over that way." He pointed left. "You know, *Rocket* and all that. It was *Rocket* that killed Huskisson, you know."

Of course, I did know. You could not help but know about the ill-fated William Huskisson if you took even the slightest interest in the history of British trains. Clive had been straight onto the subject back in Shildon. It was said Huskisson had stepped from his carriage while it paused at the now-defunct Parkside station near Newton-le-Willows – not so far from St Helens – on the way from Liverpool to Manchester on 15 September 1830 because the MP had wanted to find the Duke of Wellington, the prime minister, to patch up a political difference despite being told to stay in the carriage for safety reasons; politics taking precedence over common sense, not for the last time in Britain (but with a particularly tragic end). Meanwhile, John's reference to the Rainhill Trials was to the contest between the likes of Robert Stephenson with his *Rocket* and Timothy Hackworth and *Sans Pareil* in October 1829 to win the right to be the locomotive chosen for the Liverpool and Manchester line, during which Stephenson triumphed.

John was quite blasé referring to all of this. His assumption was that this was common knowledge; in a way it probably wasn't "down south". *Rocket*, Huskisson and much of the rest of the beginnings of trains seemed to be more widely known "up north", where industrialization began. And maybe this should have come as no surprise. No point in making all those useful new things in all those newfangled factories of the boom-time nineteenth century in Manchester and elsewhere without sending off all those useful new things to people with money to pay for them, after all. And how would all that was required to make the useful new things reach the newfangled factories in the first place?

Trains were, of course, important "down south" too. They were important everywhere, the world over. But they were possibly *especially important* in the mid-nineteenth century in the parts the 10:29 had been travelling through.

The train came to a halt at Liverpool Lime Street station and we all disembarked, safely.

From the station, the route to Crown Street Park at first took you past a Victorian pub with an ornate gold-and-black facade named the Crown Hotel, and the grand Portland stone facade of the famous Adelphi hotel – once owned by Midland Railway and widely known in years gone by for its turtle soup (with live turtles kept in tanks in the basement) and for some of its famous guests, such as Winston Churchill, Franklin D Roosevelt and unfortunate passengers about to board the *Titanic*. Beyond was a run of busy Vietnamese restaurants, the windowless Genting Casino, some vinyl record shops, the Philharmonic (another showy Victorian pub) and some student flats. After those, you came to Crown Street Park.

So this was where the first intercity train picked up its passengers on 15 September 1830.

The small, sloping park was, frankly, a mess. Litter was strewn all over: crumpled cans, bottles, fast-food wrappers. A metal sign on the gate showed a picture of *Rocket* pulling some carriages, along with the message: "This public space marks the western terminus of the world's first passenger railway" – a statement Stockton and Darlington Railway people might query given that its 1825 line had been carrying passengers for a while before then. The sign ought really to have said *world's first intercity passenger railway with a proper timetable with regular steam locomotive-pulled trains run on double tracks*. Or something like that.

Pedantry aside, there was nothing much to see other than an old red-brick ventilation tower in the grass to the left. Crown Street station was demolished in 1836 when Liverpool Lime Street station opened closer to the city centre. It had never been where the actual locomotives went. Instead, a static engine-powered pulley system had conveyed passengers in carriages through a tunnel between Crown Street and Edge Hill station, about a half a mile to the north-east, where locos would take them on the 31-mile journey to Manchester.

When I arrived at the park, a man had been relieving himself against the old ventilation tower. I waited for him to go and went over, stepping between crumpled lager cans in the grass. On the tower, someone had spray-painted the words "HAPPY F****** XMAS" (quite amusing, really). Crown Street Park seemed to be full of such homespun charms, including a section of metal fence that had somehow, spectacularly, lodged itself halfway up a tree. As I was observing the section of fence in the tree, a council employee in a hi-vis jacket, who was clearing litter by a wall, looked up and smiled and shook his head as though sharing an appreciation of the lengths it must have taken to place the fence up there.

Seeing as he seemed to be taking a break, I asked what he thought about the park's railway connection.

"What was that?" he replied, looking blank.

The first train, I prompted him.

"Sorry, mate," he said, as if to say, *I can't help you with that, mate.*

He did not know about it, and who could blame him – given the tiny sign on the gate and no other indication anywhere of the grand moment in transport history. For him, it was just another, particularly messy, park.

"The very first one?" he asked, after I explained. "Here? Bloody 'ell. I did not know that. Twice a week I clear it up here, and I did not know that. I would have thought there'd be a bit more recognition than just a gate. A monument or something."

I agreed with him and then we talked about the litter problem in the park. He told me the mess was "predominantly students: I do a quarter of the park each time I come and the following week I come back and it's the same again – bottles and the leftovers of what happens of a night."

He returned to a mini-mountain of Strongbow cans and crisp packets by a pair of discarded chairs.

I went down to Edge Hill station.

Along the way I experienced a strange episode.

As I crossed a street, a car occupied by five young men in sportswear, probably in their early twenties, sped up and honked, making me quicken my step, although the car then had to slow down rapidly a few metres further on due to reaching a traffic jam, having nowhere to go. Why the driver, with four other "lads" in the car, decided to do this, I have no idea; perhaps it was "for a laugh".

After this friendly act towards a visiting rail enthusiast on the 1830 history of British trains trail (me), the occupants proceeded to roll down their windows to observe, or you might say leer at, the visiting rail enthusiast on the 1830 history of British trains trail.

To get to Edge Hill station, I needed to walk past these five young men in sportswear, probably in their early twenties. At first, I hesitated, thinking it might be best to go another way to the station. But there seemed to be no alternative and I needed to push on to catch the 13:54 from Liverpool Lime Street to Manchester Victoria after seeing Edge Hill.

So I kept walking, acting as though nothing had happened. As I did, the young men in sportswear, all five of them, turned to regard me in a manner that suggested, *got anything to say about that, pal?* Or something like that. Perhaps they were "offended". By crossing the street, I had (inadvertently) delayed their progress in the traffic jam. As they regarded me, and I (perhaps unwisely) regarded them, I swiftly calculated the probability of what might happen if I asked something like *what was that all about?* or *can I help you?* – and potentially, as a result of such an enquiry, have to take on five Liverpool lads wearing sportswear, probably in their early twenties, while carrying a backpack full of old train books. The odds, I estimated, were not exactly stacked in my favour. So head down, eyes forward, I plodded on, the lads observing my progress and, unless I was mistaken, cackling.

Thus marked my passage from the former Crown Street station to Edge Hill station.

Pity there was no longer a train between the two.

Shortly afterwards, I was inspecting a pair of old red-stone buildings dating from 1836, according to a plaque: Edge Hill station.

A cobbled lane led to the platforms, overlooked on one side by the BUZZ BINGO hall. Most of the station windows were boarded, and paint was peeling badly on doors to old waiting rooms. No one was around and it was hard to imagine that this was where *Rocket* and all the dignitaries, including poor William Huskisson, had puffed away down the tracks all that time ago, although a useful, long information board on the main platform explained why the unlikely location was such a big deal.

This information board was a mine of information. When the station first opened in 1830, it was a hundred yards away at a sandstone cutting. You could see this spot from the current station, at the end of a platform where there were three tunnels. One of these tunnels (on the left) went up to Crown Street, another (on the right) was originally a dead end for storage and the third (in the middle) ran for 2,250 yards down to Wapping Dock. This tunnel was key to the Liverpool and Manchester Railway, as raw cotton could be transported from the docks to the factories in Manchester to be made into cotton goods.

When the tunnel first opened in 1829, before the trains started, "it was whitewashed, lit by gas and used as a promenade by visitors", said the information board. Each visitor paid a shilling to enter this strange tourist attraction, and a brass band played so music echoed throughout. It was a grand event, a major social occasion. And it was also a handy public relations stunt, as the tunnel's opening went a long way to help win over locals to the line, raising anticipation levels to fever pitch.

I had already read about this. According to the rail historian Christian Wolmar in his entertaining *Fire & Steam: A New History of the Railways in Britain* (one of the growing number of books in my backpack), the "railway pioneers needed to improve their image, being still frequently portrayed as rapacious land-grabbers, disrupting the established order of things". Much of the landed gentry, some of whom attempted to prevent Parliament from granting compulsory purchases of land, and all of the canal owners, who had vested business interests, were dead set against what were regarded by some as a bunch of ragbag fellows with their awful, noisy and smelly steam machines.

The fact that they were led by George Stephenson, a self-educated, self-made man from an ordinary background, who seemed to many to be hell-bent on grand schemes to change the way Britain ran (which he was), did not help. It was, some have said, a class thing, with mockery of Stephenson for what had been an unpolished initial presentation to Parliament in 1825, when he first attempted to gain permission to proceed with the Liverpool–Manchester line, symbolic of desperate attempts to hold back a new class of entrepreneur, or prevent "new money" rising in Britain. The historian F. D. Klingender in his book *Art and the Industrial Revolution* went as far as to describe the creation of the railways as "the final battle between two economic systems and two ways of living".

There was a huge amount of hostility towards the Liverpool and Manchester Railway, which was being proposed to Parliament in the very same year the Stockton and Darlington Railway began. However, although less ambitious, the Stockton and Darlington Railway had proved, undisputedly, to be highly effective – and, crucially, profitable (with around 10 per cent annual dividends) – becoming instantly famous, attracting headlines across the world, and making Stephenson a household name. And while landowners paid smooth-talking barristers to attempt to block him in Parliament (failing to do so, such had Stephenson's reputation risen), canal owners were also fighting a desperate rearguard action, even issuing leaflets saying steam locomotives might explode and set fire to fields and houses by tracks, and cause cows to be so frightened they would stop producing milk. Rumours spread by the anti-train lobby that travelling at 30 mph-plus might damage passengers' eyes had to be dispelled by an official doctor's report.

So the "world's first tunnel to be bored beneath a metropolis", according to the information board, and the shilling visits and brass band were all part of winning over the public ahead of the big opening, a PR campaign to show railways were exciting, modern and approachable, not scary and run by an uncouth, untrustworthy mob.

I walked down the platform to take a closer look at the weed-strewn entrance of the tunnel. A pile of old sleepers lay nearby, and the stone was crumbling on the archway leading to the depths of Liverpool. The tunnel was no longer used, having been superseded by another larger and more direct one that had later been bored to the docks on the other side of the cobbled lane to the station entrance.

Back in the small ticket office, I talked to Mark, the stationmaster, about what it meant to be in charge of the oldest working railway station in Britain and, for that matter, the world.

"I do feel proud of it," he said. "I know we've got the odd plaque and that here, but I wish there was more."

More what?

"Museum status," he replied. With a greater recognition of the heritage, he believed, extra funds might be released so the tired, old buildings could be restored.

We talked for a while, and Mark told me the train I was about to take to Manchester went along the route of the original 1830 railway.

He said there used to be a team working at Edge Hill station and that he missed the camaraderie (he was alone when I visited). He shuffled into a backroom and returned with a folder containing a few faded photocopies of photographs and drawings of how the station had looked in 1836, one depicting a locomotive called *Lion*, another, from 1959, of a grand locomotive named the *Princess Royal* emerging from the tunnel running down to Wapping Dock.

It was not that long ago, really, that steam trains were shunting around Britain. The first London to Liverpool electrified service was as recently as 1965. Until around then, all those lovely old locos had still rattled happily away down the lines. A different era, maybe, but not a million years ago. When Geoff Hurst was slotting in the winning goals in the World Cup at Wembley in 1966, plenty of old steam locos were still chugging down the lines.

Perhaps not best to dwell on altercations – but at Liverpool Lime Street station I had another run-in.

This time involving the authorities at Liverpool Lime Street station rather than a gang of lads in a car.

On arrival back at the station, I stood for a while regarding the vision ahead. This vision was the facade of Liverpool Lime Street station, which rose in a wide arch of soft-grey steel with long rows of narrow windows offering glimpses into the skylights and beams above the platforms. A grand sweep of steps led up to a row of neoclassical archways, through which you entered. On the other side of the square was St George's Hall, with its equally grand frontage featuring a small forest of classical columns. On my visit, there was also, just across the way, an absolutely enormous advertising board with a picture of the Liverpool footballer Trent Alexander-Arnold alongside the words "YOU GOT THIS".

The overall effect of the station exterior and the grand scale of what you came to outside was bold, in your face and dramatic. A statement seemed to be being made: *you have arrived somewhere important*.

And, of course, you had. The current station was completed in 1879, after replacing the 1836 station, which had to be updated as traffic grew. Liverpool had become not just a major player in global industrialization but also a major departure point for New World emigrants: many having crossed by ferry to Hull and train to Liverpool for the onward American journey. Simon Jenkins in his *Britain's 100 Best Railway Stations* was unequivocal in his admiration: "The gable end facing the square is the best railway facade in Britain… puts King's Cross in the shade."

High praise indeed from such a train station aficionado.

Inside the station I walked as far as I could from the entrance towards the tracks to admire the "spidery membranes" of the roof, as described by Jenkins.

As I was doing so, a burly station employee, who had been walking by, diverted my gaze.

"Found something interesting to take a picture of?" he said, in a manner best described as extremely sarcastic (bordering on *wind-up*). I had been taking a picture of the *spidery membranes*.

"Yes. I'm interested in the architecture," I replied. I had taken an immediate dislike to this burly station employee and estimated that this comment might rile him a bit. Why not? He was trying to rile me.

"Oh, are you now?" he replied in a "fancy" voice.

"Yes," I replied and looked at him squarely as though asking, *And?*

"The architecture," he said, in a "fancy" voice once more.

"Yes, I'm interested in the roof and those columns. They're Doric columns," I replied, estimating again that this might get up his nose.

"Oh really?" he asked rhetorically in his "fancy" voice. "Have you got permission to take pictures?" he asked, in a manner that suggested I was breaking a rule.

"I didn't know any permission was required," I replied. It was, after all, a public place.

"Just go round there and ask permission from the information office," he said, condescendingly and in the manner of an order.

"Fine," I said. The large burly station employee had been joined during all of this by another large burly station employee. I had two large burly Liverpool Lime Street station employees before me – glaring at me.

"Thanks for being so friendly," I said and turned.

"Oi, you!" said one of the burly station employees. I kept on walking. "Oi, don't walk away when we're talking to you."

I kept walking. "Don't walk away. I'm speaking to you!"

I turned and, from a few metres away, asked "What do you want to say to me now?"

"Don't raise your voice with me!" said one of the burly station employees.

I had not raised my voice and I repeated my question, though it did not seem as though either of them had anything further to say. So I walked to the information office and asked whether I needed permission to take pictures of the roof of Liverpool Lime Street station, and the attendant said "No." I asked her why the two men, who were still watching me, had requested that I ask. The attendant just shrugged.

So marked my passage through Liverpool Lime Street station. I really had no idea whatsoever what that was all about.

Nonplussed, I boarded the 13:54 to Manchester Victoria.

It was a TransPennine Express.

The train slid between high, damp black-and-green walls, passing Edge Hill station, with rain pattering on the carriage roof. It was soon passing Rainhill, Lea Green and Newton-le-Willows stations (close to where Huskisson had his accident). It crossed fields with lots of electricity pylons and passed though woodlands and beside pastures with clumps of reeds and sheep. A man left a pamphlet on the seat beside me on how "sin creates a barrier that keeps you from fellowship with the holy God that created you". Not long after that, the train came slowly to a halt in Manchester.

Journey time? Thirty-six minutes.

Back in 1830? One hour and 46 minutes.

Before the railway? Three hours by stagecoach or twelve by canal.

No wonder the trains went on to do so well.

CHAPTER FOUR

MANCHESTER TO LLANELLI VIA BLAENAU FFESTINIOG, PORTHMADOG, CAERNARFON, PRESTATYN, CREWE AND CRAVEN ARMS

VOICES FROM THE TRACKS

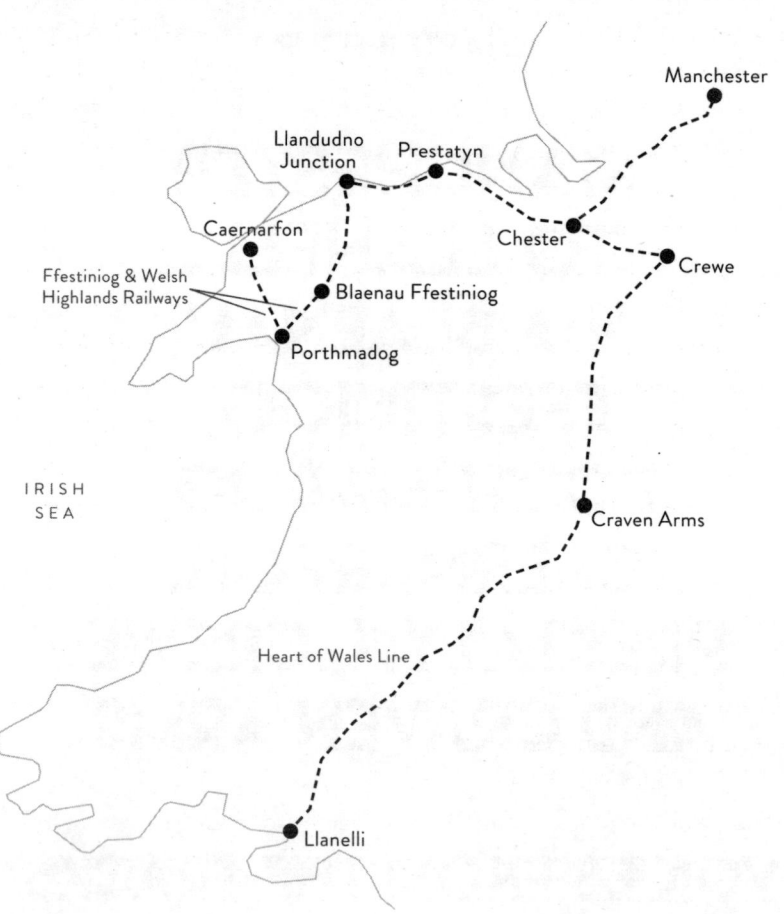

After the glory of Liverpool Lime Street – its physical appearance rather than the welcome you may receive if you take a few snaps of its old pillars and roof – Manchester Victoria was less of a showstopper from the outside, but not without its own flamboyant touches.

Inside, smart, original wooden ticket kiosks and some nice old mosaics saying, "1ST CLASS", "GRILL ROOM", "BOOKSTALL" and "REFRESHMENT ROOM" had been preserved, and there was a lovely tiled map of the old Lancashire and Yorkshire Railway (1847–1922). Rising above all this was a high, modern skylight completed in 2015, which covered these original areas dating from 1844.

Manchester Victoria was due, possibly, to become part of a "Northern Powerhouse" high-speed rail connection with Leeds and Liverpool – the word "possibly" being apposite, as many plans had been announced and slightly altered, or ditched, amended, reconsidered, crossed out, reinstated, rethought once more and generally messed about with by politicians of many persuasions. Anything seemed possible: *it would happen, or it wouldn't, or a botched version of it might, or it would all somehow work out in the end.* Yet it all, at least, seemed positive, with terms and phrases such as "High-Speed 3" ("HS3"), "Northern Powerhouse Rail" and "Integrated Rail Plan for the North and the Midlands" being bandied about.

All that said, it was difficult to get your hopes up about any government train plans after the Birmingham to Manchester HS2 link had been so unceremoniously dumped.

To complete the other half of the Liverpool and Manchester Railway, I set off past the front of Manchester Victoria, with its restored old signs advertising destinations such as Hull, Harrogate, Leeds, Bradford, Blackpool and, weirdly, Belgium (presumably by ferry from Hull), on the way to Manchester Liverpool Road station.

This was not that far away, past the shiny National Football Museum, a statue of Gandhi, Waterstones Dean Street and a man who approached with a clipboard asking, "Excuse me, sir, we're just doing a survey to tackle knife crime in the country, sir, can you take part, sir?" And who looked slightly upset when I said, "No thanks." Not that I was against tackling knife crime, just I didn't think anything I might add could help in the slightest, and I was in a hurry to get to Manchester's Science and Industry Museum before it closed.

This I did – and headed straight to the rear of the museum to see Manchester Liverpool Road station, where I met Gemma Gibb, the museum's head of communications.

Gemma wore a green cardigan and glasses. I had not made an appointment. I had just turned up, discovered that the Manchester Liverpool Road station section of the museum was closed due to temporary works, and (pleadingly) phoned the museum's admin office. Gemma was before me 10 minutes later, smiling and, luckily for me, free to show the old station, which has been preserved at the back of the museum along with an 1830s warehouse full of steam-age locomotives, though this was closed too.

"This is the world's oldest surviving intercity passenger station," were just about the first words to come from Gemma's mouth, spoken carefully. "Or I should say *inter-urban* as that's more accurate."

I asked her what she meant by this – which I guessed had something to do with remnants of stations along the Stockton and Darlington Railway, although there was nothing there to match Manchester Liverpool Road station.

Gemma said, almost as an aside and with some reverence, "Well, that's what the train experts say."

She pointed at a warehouse. "That's the world's first railway goods warehouse. The station and the warehouse are Grade I listed, although that track there is 1980s." She was pointing at a section of railway by the station's old, wooden-planked platform with its red-bricked waiting rooms with barred windows and a timber-beamed roof supported by iron columns. Steam trains used to offer rides on this tiny section of track for museum visitors, although this had been discontinued years back.

"The viaduct is by George Stephenson," Gemma said. The station was raised above the street below with a townhouse-style exterior on Liverpool Road and tracks designed by Stephenson curving off to one side and leading to Stephenson's Bridge over the river Irwell. After crossing a cobbled yard, Gemma stopped as we reached the platform, which had a strangely Wild West frontier feel with its scuffed wooden floorboards. She said, with reverence again, "Manchester was the first industrial city. Here, amazingly, this is where it all happened. We all love working here." She gestured towards some modern buildings rising beyond the platform. "From here, you can see the changing style of Manchester – tall residential buildings past the old station, then you've got the HQ of Booking.com. You've got residential and offices. This is the heart of it all, really – the museum."

Just like Sarah back at Locomotion, Gemma was clearly passionate about her museum and its setting sprawled across six and a half prime acres of old industrial Manchester.

Originally, back in 1830, there had been no platform. "Passengers had to yank themselves up, it was a bit undignified. It was cobbles and rails and no platform. They hadn't been invented yet," she said. Ladders were provided.

We walked along the platform, added later, and inspected the first- and second-class booking halls (first-class carriages had been plush and covered, second-class open to the elements), and then we went out onto the road to gaze at the old station agent's house: a Georgian building (turned into a holiday let) attached to the townhouses that fronted the station itself. "It doesn't look like a station as there was no blueprint for one back then," said Gemma. You could easily walk past thinking it was the former home of some industrial age Mancunian bigwig, not for a moment suspecting the *world's oldest surviving inter-urban station* lurked within.

Across the road, scaffolding clung to a building that Gemma said was the world's oldest railway hotel, the Commercial Hotel, which was being done up. A ramp down from the tracks was for herding animals off trains, as many as 80,000 pigs a year in the 1830s, to feed the hungry factory workers. By 1844, however, passenger travel had been shifted to Manchester Victoria station. Freight trains continued until 1975, when Manchester Liverpool Road station closed for good, with the museum opening eight years later due to local recognition of the site's importance in industrial history.

This stood out, especially compared to Liverpool.

Back on Merseyside, the council worker clearing litter from a park where the former western terminus of the Liverpool and Manchester Railway had once stood had been unsurprisingly oblivious to its historical significance. Manchester, by contrast, had gone to town, highlighting the importance of the line. (Admittedly, its terminus had not been demolished in 1836 as Liverpool's Crown Street station had.)

The irony is that when the train, after the sad hold-up caused by Huskisson's accident, reached Manchester on 15 September 1830, it did not receive a universally warm welcome. While some onlookers cheered, others hurled stones, shouted insults and waved banners saying, "VOTE BY BALLOT" (only 11 per cent of adult males then had the vote, and especially few in the industrial north) as well as "NO TO THE CORN LAWS" (which had been raising bread prices while bolstering landowners' incomes). What was going on?

The answer was the presence of the prime minister; itself a sign of how far Stephenson had advanced in public awareness and acceptance since the solitary *Experiment* carriage of 1825, back on the Stockton and Darlington Railway. The Duke of Wellington was unpopular in Manchester and he wisely stayed in his carriage before the return of that inaugural ride to Liverpool, wary of sparking unrest; he had earlier requested that the train turn around after Huskisson's accident, but there had been fears that doing so might lead to riots among thousands in Manchester lining the track, patiently awaiting *Rocket*'s arrival.

There was another political side to these concerns.

It was not all that long after Peterloo, when eighteen people died and between 400 and 700 were injured after cavalry charged a gathering of 60,000 working-class people demanding a fairer voting system at St Peter's Field, close to the railway terminus, in Manchester in 1819. The very name "Peterloo" was a bitter reference to the battle of Waterloo at which the Duke of Wellington had led the successful defeat of Napoleon.

On 15 September 1830, some of the most vociferous protesters were even wearing tricolour ribbons in support of the egalitarian principles of the French Revolution. The atmosphere was extremely tense when the first Liverpool and Manchester Railway locomotive rolled in, though to be fair to Stephenson, it had absolutely nothing to do with him or his railway.

Interestingly, the Duke of Wellington, so widely unpopular he resigned as prime minister two months later to make way for the less detested Earl Grey, did not board another train for thirteen years. The historian Christian Wolmar, connecting the events, has said "perhaps he could be called railway's first political casualty".

Politics aside, however, the railway proved a massive hit. Instead of the expected 250 passengers a day, within a month 1,200 were making the journey, which was half the price of stagecoaches. The actress Fanny Kemble, an early passenger (who admitted to being "horribly in love" with Stephenson), matched the reaction of many: "You can't imagine how strange it seemed to be journeying on thus, without any visible cause of progress other than the magical machine, with its flying white breath and rhythmical, unvarying pace... when I closed my eyes, this sensation of flying was quite delightful, and strange beyond description; yet strange it was, I had a perfect sense of security, and not the slightest fear."

She had, it seemed, enjoyed herself very much – and captured the feelings on those first rides wonderfully too.

Victorian scandals and pounds per mile
Manchester to Caernarfon via Blaenau Ffestiniog and Porthmadog

It was time to switch from the north of one country to the north of another: Wales, where a joyous journey on some old slate mine trains in the mountains awaited. My mission to mooch around Britain on trains was (pleasingly) taking me to places I would never otherwise have visited. Just as I always hoped it would.

In the morning, after a night at a football-themed hotel facing Manchester United's Old Trafford stadium, two Manchester Metrolink trains were required to reach Manchester Piccadilly, the city's cavernous, frankly rather unattractive main station.

On board these above-ground Metrolink trains, I listened to commuters discussing holidays in Croatia and high local property prices and watched mini-Manhattans of gleaming glass and steel shooting upwards from the red-brick lowlands of the nineteenth century – one form of civilization rising from another – while Roman remains, another still, lurked down by canals and the river Irwell, not far from Manchester Liverpool Road station.

Then the 10:44 to Llandudno Junction left platform fourteen, a messy corner of the messy station, reached by a moving walkway. It duly arrived: a Transport for Wales service operated by the Welsh government. I boarded the red, white and grey train with its red, white and grey seats, sitting across the aisle from an elderly man in a grubby hi-vis jacket who was fast asleep with his head tilted forwards, his mouth open and his ticket on the fold-down table before him. Announcements were made in both English and Welsh – Llandudno was pronounced "Shan-did-no", or at least that was how it sounded – and we moved away, passing building sites of half-constructed tower blocks. The train, a smooth one, purred back towards Liverpool, stopping at Newton-le-Willows, where a cheerful station sign read "TREAT PEOPLE UNITED WITH KINDNESS AND LOVE", although I was reading a front-page story in the *Manchester Evening News* that involved little of that: "MASKED RAID TERROR AT TOP RESTAURANT".

A power station rose in the distance, looking like a ghost ship beyond the Manchester Ship Canal. Onwards we softly purred to Runcorn and the river Mersey, skirting wind farms and industrial estates before arriving at Chester (where the man opposite woke with a start and began eating sandwiches from a Tupperware box).

Shortly afterwards, we crossed the river Dee and passed into Wales, stopping at a place called Flint, where the station was daubed in red paint, seemingly to assert the new national surroundings. The wide mouth of the river Dee opened into the Irish Sea, and the train curved by static holiday home camps and a golf course, pausing at Prestatyn and an advertisement saying "DISCOVER RETIREMENT LIVING TO THE FULL" before continuing beyond bungalows with solar panels and satellite dishes to a bingo hall the size of a large church near Rhyl and arriving at Colwyn Bay, where the man with the hi-vis nodded at me and got off. The surface of the Irish Sea had an unexpectedly turquoise gleam at Colwyn Bay, striking a vivid contrast with the luminous grey sky.

Shortly afterwards, we arrived at Llandudno Junction, where I had a good cup of tea at a platform café and the assistant said, "Oh yes, it's nice in Llandudno. It's still very Victorian, what they've kept of it, that is. Colourful, the houses. You've got Alfred Wainwright things, and Lewis Carroll came on holiday here. Did you know that? All in all, it's nice in Llandudno." Then I boarded the 13:28 to Ffestiniog Blaenau and another Transport for Wales train moved away, following the river Conwy, entering emerald hills with little settlements and farmsteads featuring corrugated barns and cattle. Through woodlands covered in thick green moss, past rocky escarpments and tangles of brambles, alongside rusty-coloured streams, we slowly rose, eventually plunging into a tunnel and emerging amid slate slopes dotted with rhododendron bushes and topped by misty, craggy cliffs. We pulled into a little station of Blaenau Ffestiniog at 216 metres above the Irish Sea. It was 2.30 p.m.

You felt well away from the Big Smoke up in Blaenau Ffestiniog. The small town (population 4,000) was a former slate centre established in the mid-eighteenth century for quarrymen and their families, nicknamed "City of Slates" back then. It had begun to boom in 1836 after the arrival of the Ffestiniog Railway covering the dozen miles southwest to the port of Porthmadog on the Irish Sea, with its population peaking at 12,000 following the introduction of steam locomotives in 1863. Before then, the railway had relied on gravity for downwards passage, with horses pulling up empty wagons. Blaenau Ffestiniog, thanks to the steam locomotives, was said to have "roofed the world". Yet another place, like Middlesbrough and Grange-over-Sands (and just about everywhere I had been so far), that would be completely different without trains.

You could not help but like it. I walked down a narrow, winding high street. All around, craggy slopes rose, shrouded in fog, mysterious and no doubt dangerous, yet somehow reassuring too. Up in the misty hills, Blaenau Ffestiniog felt like another world, with its quaint little bookshop full of second-hand mountaineering books (the town is a base for climbers and walkers, with Snowdon, or Yr Wyddfa, close by), a little knitting shop and a "Traditional Turkish Barbers". A clutch of pubs included the busy-looking Meirion Vaults and the Queens Hotel (right by the station). Other businesses included a tanning parlour, a tattoo parlour, a Chinese restaurant, an Indian restaurant (Red Chillies), a fish 'n' chip shop and a sports massage centre. All par for the course, it seemed, in a former industrial village in the hills in twenty-first-century Wales.

Waiting for the train to Porthmadog, I went for a pint of lime and soda (70 pence) at the Queens Hotel bar, causing a couple of old-timers drinking pints of lager, the only other clientele, to pause in conversation and gaze my way. It was not, I gathered from their glances, a regular order.

The Queens Hotel was a relaxing place, with a lounge at the front with comfy grey armchairs. I sank into one of these close to a television with snooker on silent, pleased to be up among peaks and clouds and mountain paths.

The old-timers resumed their conversation. It was almost therapeutic listening to them; their chat mainly in rich, lyrical-sounding Welsh with the odd English word punctuating the flow.

This was how it went: long flurry of lyrical Welsh... "chicken stir-fry"... more softly flowing Welsh... "Pot Noodles"... another mellifluous Welsh stream... "fish fingers"... Welsh... "chips or pizza"... Welsh... "five hundred pounds"... Welsh... "f*** that!"... Welsh... "twenty-five quid" [spoken by a younger man who had joined them]... more gentle Welsh lilt... "chicken and mushroom, curry sauce"... Welsh... "f***in' 'ell"... "stir-fry"... Welsh... "f***in' 'ell, f***in' 'ell"... Welsh... "dancing" [younger man]... Welsh... "f***in' 'ell, f***in' 'ell, f***in' 'ell, ha ha ha, aargh!" Some conclusion seemed to have been reached, or story completed, and the younger man parted, with dinner plans, business arrangements of some sort and perhaps a night on the tiles apparently decided.

I returned to the station and, from a platform opposite the main line from Llandudno Junction, boarded "The Quarryman" service to Porthmadog, pulled by a green locomotive named *Linda* and part of the Ffestiniog & Welsh Highland Railways, yet another heritage organization, though this one had nothing to do with Dr Beeching. The original railway closed to passengers in 1939 and slate traffic ended in 1946, due to a fall in demand. Rail enthusiasts, as you so often found with all these lines, had stepped in and performed stoic heroics, and the narrow-gauge railway (1 foot 11½ inches wide, precisely) had reopened fully by 1982, to be joined by yet another narrow-gauge train onwards from Porthmadog to Caernarfon covering 25 miles in 2011. The first journey was officially on Ffestiniog Railway, which laid claim to being "the world's oldest narrow-gauge railway". Meanwhile, its sister railway, the Welsh Highland Railway, which had been a commercial failure when it originally operated from 1920 to 1937, laid claim to being "the UK's longest heritage railway".

In short, you were in narrow-gauge railway heaven, up in the hills of Wales.

The famous Ffestiniog & Welsh Highland Railways was why I had come this way in the first place. How could any embryonic Train Nut not want to go and check out the Ffestiniog & Welsh Highland Railways?

It did not disappoint. The train snaked away out of the little town, clinging to the tiny tracks, and it was relaxing simply letting the wheels roll and the dramatic scenery unfold. You do not have to be a hardcore rail enthusiast to enjoy sitting back on a small, red moquette seat, with the letters "FR" in a pattern in the fabric, watching the slate slopes slip by, feeling the sways and the rattles as the carriages roll above slate rooftops of terraced former quarry-worker houses into a great swirling mist above valleys with ink-black reservoirs and enormous folds of rock. The train pulled into small stations. Then it pulled out of them. Hoots echoed across the hills and we moved into an ancient oak woodland.

Two female hikers were sitting in the seats in front of me. From time to time, one would say to the other "That's gorgeous" to which the other would reply "That's lovely". There would be a pause for a while as they fell into contemplative silence. Then one would say "It's beautiful" to which the other would reply "Yes, gorgeous". They kept going like this for 13½ miles, and their observations were invariably correct.

A guard with a neat goatee beard, a blue waistcoat and a gold chain came by and informed me that the forest was a "Celtic rainforest from the Middle Ages – some of those sessile oaks are nine hundred years old". He also told me that an engineer named Robert Francis Fairlie had made steam trains possible on the steep, curving railway, which rose more than 200 metres, by inventing a special locomotive with "double engines and swivelling bogies that could navigate the twisty turns. He sold them all over the world and they're still used in India." When the first loco was demonstrated in 1863, it had been a "major event", attracting interest from across the globe, with counts from Russia and Hungary, Polish viceroys, plus Turkish, Swedish and Indian railway representatives in attendance, as well as the Duke of Sutherland and journalists from *The Times* and the *Engineering Gazette*.

The guard told me a story involving Fairlie, who had clearly been a larger-than-life Victorian character. Eight years before his big breakthrough, he had eloped to Spain after marrying the 17-year-old daughter of a fellow railway engineer named George England without her father's consent. This, at the time, was a crime for which he could be sent to prison, and England pursued this, the case being reported in *The Times*. Fairlie, aged 30, had falsely signed documents saying permission had been given but was let off on a technicality as it was subsequently discovered that England was not legally married himself and so his daughter had been born out of wedlock and could do as she pleased. Fairlie and England, to add a final twist, settled their differences and England helped build the "double engines with swivelling bogies". The whole affair, the guard said, was "a Victorian scandal that could make a good Netflix film".

As he finished this story, the train began to traverse a long, especially beautiful section of the line on a mile-long embankment, with the Irish Sea rising in a silvery expanse beneath a sky of exploding clouds with pockets of defiant blue to the left and a reedy salt marsh on reclaimed land that formed a plain between mountains running inland to the right. This embankment was known as the Cob, the result of the exploits of an early nineteenth-century landowner named William Madocks, who wanted to establish farming inland. The train seemed to float along it, as though the scenery had been laid before the passengers for their eyes only, before ending at Porthmadog station, where we all disembarked and I went to look at *Linda*, our steam engine, only to discover it was not a "double engine with swivelling bogies", but it dated from 130 years ago nevertheless, built by Hunslet Engine Co in Leeds. Good enough for me.

Porthmadog was yet another whirlwind stop.

The station was a hotchpotch of rooms, with a gift shop selling model trains and (many) railway-related books and a restaurant/bar named Spooner's after James Spooner, who built the Ffestiniog Railway between 1832 and 1836 (nothing to do with Wetherspoons).

On a terrace by the platforms, I ate a sandwich and had enough time to talk to Osian from the marketing department of the Ffestiniog & Welsh Highland Railways. Osian was young, dynamic and full of ideas for the business. He gave me a crash course: "We get one hundred and forty-five thousand passengers a year. In 2019 we had more than one hundred and eighty thousand. But then we were running five hundred thousand seats. It's two hundred and fifty thousand seats now for one hundred and forty-five thousand passengers. Better efficiency. We want to avoid ECS, you see."

He looked at me as though waiting for me to ask what ECS was, and so I did.

"Empty Coaching Stock," he replied. "We don't want empty seats running up and down. That will kill us. We're looking at the PPM, you see."

He waited for me again.

I asked what PPM stood for.

"Pounds per mile," he replied. "We need to push that up. We're currently running at one hundred and twenty-five pounds per mile. We hope to get that to one hundred and fifty pounds. Maybe that's optimistic. Maybe around one hundred and thirty pounds is a more realistic target… 2019 was probably terrible – five pounds a mile or something. There were loads of trains but at what cost? How much coal were we burning?"

There was clearly more to running a heritage railway line than met the eye.

I boarded the Snowdonia Star service to Caernarfon pulled by a large green locomotive from 1958, built in Manchester (said a plaque). Again, no "double engine with swivelling bogies" designed by an eloping Victorian engineering legend, somewhat sadly. It seemed to be the luck of the draw whether you got that.

We rolled away, slightly jerkily, across a road, over a bridge and past a Premier Inn, a Londis and a Shell garage. Oystercatchers and egrets were flitting about in the salt marsh, fluttering one way and another like handkerchiefs floating in the wind. Black cattle stood sentient in fields beyond the town boundary, with mountains rising across a valley plain. The carriage interior had stiff, burgundy-coloured seats with wooden fittings and small tables, looking prim and proper in an old-fashioned way. It was still misty. A sulphury smell of soot from the loco had found its way into the carriage.

Rising into woodland from a bend with a crystalline river, the landscape turned more rugged. Scree tumbled one way. Cliffs plummeted another. There were some old tractors. There were some old farm carts. We went very slowly up, up, up via some pine trees. A wide area of meadows with springy-looking turf emerged, with spiky ridges rising on the horizon. Snowdon (Yr Wyddfa) arose in a bulge to the right. I settled into the rhythm of the ride, only leaving my seat once to stroll to the end of the carriage to gaze down the line out of the back window. There was something reassuring about watching the sleepers flowing from beneath the train as the shiny parallel tracks curled away. On a railway you knew where you were going, and you knew where you had been, quite precisely: the evidence was there, hammered down in the soil, often many years gone by.

I returned to my seat through a doorway that said, "GWYLIWCH EICH PEN" (MIND YOUR HEAD). All the instructions were in both languages; around 80 per cent of locals in the county of Gwynedd were fluent in Welsh, compared to a national average of 30 per cent.

The train entered a tunnel and began to descend. The only other passenger in my carriage (poor "ECS"; Osian would be less than impressed) was a woman who was fast asleep. She had boarded the train, glanced out of the window at the platform at Porthmadog and promptly closed her eyes and begun to snooze. Maybe she would stay on board for the return, whether she planned to or not.

A castle arose with turrets and flags, a vivid silhouette in the distance: Caernarfon Castle. The Snowdonia Star service rolled onwards towards it, down to a cutting by a high wall and Caernarfon station. We all disembarked, even the snoozer. I went up the hill, admiring the castle and a statue of a pugnacious-looking David Lloyd George, a former local MP, found my digs round the corner on a cobbled lane, ate dinner at another gloomy-but-good-value Wetherspoons pub (I was getting to know this chain) and wandered around the colourful narrow streets of Caernarfon for a while, occasionally being dive-bombed by gulls.

Larkin and Kevin
Caernarfon to Crewe via Prestatyn

That was Caernarfon. No time to dwell on it, sadly. I liked it. Nice place, aside from the kamikaze gulls, but time was of the essence. I was about to move south; in three nights I would be in Penzance in south-west Cornwall, all being well with the trains. That was the plan. This railway journey round Britain – which was sometimes to have a snakes-and-ladder quality (the journey down to Penzance being a "snake") – was now heading south-west. Something about Penzance, all those miles down there, caught the eye. It had always been my intention to go that way; why not drop down in a couple of days? Some strange inner urge made me want to go to Penzance in south-west Cornwall, all of a sudden. Who was I to fight it? Let strange inner train urges run loose. This was your right as a train rambler with two months free to ramble. You could look at your National Rail map and ramble. Nobody was stopping you. You made your decisions. You booked your tickets.

And off you went.

The freedom of the tracks meant anything was possible.

To begin this manoeuvre, the way I hoped to go, first required a short burst north on a morning bus to Porthmadog (no suitable train was available), followed by a return "Mountain Spirit" service to Blaenau Ffestiniog, a connection to Llandudno Junction, with its lovely, friendly little platform café, and then another train to the seaside resort of Prestatyn.

Why? You might well ask. Why Prestatyn? Well, the answer was that I had always been curious about the resort that featured in a Philip Larkin poem entitled "Sunny Prestatyn". Being a big fan of Larkin and seeing Prestatyn on the map – and half-remembering the poem – I had booked a place to stay on the spur of the moment: a chance to enjoy the Welsh seaside and also be a Larkin tourist, which I was intending to be later at his former adopted city of Hull.

The poem, comprising three stanzas, was, suitably enough, all about a railway poster depicting an attractive, happy, smiling woman drawn on a beach in front of a hotel with palm trees beneath the words "Come To Sunny Prestatyn" – except the figure had been attacked by puerile-minded graffiti vandals, and the poem progresses with the damaged poster being replaced with another advertising a "fight cancer" campaign. "She was too good for this life" writes Larkin, with his characteristic deadpan take on matters, and you are left slightly wondering, *What was that all about?*

That said, the words "Come To Sunny Prestatyn" had somehow stuck at the back of my mind and I was going to Prestatyn, and it was even quite sunny. Again though, it would be a fly-by visit. Again though, that did not matter. I dropped my backpack in a small single room in a popular rugby-oriented pub/hotel and walked down a long, sloping high street that had a similar eclectic feel to the one in Blaenau Ffestiniog but a more upmarket sideline in boutique clothes shops and cocktail bars mixed in with an Iceland, a Subway and a Domino's pizzeria. From a churchyard came a smell of dope. An accountancy office advertised itself as being a "tax-driven accountants, driven to keep your taxes down". The street led back past the station and the playing field of Prestatyn Town FC to a wide, golden sand beach with hard-packed sand knotted with ripples, crunchy underfoot from razor shells. A few dog walkers were about; the summer season and the swimming costumes and railway-poster smiles were months away.

This was where the 177-mile Offa's Dyke Path National Trail began and ended, criss-crossing the Wales–England border all the way down to Chepstow by the Bristol Channel, named after Offa, an Anglo-Saxon king from the eighth century CE. It was believed that Offa built his dyke (defensive ditch) to keep out the enemy Princes of Powys. I had inadvertently wandered to a significant Welsh place. I sat with a coffee at the Nova Leisure Centre and thought about Offa and Larkin, singular characters in their own ways: one building miles of defensive ditches across Welsh wildlands, the other penning pages of pithy odes in Hull.

I flicked through the *Daily Post*, billed as "North Wales' Best Read Newspaper": money was being spent on an "antisocial hotspots crackdown", it was a "dark time" for council tax rises, a Barclays Bank was closing and businesses were "pleading for a rethink", there were fears of "stagflation" (not just in North Wales, across the country), and a report focused on the demise of Pontins, a local holiday park that had opened in Prestatyn in 1971 but which had "closed suddenly" a few months earlier. Not the cheeriest of times, and the Pontins shutdown seemed weirdly to echo Larkin's bleak, odd poem.

I walked back up the hill to my rugby-oriented pub/hotel, passing a red-faced man by the station who was yelling to an acquaintance, "I've just been getting leathered out my head, mate." I ate a Subway submarine sandwich. I watched a film at the Marlin cinema. And fell asleep listening to rugby chatter rising through the floorboards.

In the morning, of course, another train awaited.

Prestatyn's little station was a particularly pleasant one, maintained in part by the Friends of Prestatyn Railway Station. It had done a fine job, with troughs of purple and pink hyacinths, old black-and-white pictures of trains in the ticket office and the commissioning of an unusual wooden sculpture of a rambler, known as the *Prestatyn Walker*, by the artist Simon O'Rourke, which dwelled at the end of one of the platforms and had been erected to signify that "Walkers are Welcome" in the seaside town. A sign informed that the station had opened in 1848 and an incredible 22 million rail passengers passed along the line each year. Many of these were en route to and from Holyhead station at the end of the North Wales railway, from where you could catch a ferry to Ireland.

The 09:02 to Crewe pulled in and departed on time.

This was an Avanti West Coast service: shiny, red-and-grey, smooth and almost empty.

A solitary man sat nearby, the only other passenger in sight. He had a camera and a small canvas bag. My increasingly acute trainspotter radar was saying *trainspotter*. But we kept ourselves to ourselves for some time before I could not resist and asked him, using less potentially pejorative terminology, "Are you a rail enthusiast?"

Of course, he was.

I was about to receive my first rail enthusiast/trainspotter briefing of the day on my journey to Llanelli in South Wales via Crewe in the county of Cheshire (my own surname is an old variant of this, though I have no family connection to the area) and a place I had never previously heard of named Craven Arms in Shropshire. A service from Craven Arms known as the Heart of Wales Line ran as advertised south to Llanelli, yet another random stop-off; I didn't even have an old, strange poem reason to go there.

His name was Kevin. He was going to Crewe to meet his 28-year-old son and then they would travel together to Kidderminster to go on the Severn Valley Railway, a heritage line. When you kept your eyes peeled and ears open, attuned your "rail enthusiasm radar", and generally had your railway wits about you, there seemed to be people like Kevin lurking just about anywhere and everywhere on Britain's train network, most of the time. You simply needed to "get in the train zone". And I was beginning to sense I was attaining this higher state of train being. At least, I may have been a little bit closer.

Kevin was a retired civil servant, aged 67, and preferred diesel and electric trains to steam trains. After telling me these basics – railway enthusiasts tend to be quite open about their lives, in particular their inclinations regarding rolling stock – this is what he said, with little prompting, when asked about his enjoyment of trains: "Well, for me it's largely about nostalgia, the old days and all that. But I also like to travel, to get about and take photos and meet people. Have you heard of Woodhead Railway?"

I said I hadn't.

"Well, it was shut in the 1980s, Manchester to Sheffield. It was an electric railway but because of the lack of demand it closed down. I lived very close to that railway, in Hyde in Cheshire."

This was what had got him into trains in the first place – yet another railway that had been squeezed out during Dr Beeching's cuts, although Kevin was a bit down on trains in general these days.

"Nowadays, I don't find train travel relaxing," he said. "You mainly get trains with two carriages, jam-packed full of people, and not comfortable at all, especially at weekends. I do avoid travelling by trains, though deep down I do like it." He paused, thinking about this. "Obviously, I love trains, but the new modern trains are too stressful. There are very often delays and cancellations. I find it very stressful. But I still like taking photos of them."

Kevin showed me his Samsung camera.

"I have something like nine thousand pictures of trains and two thousand of stations," he said, as though this was really nothing.

What were the best places to go to take pictures of trains?

"Clapham Junction because it's so busy and lots to see," he answered, quick as a shot. "Then Crewe, again because there's lots to see. Then Doncaster because you get to see different trains and a lot of freight."

Did he take numbers?

"Yes, only so I can look them up."

Did he know anything about the train we were on?

I thought there was a chance I might just catch him out with this. But I was, of course, wrong, and deep down I knew he would know.

"Voyager. Class 221, run by Avanti," he replied. "Transport for Wales, to my mind, are rubbish as they're always late and crowded. I've lived in Prestatyn for five years, I've been on enough of them."

Transport for Wales also ran trains along the line, but Avanti West Coast's did not usually have as many stops.

What were his favourite heritage railways in Britain?

"Number one, the North Yorkshire Moors," he said, making me feel pleased that Clive had got me to go there after Darlington. "Two, East Lancs Railway. Three, Severn Valley Railway."

Sadly, it seemed, I would be missing these.

Was there, for him, a Penny Black of trains that he was always quietly hoping he might one day spot?

"Now, that's difficult to say as it's personal," he replied with great seriousness before giving me not one but two answers. "First, the Deltic, British Rail Class 55. It's a Co-Co."

He looked at me enquiringly as though ascertaining whether I understood what a "Co-Co" was. I did not, naturally, and felt I was letting Kevin down about this paucity of train knowledge. I had no idea what a "Deltic, British Rail Class 55" was either. But Kevin was patient, and seemed happy enough to fill me in.

"Co-Co means that there are six wheels on each bogie, with two bogies and three axles, and each axle is driven by an electric motor," he said, to which I nodded as though I completely followed what on earth he was exactly saying. "For any rail enthusiast who likes diesel, the Deltics are top. Built in the 1950s. They are withdrawn. But six are in preservation. In Crewe you can see them. You may actually see me in Crewe trying to spot them later. On the North York Moors, you can see them. You can see them on the main line. At Shildon, you'll see the original."

We paused and I looked this up on my phone. I had indeed unwittingly seen the original Deltic, British Rail Class 55 Co-Co when at the Locomotion museum. It was a big gleaming blue one with a flurry of yellow stripes at the front and a streamlined, art deco look to it (at least to my eye). It had been in pride of place by the entrance. I had considered it one of the best of the lot at Shildon in terms of sheer impressiveness.

Kevin was pleased I was in line with his thinking regarding the Deltic, British Rail Class 55 Co-Co.

He gave me his second most-desired "train spot".

"This is where I'm a bit strange," he said. "I like Class 76. They're electric. They're Bo-Bos, they've got four sets of wheels on each bogie and two axles on each bogie and each axle is driven by an electric motor." He did not bother to see whether I knew this on this occasion; he had already ascertained the depth of my train knowledge. "There were 58 of them and now there's one at York Museum. I've got two photographs. They collect electricity from overhead lines. You'll see a number on it, 26020. It's shiny black, electric, and you don't get many of those."

I told Kevin I would keep an eye out.

Seeing as I had a true expert on my hands, I asked what he considered to be Britain's best rail operator?

"Number one, Avanti. Well, actually, Virgin, I used to like them more. They tended to run on time…" Virgin Trains had lost its franchise to run West Coast Main Line trains a few years back. Kevin was about to tell me the rest of his rankings, but he became distracted by a thought and asked me whether I had been past Prestatyn station on the line towards Holyhead. I explained I had only been as far as Llandudno Junction before heading inland to Blaenau Ffestiniog.

"Ah, well you'll have missed out then on the station with the longest name in Britain," Kevin said. This station was, ridiculously, named Llanfairpwllgwyngyllgogerychwyrndrobwllllantysiliogogogoch (58 letters, to save those inclined a count), and it was just across the Menai Strait on the island of Anglesey, although it was sensibly shortened and referred to as Llanfairpwll on timetables and it served the village of Llanfair Pwllgwyngyll, just to make things even more confusing.

The crazy long name had, in fact, just been a joke/stunt to attract Victorian tourists, an 1869 wheeze of a local tailor, it is said, who squeezed the names of extra local sights into the station name in the hope of attracting a tourist stampede to visit the station with the longest name in Britain. So all along it had been a prank. The station with the longest name in Britain was not really the station with the longest name in Britain, but you could go there (as many did) and stare at a station nameplate with the full 58-word name, which meant in its entirety *Saint Mary's Church in the hollow of the white hazel near a rapid whirlpool and the Church of St Tysilio of the red cave.*

Sometimes "railway knowledge" could be quite infuriating.

As Kevin explained this, we were pulling into Crewe, past an electric train depot run by DB Cargo and yards full of old carriages and locomotives at Crewe Heritage Centre.

We both looked across at these old carriages and locos, and I was expecting Kevin to fill me in on some aspect of their technical origin, but instead he just looked a bit dreamy-eyed and said, "I've driven that blue one." He was pointing at an old blue loco. He said no more for a moment or two as though revelling in the memory. Then he said, in a completely disconnected stream of thought, "My wife comes from Crewe."

Did he marry her because she was from one of his favourite stations? (I asked this as a joke.)

"Oh no!" he replied. "Ha ha ha!"

The train stopped at Crewe station.

It felt as though we were arriving at an important "train place".

After all, Crewe had been nothing more than a few fields a couple of miles from a country house named Crewe Hall before the opening of Crewe station on the Grand Junction Railway in 1837. When its location was picked for railway works by the prominent Victorian engineer Joseph Locke (who had been crucial to the building of the Liverpool and Manchester Railway alongside George Stephenson, and who had been driving *Rocket* when it tragically ran over poor old William Huskisson), its fate was sealed and a "railway town" sprang up, with town planning overseen by Grand Junction itself.

From population zero, Crewe had risen to a population of 76,437 at last count. Railways were still an employer locally, at DB Cargo UK and also at a heritage train maintenance depot named Locomotive Service Limited, but this was minor compared to the railway influence of years gone by, when thousands were employed in train yards. Local employment had moved on to include work in a Bentley car factory, a BAE Systems Land and Armaments factory making ammunition for the army, an ice-cream manufacturer and the headquarters of the chain Bargain Booze.

Nevertheless, the local football team was still nicknamed The Railwaymen, and the Crewe Heritage Centre, although almost entirely devoted to trains, did not need the word "trains" in its title, as the "heritage" of the town was, more or less entirely, "trains" so this did not appear to be necessary to state outright.

"We're still enthusiasts, despite everything"
Crewe station

Crewe station was Trainspotter Central. Everywhere you looked: trainspotters. The place was crawling with them.

There were young trainspotters. "I find trains interesting and different. Varied. I like locomotives when they're lovely and slick," said Ben (not his real name), aged sixteen.

There were thirtysomething trainspotters. "I like taking videos of trains. The variety of locomotives. Doing this [trainspotting] allows you to explore places," said Patrick, aged 33.

There were a great many middle-aged trainspotters, many of whom were on platform 12.

Richard was aged 58, a civil contractor from Telford. He was with his mate David, aged 61, an engineer from York.

I was about to receive my second trainspotter briefing of the day, delivered in tandem. Both Richard and David, however, seemed slightly down about their hobby.

Richard: "There's not a lot to see these days. Some heritage stuff. Some new stuff. I suppose it's still nice to see the new ones."

David: "I can't get the love of trains any more. I never look at 'em all. They're just plastic junk. They don't really build proper ones any more."

Why had they come to platform 12 then?

David: "East Coast Main Line Class 91. They're the sole survivors. 1991. That's the best. That's from before all the buying plastic from abroad."

Richard: "Now trains are built to a price and they're not reliable."

David: "Not comfortable. Cheap."

Richard: "I do like Stadler 777s."

David smirked at that as though he certainly did not like Stadler 777s.

Richard: "But they've got some door problems at the moment, modifications."

David looked across the track and sighed: "That's a good British product."

It was a purple-coloured East Midlands Railway train. "That's a Class 170," he said. He seemed to approve of Class 170s.

Richard: "Mainly you get Spanish rubbish, you get them going to Caernarfon, Cardiff… two carriages. Twenty years ago, there'd be five. Now you'll have to stand up probably."

Richard turned and regarded a passing train: "That's a 197, built by CAF, assembled in Newport." CAF stood for Construcciones y Auxiliar de Ferrocarriles, a Spanish company.

David: "Like a jigsaw." Referring to how the 197 trains were assembled. He sounded disparaging about this technique.

A bullet-nosed London North Eastern Railway (LNER) train zoomed by platform 12.

Richard: "That's an Azuma, built in Japan… Hitachi. Assembled in Newton Aycliffe."

Their feelings on Azumas were not made clear, though they did not seem especially enamoured.

David: "If you could find a time machine and go back 30 years. I'd have it. It were proper back then."

Richard: "Exeter to Newton Abbot, you could have the window down. Salt air in face and wind in hair. That's all you want. The railway is very sterile, health and safety conscious now."

David: "OTT."

Richard: "And boring."

David: "We used to go every week." He was referring to trainspotting.

Richard: "Grantham, Peterborough, York, Doncaster, Manchester, Bristol."

David: "Clapham Junction, to sit and watch trains. Doncaster."

Pause (and contemplation of better times).

Richard: "But we're still enthusiasts, despite everything."

Pause (and contemplation of current times).

Richard: "Signal failures, mechanical failures, strikes, delays to services. You can't rely on 'em any more."

David: "Twenty years ago, if there was snow, the roads would shut and there would be no buses. But the railway said, *Don't worry, we'll get you to Leeds*. Now?" He left this hanging with an unspoken answer of: *Forget it*.

Richard: "Transport for Wales two years ago cancelled the trains because of the threat of snow." He put particular emphasis on the word "threat". In the event there had not been any snow. "Health and safety for the staff," he said.

David: "The railways are not run for the passengers any more."

Richard: "It's a business. If a train's late or cancelled now, *It's your problem, mate*. Before it was *We'll get you there*. Remember British Rail? In the last ten to twenty years, it'd been steadily deteriorating." British Rail had ceased trading in 1997 as privatization of BR, planned under Conservative Prime Minister Margaret Thatcher, was put into action by her colleague and successor Prime Minister John Major.

Richard: "Health and safety. If you're on platform six and on the wrong side of the yellow line, just walking along by it without a train in sight, you'll be told to move."

As Richard said this, a cancellation was announced over the station speakers.

David: "Oh, a cancellation!" He said this in a mocking voice. The announcement said the cancellation was because of a broken-down train.

David: "*Broken-down train*, that's what they just said. But it went through just now empty. Probably a guard hasn't turned up. Cancelled due to more trains than staff."

David: "Why lie to people? Seriously. The whole time. They're up their own a***s."

A train went by.

Richard: "That's a Class 70."

I could not detect from his tone of voice whether that was good or bad.

As we parted, as though to confirm their gloom, another announcement began explaining a delay: *This is due to a broken...*

Richard and David looked at me with expressions that suggested *You believe that?* Then they shuffled off. "See you later, ta-rah," said Richard. They shuffled away clutching satchel-style bags with multiple zips and wearing heavy jackets and aviator-style glasses: proper old-school trainspotters.

On another platform at Crewe there was a kerfuffle.

This was because a heritage train run by a company specializing in heritage journeys had drawn in.

Crewe was a veritable hive of activity: trainspotters and trains.

The heritage train had well-polished, brown-and-cream carriages with "PULLMAN" written on them – named after the flamboyant American railway entrepreneur George Mortimer Pullman (1831–1897) – and crisp, white tablecloths with well-polished cutlery and well-polished wine glasses set at the tables inside. Everything was spick and span and generally well polished and in good order, with staff from a company called Statesman Rail in smart uniforms preparing for passengers to arrive for a journey. I asked one about the train, which was pulled by a two-tone green diesel locomotive with *Roger Hosking* on the nameplate – and which was driving a cluster of trainspotters wild by rumbling and occasionally hooting.

"Dining is three hundred and fifty pounds a head including drink. We're going to Carlisle, eight carriages," said the train manager.

A station "safeguarding officer" was on the platform, running about in a state of high nervousness with so many trainspotters about, making sure no one crossed the yellow safety line.

One of these trainspotters (only one out of about 30) was female. She was in her teens and in a jubilant mood as she admired *Roger Hosking*. "I've been inspired by many people, taken it up as a hobby," she said.

"I'm obsessed, to be honest. My friends don't know any other women trainspotters, but they are happy to know me."

What did she like about trains so much?

"Everything really… classes and liveries," she said, adding that her favourite was a "Castle HST, a Class 37."

I thanked her for this information and went to platform five to catch the 12:10 to Craven Arms.

Football lads and a Welsh party train
Crewe to Llanelli via Craven Arms

All was not well on platform five. Several trains were being delayed or cancelled to Liverpool Lime Street and Glasgow Central. The operating company involved, Avanti West Coast, was, however, at least admitting that these problems were "due to a shortage of train crew", not blaming something else.

The 12:10 was not, however, delayed. I boarded, and shortly afterwards so did a large number of Wigan Athletic football fans, who were travelling to watch their team play in Shrewsbury. I was lucky to have a seat. The Wigan Athletic FC lads (they were all blokes, mainly in their late teens and twenties and thirties, though some were older) had filled the aisles and the doorways: standing room only. An Avanti member of staff with a trolley with teas and snacks was stuck by the doorway, unable to move anywhere for the time being, though the football lads, who numbered at least fifty and who wore a fine line in jeans and mint-condition casual sportswear, with Adidas and Puma among the favourite brands of footwear, were not giving her any other trouble. She was simply stuck.

"Has anyone got a bottle opener?" asked one. He had a box of Super Bock bottled beers in a plastic bag.

"B******s!" said one of them. I did not think this was in reply to the question.

"Give me a Super Bock!" said another.

Then they all started singing, over and over, for a while, "Blue and White Army!"

A middle-aged woman was sitting next to me. She was travelling beyond Shrewsbury to collect a horsebox to replace one that had burned in a mysterious fire caused by a faulty battery, and was having trouble with insurance paying out (she had rapidly conveyed all this). She raised an eyebrow but smiled. She did not seem to mind the lads but was unhappy with her seat. "No good for my dodgy knee," she said.

We rolled away, and the Wigan lads began singing, "Di-di-di-di-di-der-der-der... Do-do-do-do-dah-dah-dah-dah" before pausing and adding, "Whoah! Whoah!"

Football lads, again, singing: "Who gives a f***? I like it, I like it... [name of a player mentioned] Super sub! Whoah! Whoah!" Repeated a few times.

Pause briefly.

Football lads: "Oh, Wigan Town is wonderful. Oh, Wigan Town is wonderful. It's full of tits, fanny and football. Oh, Wigan town is wonderful."

The middle-aged woman sitting next to me was smiling and looking out of the window in a manner that suggested, *Lads will be lads, they're harmless really.*

"You got some Super Bock?" said a lad.

"Yeah," said the Super Bock lad.

"That's Portuguese, that is," said the lad wanting the Super Bock.

"Yeah," said the Super Bock lad.

Football lads singing again to the tune of the Beatles' song "Yellow Submarine": "We all live in a tub of margarine, a tub of margarine, a tub of margarine." Over and over, for a while. I quite liked that one.

Another song: "When I see you Wigan, I go out of my head... I just can't get enough! I just can't get enough!" Repeated several times over to the tune of Depeche Mode's song "Just Can't Get Enough". Another decent Wigan FC ditty.

Another song: "All in all, drinking all the Guinness!" Repeated to the tune of "September" by Earth, Wind and Fire. Not bad either.

Somebody burped loudly.

The middle-aged woman turned to me and said, "I'm glad they're only going to Shrewsbury."

Football lads, as though having heard her: "Que sera sera, whatever will be will be, we're going to Shrewsbury, que sera sera."

Then: "Oh ah, oh ah, oh ah, you should be a Wig-an-er!"

Depeche Mode again: "When I see you, Wigan… I just can't get enough… I just can't get enough."

Football lads, going a bit *Clockwork Orange*: "Karen's f***in' fumin'. Karen? Karen? Who the f*** is Karen? Que sera sera, whatever will be, will be… All the ****in' tits [repeated three times]… I need a piss [repeated three times]." Loud fart.

Middle-aged woman, changing her attitude: "It's just intimidating, isn't it?"

Loud fart again as the train pulled into Shrewsbury.

Football lads: "I wanna go home, I wanna go home, Shrewsbury's a s***hole, I wanna go home."

The football lads all got off the train, where a dog waiting with a passenger cowered from them.

The trolley woman continued her service. As I bought a cup of tea, she said, "I'm used to it. But that was a big crowd."

You could not but admire her nerve.

Middle-aged woman, whose name was Sue: "This is the problem really, trains get a bad press and people want to go in their cars."

Not long afterwards the Avanti West Coast service pulled into Craven Arms.

This turned out to be yet another railway town – what corner of the country you may soon find yourself asking, if you go around it messing about on trains for long enough, has not been at least touched, if not completely transformed, by your mode of transport?

Craven Arms had once been a small village named Newton – until the railway came in 1852, that is. Suddenly, a market town sprang up and the name was changed to Craven Arms after the Craven Arms Hotel, a red-brick structure close to the tracks. I had stopped in a place named after a train hotel. Or to be more accurate: a town named after a former train hotel that was now derelict and boarded up with metal vandal-proof sheets across its windows (on my visit).

Nearby, I had read, was a local museum named the Land of Lost Content, which was billed as a "national museum of British popular culture" and was said to "chronicle twentieth-century life". Intriguing. With two hours to kill till my next train, I walked down a terraced street to find this "national museum", but the national museum of British popular culture was permanently closed too, looking in a sorry state, with peeling paint and a few piled-up empty boxes visible through the window in a dusty, otherwise empty front room. The "lost content" from the lost content museum seemed to have been lost (or taken somewhere else).

I ate a decent chilli con carne at a pub that was open named The Stables, sitting near a lit fireplace at a table that was also occupied by a red-faced man drinking lager, who told me he used to be centre-forward for the pub football team.

"Thirty-six goals in one season, I'd just put the ball ahead of me and boom! I was that good," he said, thrusting a foot forwards as though showing how he used to score. He went to the bar to fetch another drink.

Then I walked back to the (unstaffed) station and boarded the 15:52 to Llanelli.

So began a journey on the Welsh party train.

The 15:52 was a single carriage Transport for Wales service and it was packed.

This train, travelling along the Heart of Wales Line, passed 30 stations, with quite a few of these beginning with "Ll", as it wound its way for 90 miles to the final "Ll" of Llanelli. The journey would take 3 hours and 9 minutes at about 30 mph. On the trusty National Rail map, the route slashed across the middle of Wales in a thin blue line at 45 degrees.

The Heart of Wales Line had survived the Beeching cuts, being too important to local communities. So the single-track service remained, running about a dozen times directly in each direction daily.

I boarded the 15:52 and it set forth slowly but steadily across brown ploughed fields beyond Craven Arms as solitary clouds scudded above and lazy sunbeams fanned recently cultivated fields.

The Heart of Wales train felt like a trip off the map, despite being so clearly on it. Once the junction for Broome and then Hopton Heath and Bucknell, Knighton, Knucklas, Llangynllo and Llanbister Road was taken (those were the first stations), it seemed as though you were heading deeper and deeper into remote landscape, more isolated and removed than the Yorkshire Dales, even, if not as bleak.

This was rich, fertile farmland. You crossed into Wales between Knighton and Knucklas, where – at around this point – the first sound of beer cans fizzing open began. My neighbours, two middle-aged couples in the rows ahead, launched into Cobra lagers (for the men) and Chardonnay (for their other halves).

Fizz. Tinkle of bottle cap. "Wahaay! Cheers to you, Stuart!"

"Cheers, Gav!"

"You OK there, Jane?"

Jane, sipping Chardonnay from a plastic glass: "I'm OK, Gav."

"Glenda?"

"Yes, Gav?"

"You OK?"

She had Chardonnay in a plastic glass, too. "Yes, Gav." In a tone to suggest *Could you pipe down a bit, Gav, everyone can hear you.*

But they were not the only ones; further down the carriage, similar scenes were afoot. I had joined the Heart of Wales party line.

Outside, rain began to lash down almost the moment our happy little red train entered Wales, clicking and clattering along the line, hooting now and then. The scenery became green and hilly, as though the 15:52 had entered a wet green dunescape; a Welsh Sahara; a very damp Welsh Empty Quarter.

The tracks rose. Farmsteads came and went in an increasing gloom. Extremely muddy fields appeared and went. The hills loomed. The rain persisted. Jane said, "Come on then. Let's have a sing-song. Let's do it in Welsh."

She started singing but the others did not follow, so she kept going for a while and it was extremely charming and almost haunting as the rest of the carriage fell silent as she sang, pausing in the pouring of wine and opening of cans. I could not understand a single word but it was quite lovely.

She stopped. Bottles resumed clinking. Rain ran in rivulets down the carriage windows. It got darker still. We went by the river Wye, which looked glossy and brown and as though many trout probably lurked below. A long, wobbly ridge rose with copses that looked stuck on like fake moustaches.

Stuart, Gav, Jane and Glenda talked about all sorts.

Jane, on her daughter's hair: "I can't do nothing with it. I can't do her hair myself. Twenty pounds I give her to get it done. Twenty!"

Gav, in response, in mock seriousness: "Shocking."

Glenda and Jane talked in Welsh between themselves for a while, at the end of which Glenda said, in English, "Well, he's not in my family, he's the father of my granddaughter, that's it. Not my family. He's a right…"

Glenda used some colourful language.

Gav, who had been ignoring this, muttered at his phone and waved it about as he switched subject to technology: "You know, I'm glad I'm not on Facebook."

Stuart, who was not either he said, nodded in agreement: "I'm with you, Gav. TikTok. Do you know TikTok? What is TikTok? Do you know, Gav?"

Gav said he did not know. Glenda and Jane kept quiet, and I got the impression they did not know either.

Then Jane, breaking a temporary silence, said, "It's Alexa I worry about. You know it's listening to you? Have you ever had it ask you something that you never knew it knew about you?"

Stuart: "Does it know your bank details?"

Jane: "I should hope not."

Gav, peering out of the window: "Look at it now. It's absolutely chuckin' it down."

The rain had intensified. It was like a monsoon.

Glenda, introducing another topic: "Have you seen Neil lately? When he's up to 17 stone, he knows it's time to go on a diet. He's going to have a big heart attack."

Gav: "Shocking."

Jane, on another male acquaintance and his behaviour at a party she had been to with him, at what sounded like a nightclub: "He says to me, 'I'm going to turn a straight man gay.'"

Stuart, replying: "You can't do that."

Jane: "Well, I asked later where he was and someone said, 'Oh, he's having sex in the toilet.'"

The gay man had turned the straight man gay, according to Jane, despite Stuart's thoughts on the matter.

Stuart: "Was it consensual?"

Gav: "What does that mean? Get me a dictionary!"

Stuart: "Did he want to do it?"

Glenda: "Was the other man married?"

Jane: "Yes."

Glenda: "Well he must have been a bisexual then."

They all moved on to red wine. They were clearly enjoying having a good gossip and pushing the boundaries of topics as the train rattled on and darkness began to fall.

Gav: "Are there any empties there? Yes? Give them here."

Jane, pouring herself the rest of the Chardonnay and handing over the bottle: "I can't drink red wine anyway."

Gav: "It's good for you!"

Stuart: "Red is always stronger, isn't it?"

Glenda, who had tasted it: "It's a cheap wine."

Gav, pretending to be offended and reading from the label: "It's spicy, well-balanced wine with a rounded taste that fits most dishes – Italian and spicy Asian foods."

There were pouring sounds, both inside and outside the 15:52.

They discussed holidays.

Jane: "Seven nights, Rhodes, four hundred and eighty-five pounds, all-inclusive, October twenty-fourth."

Gav: "Where's Rhodes?"

Jane, with mock disdain at his played-up ignorance: "Greece."

Stuart: "'Sex on the Beach', you'll enjoy that."

Glenda, ignoring this comment directed at her: "It's an island, isn't it?"

Jane: "Rhodes, yes, you go to Faliraki... then you've got Ios."

Stuart: "That's the smallest island."

Gav: "If it's all-inclusive, you don't get out and about."

Glenda: "I bet these deals get booked up quickly anyway."

Jane: "Another one here, Dalaman. Two hundred and ninety-three for five nights."

Gav: "Where's that?"

Jane, with mock disdain bordering on real disdain: "Turkey."

Glenda: "We've got to look cheaper than that."

Gav, to Stuart: "You've got money."

Stuart, reflectively: "Well, yes, I've got a few bob."

The subjects swirled. Wales turned black. The red wine was finished. We arrived in Llanelli in the south-west Welsh county of Carmarthenshire. We all got off.

The 15:52 from Craven Arms to Llanelli was one of the best rides yet. Not for any particular Train Nut reasons. Just because it was a whole lot of fun.

CHAPTER FIVE

LLANELLI TO TAUNTON VIA PENZANCE, ST IVES, TORQUAY, EXETER AND OKEHAMPTON

BRUNEL'S BRITAIN

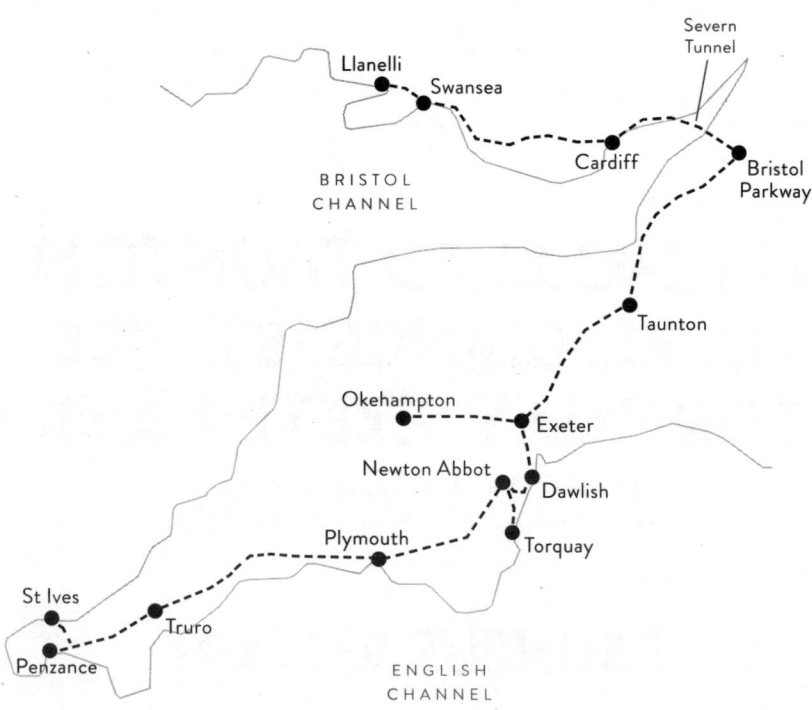

The purpose of these train travels was not to do places down – it was to celebrate British trains on a grand, meandering and admittedly somewhat whimsical tour that also happened to be a great excuse to hit the tracks and "escape" in a "railway world" for a while. I could not deny that. (And what could possibly be wrong with, or the slightest bit unusual about, that?). All perfectly normal… quite perfectly normal.

On the other hand, no point in keeping your thoughts to yourself about stops along the way: tell it how it was. Even on the briefest of visits to Llanelli, impressions were that it had seen (much) better times.

A terraced street scattered with litter by the railway led down from the station to what seemed to be the centre of this South Wales market town, once a thriving tin- and steel-making hub. It was Saturday night and I was expecting lively scenes, especially after the Heart of Wales party line. Instead, I entered a warren of empty, windswept pedestrianized streets where the only place that seemed to be open was a bookmaker, although I kept on walking and at the edge of this warren you came to an opening with a solitary pub, The New Stepney, opposite an arts complex (with nothing on that evening).

A woman standing outside the pub was smoking a cigarette. Considering going in, I asked if I was in the centre of Llanelli.

"Yes," she replied, taking a drag and pausing to blow out a plume of smoke. "You're in it."

Was there another bit that I was missing?

"There's nothing here really," she replied. "It's just gone from worse to worse round here. It's all closed. Closed over there." She was pointing back to the pedestrianized area. "There's not much point in coming here. Not here," she said. "You could try Carmarthen. Carmarthen's on the rise." Carmarthen was the county town of Carmarthenshire, fifteen miles to the north.

"Not here. There's nothing here. I wouldn't bother," she said, reiterating her earlier observation. She would not have made the greatest local tourist board official, but she was the only "local guide" (just about the only local at all) seemingly around.

I took her advice, returned to my hotel and got an early Saturday night. Best to cut your losses sometimes.

"We are very sorry to announce that…"
Llanelli to Penzance

Sunday morning in Llanelli was even quieter still.

I was due to catch the 09:59 to Swansea and arrived at the station early to get breakfast at an inviting little corner café I had spotted the evening before: The Coffee Pot.

But first I went to the station platform and gazed across the tracks. For Llanelli station was the scene of high drama and tragedy in 1911.

On 19 August that year, railway workers seeking better pay had staged demonstrations as part of the first national rail strike, a two-day strike that had begun the day before. It was a highly sensitive occasion across the country, and around 60,000 troops had been mobilized by Winston Churchill, the home secretary, to keep the peace. Many, Churchill included, feared troubles could flare and have wider consequences – a breakdown in national order – not just causing great harm to the economy.

In Llanelli, 370 troops had gathered, while strikers had formed a picket by the station and taken to the tracks to block a train run by "blacklegs" (strike-breakers). This they had achieved, and by putting out the fire of the furnace, the locomotive had become immobilized, with the unrest escalating as stones were thrown at troops, who opened fire, tragically killing two young men, supposedly the result of warning shots that had gone astray. The reaction was rioting across town as well as an explosion in a freight carriage that resulted in four others dying.

It had been a dreadful day. The two men shot dead were John "Jac" John, a 21-year-old millworker supporting the railway strike, and Leonard Worsell, a 19-year-old from south London who had been visiting the town and merely watching what was happening from a back garden. A plaque on Union Bridge at Queen Victoria Road remembered them:

"On the track below a train was stopped by strikers. Two bystanders were shot and killed by troops."

It turned out that while this had been going on, negotiations to resolve the dispute had already begun in London; the news had not reached the Llanelli demonstrators.

The background to all this was that rail workers had long been underpaid, but railway companies had been clamping down on wages as costs had been rising, and they were also under pressure to maintain dividends for shareholders. At the time, around 650,000 people out of a population of 45.2 million were employed on the railways, and the strike did indeed lead to positive change for rail workers, with the 1912 Light Railways Act permitting train companies to increase ticket prices, which had previously been capped, to cover higher wages.

Plenty to think about over breakfast at The Coffee Pot.

And what a great breakfast it was: a Full Monty Welsh breakfast, a veritable pile-up of a fry-up, with sausages, eggs, bacon, beans, the lot, served in a light and airy room with four other diners in attendance, all eating Full Monty Welsh breakfasts too.

No one said a word. Yet somehow we were united in silent solidarity, content with our Full Montys, no conversation required. It was peaceful and quiet. There were simple tables and chairs, whitewashed walls, an ordering kiosk and a menu offering steak pie, potatoes and peas (£9) or chicken curry with rice (£7); the café's hours were 7 a.m. to 3 p.m., so presumably these were for lunch.

A picture of a glamorous couple on a platform with a train that looked like the Orient Express waiting to depart hung above a fireplace on the right. There was no other ostentation. There was no need for any. We ate our excellent Full Monty Welsh breakfasts. The food did the talking at The Coffee Pot, my favourite station café of the trip so far.

Then I walked over to the station to catch the 09:59 to Swansea.

The "train plan" for the day involved this short trip of about a dozen miles, followed by a connection to Bristol Parkway, another to

Plymouth and a final train to Penzance in Cornwall. A total journey of 7 hours and 6 minutes. Madness, you might say. Yet there was only a single line down to the far south-western tip of England, and I figured I would be returning along the south coast of Cornwall and Devon anyway. So the journey to Penzance was an act of "relocation" ready for a swoop across southern England, heading in the direction of Kent.

Yes, 7 hours was a long time, but I had plenty of reading material for the rides.

However, the journey began, nevertheless, to take on an epic quality that might be summed up thus: *When It All Goes Wrong*.

Though it all began smoothly enough.

OK, the first train was slightly late – an announcement at Llanelli had said, "The 09:59 to Swansea is delayed by six minutes due to crew being delayed" (no reason given for that) – but we were soon trundling beyond rows of pebble-dash houses with satellite dishes on the way to Swansea. This was when a message flashed on my phone. It was from the company I had bought my ticket from. It read: "CHANGE AT SWANSEA. NOT ENOUGH TIME TO CHANGE."

Oh, I thought for a moment, not sure what to make of this.

The train was going fast with the Severn Estuary looking vapoury to the right, where fishermen on fold-up chairs were trying their luck. A few passengers near me were worried about the connection too and were asking the conductor about it.

"It's fine," he said. "They're going to hold it, the one to London. We've been on the phone to them."

This was when another message from the company I had bought my ticket from flashed up: "Major disruption between Bristol Parkway/Chippenham and Swindon expected until 12:00."

Oh, I thought to myself, *at least that won't affect me*.

The train passed a FedEx depot, crossed the river Loughor, skirted terraced rows on a hill on the edge of Swansea and arrived at Swansea station. Several of us disembarked and rushed onto the 10:22 to

London, due in at Bristol Parkway at 11:55. This was a chrome-green Great Western Railway (GWR) service, stopping at Neath, Port Talbot Parkway, Bridgend, Cardiff Central and Newport before Bristol Parkway. It rolled away past Swansea City AFC's stadium. A fellow passenger was eating crisps noisily nearby, but I could handle that. The train had left on time – I would make the connection in Bristol.

The line followed the M4 for a while, with houses rising on a hill before the stop at Port Talbot where you got a decent view of the old, closed steelworks with their cooling towers and pipes on the right that were said to have inspired Ridley Scott's hellish vision of the future in the film *Blade Runner*. Into and out of Cardiff past its striking Principality Stadium and across the river Taff we went, and an announcement was made over the speakers: "We will be making additional stops on this route due to heavy flooding during the night where we are passing. So we are stopping at extra stations and diverting so it will put time on – at least thirty minutes."

Oh, I thought for a moment, but all of this was happening after Bristol Parkway, so, frankly and admittedly selfishly, *what did I care?*

The train plunged beneath the river Severn, rose into England and stopped soon at Bristol Parkway, where I disembarked... and began to listen to a long string of announcements. Each one concerned delays that were being blamed on *waiting for a part of the train to be attached*, *flooding* and *a fault on the train in front*. The announcements began with *we are very sorry to announce that* – and because the delays kept slightly increasing in length, whoever was in charge of the announcements felt obliged to issue updated announcements beginning each new message with *we are very sorry to announce that*. These happened with such regularity that I began to count the time between them and never made it beyond 60 seconds. Very quickly, the phrase *we are very sorry to announce that* was humming through my brain on repeat, whether coming from the speakers at Bristol Parkway station or not.

I boarded the 12:39, which was actually departing at 1.06 p.m. – so only 27 minutes late (not too bad; others had been over an hour).

This was a CrossCountry train, delayed due to *a fault on a train in front of this one around Derby*. So not CrossCountry's fault, as the tone of voice of the announcer made abundantly clear.

After stopping at Bristol Temple Meads, the main Bristol station, the train rolled on through classic English countryside. Solitary oaks rose in fields. Hedgerows meandered. Horseboxes stood in drives next to Range Rovers beside stables. Bedraggled sheep munched turf in boggy pastures while clusters of starlings circled above mossy-roofed barns as sunlight broke through in long thin beams onto the stubble of hayfields below. The silhouette of the train sometimes fell in shadow beside the tracks, hypnotic to watch until the next cloud broke the "show".

The countryside was not untouched by the awfulness of twenty-first-century human beings. There were electricity pylons, solar panel farms (awful-looking yet not without their merits) and an extremely long, large Morrisons supermarket depot between Burnham-on-Sea and Bridgwater. But nature seemed generally to be "winning" on this stretch, and we pulled into Taunton station, where my seat was, conveniently, beside a plaque that said the station had opened in 1835 and that the Bristol and Exeter Railway had first arrived on 1 July 1842, seventeen years after the Stockton and Darlington Railway.

As I gazed at this plaque thinking about how incredible that seemed, an announcement was made that we would be delayed for a while longer at the station due to traffic on the track.

Oh, I thought to myself, *no surprise there*.

But I did not mind one bit.

Because this seemed an appropriate place to pay homage to the man who had made the railway to Taunton possible in the first place.

This line had been the work of the brilliant engineer Isambard Kingdom Brunel, who had opened the famous Great Western Railway from London to Bristol a year earlier (having personally surveyed the 104 miles between the two, working 20-hour days at the task) and whose tracks were to reach Exeter (in 1844) and Plymouth (1849). His plans were in place to continue a main line with through trains to Penzance at the time of his death (1859), a feat eventually achieved across the challengingly hilly Cornish landscape in 1867; although, happily, the Portsmouth-born genius had been alive to witness the key opening of the Royal Albert Bridge across the river Tamar into Cornwall from Devon (to his design) five months before his premature departure from a stroke aged 53.

Genius is not too strong a word – genius combined with drive. Brunel's creations rapidly and effectively opened up the west and the south-west of England to trains, the invention that was transforming Victorian Britain. No doubt trains would have happened if Brunel had not been around, but his sheer force of personality, attention to detail and talent, despite having no previous railway experience, raised the railway-building game in the country. The Stephensons had for once been pushed to one side by a parliamentary decision to try out the daring newcomer, who had formal training in engineering, unlike his self-taught rivals.

Brunel's acumen at building tunnels (including the first under a navigable river at the Thames in east London) and bridges (including the Royal Albert Bridge, the important Maidenhead Bridge over the Thames and the spectacular Clifton Suspension Bridge across the Avon Gorge in Bristol) was second to none. Meanwhile, as no small sideline, he was to create a series of pioneering steamships, including what is considered the first truly modern ship (one driven by a propeller, with an iron hull), the *SS Great Britain*, which first crossed the Atlantic to New York from Liverpool in 1845. Put together, which he intended them to be, his steam-powered trains and steam-powered boats effectively shrank the globe forever and were vital to many of the successes of the Victorian era that bolstered Britain's wealth.

He was an engineering revolutionary who pushed boundaries. When Brunel's line from Bristol to Exeter opened on 1 May 1844 – departing at 5.20 p.m. and passing though Taunton station – one of the passengers, Sir Thomas Acland, Member of Parliament, had on arrival in the capital headed straight to the Houses of Parliament to tell the assorted members in attendance at 10.30 p.m. where he had been just a few hours earlier. His colleagues were amazed, but not completely astounded; Brunel had already wowed them all enough times.

By the following year, Brunel's Bristol express trains were powering along from London, achieving speeds of more than 70 mph. A mere 20 years after the crowds had gathered at Darlington to cheer on *Locomotion No 1* puttering along at 15 mph and 15 years after the *Rocket* had slid into Manchester with the cowering Duke of Wellington on board, reaching a similar speed on that journey (although *Rocket* was capable of 30 mph), Brunel had trains running at Britain's maximum speed for cars on roads in the 2020s.

The days of stagecoaches and canals seemed to belong to another era, and cartoons in satirical magazines showed horses busking with violins, prancing on two legs and holding out hats for tips, with speech bubbles saying "Please to remember old Paddy the trader on the Liverpool Road" and seeking handouts from corn warehouses: "Four pennyworth of corn for me and my brother sufferers."

In short, Brunel had taken what the Stephensons had dreamed up and run with it. No wonder in a major poll in 2002 of the "100 Greatest Britons" Brunel had come second, behind only Winston Churchill (George Stephenson, rather unfairly, came in at number 65, two behind George Harrison, guitarist for the Beatles). Not only had Brunel excelled in his field of endeavour, but the public also loved him, even 143 years on.

His only real mistake – quite a big one – was to have opted for a broad gauge of railway track (7 feet, ¼ inch) rather than the Stephensons' lesser standard gauge (4 feet, 8½ inches). Brunel, with arrogance springing from his usual Midas touch, believed that all the other railways would be altered to his wider gauge when they realized how smoothly his trains ran. He got this completely wrong; although it did not matter too much as the tracks were altered after his death so all Britain's railways would easily connect without tiresome waits for those transferring to/from GWR services.

What a character he must have been.

No harm in letting a little blue plaque on a station wall let your mind wander.

An announcement warned us to stand clear of the doors.

The train moved on to Plymouth.

More classic English countryside appeared outside: hedgerows and paddocks and fields of ploughed earth, with solitary oak trees dotted here and there and tractors puttering along. There were cows and pigs and sheep and all seemed well with the world. The train was moving smoothly, so gently yet swiftly we seemed to be levitating across this distinguished stretch of West Country.

Further on, wide plains arose and the landscape became wetter and muddier as though a particularly heavy band of rain had just passed through, evidence of the aftermath of the downpours hampering journeys beyond Bristol to London. We pulled into Exeter, took on a lot more passengers and continued past a church spire and along the river Exe, passing a half-sunk boat and moving to a seawall along the English Channel. This was one of the loveliest sections of ride yet: golden, red-tinted sand on beaches, crumbly cliffs and the metallic sweep of sea leading across the horizon to France.

It was also the section, at Dawlish, that sometimes closed in heavy storms. Ten years previously, a particularly severe storm had wiped away part of the station, causing the line's closure and requiring Network Rail to spend £165 million fortifying the seawall and patching up the line, the only one connecting to parts of Devon and all of Cornwall, so that it could be used again within two months, although the economic impact of the closure was estimated to be as much as £1.2 billion. This seemed rather steep, but if accurate showed just how important railways remained.

Anyway, around Dawlish some GWR staff, a whole crew from a train, sat down near me in the carriage and I listened to them for a while.

Their train had been cancelled and the "resources department" had sent them home to Plymouth; though one of them was worried their supervisor would be upset that she had listened to the resources department and was concerned that "I'm gonna get sacked".

A colleague reassured her: "No one will do that. I'll ring them to cover you."

And I listened to this GWR crew discussing senior colleagues in a colourful way for a while.

At Plymouth, where I was due to change, different GWR staff on the platform told all of us going to Penzance to get on one train. All of us going to Penzance did that. Then there was an announcement: "Sorry, just waiting for some crew issues to be resolved."

Oh, I thought to myself, *well at least we're on the train and ready to go, maybe that GWR crew I was eavesdropping on will be called back into action.*

We all sat on the train and waited. Then all of us going to Penzance were told to cross the platform and join a different train that would be going to our destination. This train was much smaller than the other train, but luckily, as I was one of the first across, I found a seat.

On board this train, another GWR service, there was a further announcement, made by a harassed-sounding guard: "There's been a lot of bad communication here at Plymouth. The train at the other platform was cancelled. Why no one told me I do not know. Please accept my apologies. It's an absolutely disgusting situation. Why they thought they could do this, put a nine-carriage train in a three-carriage train, I do not know."

This was what had happened. We all waited for a while, dealing with the "absolutely disgusting situation" the best we could – a lot of people were standing in the aisles due to the switch from a nine-carriage to a three-carriage train.

There was another announcement: "Please accept my apologies. I cannot physically move this train with so many people on it. I can't get on the train. I cannot move within it as it is now." Chaos seemed to be descending.

"Why they cancelled a nine-carriage train and put it on a three-carriage, I do not know," he said.

However, the doors made a beeping sound and the train moved away. The harassed guard came on again: "This train is seventeen minutes late. This is due to legally not being able to run the train. I understand that you are badly delayed already. I hope you understand that to put a nine-carriage train in a three-carriage train, the laws of physics could not allow."

Other passengers were getting sick and tired of it all.

A woman in the row in front was on her phone: "It's ridiculous, we were just kicked off a nine-carriage train onto a three-carriage train…"

Another passenger was saying to a friend, "Jess has just texted to say they've landed in France. It's quicker to get to France than Cornwall."

The GWR train passed the Plymouth docks, with glimpses of funnels and radars on some naval ships, and then we crossed the solid metal frame of Brunel's fantastic Royal Albert Bridge, looking at the little sailing boats moored on the river Tamar below. This took us to Saltash station, where the train stopped and did not move again for some time.

There was an announcement. It was the harassed guard once more: "Apologies but we do now have a problem with a door. We are still trying to figure it out. We do not understand what's going on. We do understand that this is awful with all the delays caused by the floods." Other passengers, many coming from London, had been badly held up by them.

Annoyingly, a recorded message began repeatedly saying: "Welcome aboard. Safely store your luggage…" Then there were some loud grinding sounds, which all of us going to Penzance assumed was an effort to resolve the problem with the door near the back of the train. After half an hour or so, the doors made a bleeping sound and shut. There was no further announcement and we continued across rolling green Cornish countryside, passing the remains of a fine old stone viaduct near Liskeard, to Truro.

As we were pulling into Truro, however, the harassed guard was back on again: "This service will terminate at Truro."

He informed us we must change onto the train behind.

"Nobody has called to tell me this," he said. "I have just seen this on the app."

The GWR app, we assumed.

The harassed guard, who was sounding more exasperated than ever, added, "Go to 'Delay Repay' on the website and claim as much back as possible as it's been a bit of a mess today. Again, I apologize."

Oh, I thought for a moment, wondering how long we would be held up in Cornwall's capital. Then, along with all the other passengers for Penzance, I disembarked and waited on a crowded platform, where there was a station announcement: "Welcome to all our unexpected guests at Truro station today due to trouble up the line."

People were on their phones again on the platform. "It's been awful…" one passenger was saying as I walked by. "Absolute madness…" said another, their voice trailing off as I came to a free space to stand.

A train was coming into the station, and as I happened to be beside a different harassed guard, I asked what type of train we were boarding. His eyes lit up at a question that was not about the delays: "A Class 158."

Electric or diesel, I asked, as I knew by this stage that things like this mattered in such discussions.

"Electric?" he replied rhetorically. "No, no, it's diesel. We only just got electricity round here." He was making a joke about Cornwall in general.

On board, there were no initial announcements. Old sandwich wrappers, cans and empty bottles were scattered all over the place. A digital display said, "THE NEXT STATION IS TAUNTON." Which it obviously would not be: that was 130 miles or so back. Then we rolled onwards into the darkness, arriving in Penzance, the southernmost railway station in Britain, at 6.55 p.m. The journey from Llanelli had taken 10 hours and 54 minutes rather than 7 hours and 6 minutes – 3 hours and 48 minutes longer than expected.

Oh well, I thought for a moment, *at least we made it*.

"You can feel quite cut off down here"
Penzance to St Ives

My room at The Longboat Inn in Penzance could not have been much closer to the station – just round the back, across a street. If I had needed to rush to a train, I could have made it in a couple of minutes.

I left the backpack in a small, plain room and returned to the wide bar with low beams and a scuffed wooden floor scattered with carpets. A television near the bar had been placed within a gilded frame, as though the weather forecast being shown was "art". A yellow cone warned that the perfectly dry floor was wet. I asked a barman for the whereabouts of the Penlee House Gallery, which I intended to visit in the morning, and he replied, "Oh, I don't know about that."

He regarded me for a moment. "Are you a guest?"

"Yes," I replied. He had not been around when I entered a few minutes earlier.

"Do you want breakfast?" he asked, quick as a shot.

I said I was not sure as in the morning I was intending, before going to the Penlee House Gallery, to take a long early morning walk, 4 miles each way, to the neighbouring village of Marazion, to inspect the famous, pyramid-shaped little island of St Michael's Mount. I might, depending on how fast I went, eat breakfast in Penzance or Marazion.

"I do need to know this evening so we can order food in," he replied – conjuring up visions of a message being sent beyond the county borders and a delivery of sausages, bacon and beans being made along the tracks overnight, though I did not mention these thoughts. Instead, I said I would not be having breakfast, ordered a drink and sat in a corner, simply relieved to no longer be on a train, as heretic as those thoughts might be on a long railway journey round Britain.

Penzance was quiet. I wandered up Market Jew Street, cut down a narrow lane to The Globe pub and listened to "Dylan and Josh" play some live acoustic guitar and drum songs while golf flickered on a television and a man with a St Bernard dog came in, drank a pint of

Guinness Zero in 5 minutes flat and left. There were only a few people in, some dancing animatedly to Dylan and Josh's music near the bar.

Food was not being served, but it was up the hill at The Tremenheere, which I was unsurprised to discover was a Wetherspoons pub (yet again, my third). What could you do? They seemed to be everywhere. I raised a glass to Paul and David and their quest to visit all 805 Wetherspoons. They were like medieval pilgrims but without any religion and with the benefit of trains invented in the early nineteenth century to transport them to their "holy" watering holes. As challenges went, it was a good one, though they had not mentioned raising money for charity. If either Paul or David were ever to make *Who's Who,* their "hobbies" listing would stand out: *Visiting every single Wetherspoons pub by train.* At least it would be an honest one.

The Tremenheere was a large room on a couple of levels, and I ate my dinner near a Space Invaders the Next Level fruit machine while learning that the name of the pub came from a prestigious local family of former mayors and that "Penzance" came from "Pen Sans", Cornish language for "holy headland". Others in The Tremenheere appeared to be locals and it was enjoyable to be in Cornwall without being surrounded by tourists… or stuck on some platform listening to messages beginning *we are sorry to announce* for several hours on end.

The town of Penzance (population 21,382) made an excellent train terminus. You could arrive there and feel sufficiently removed from the rest of the madness of twenty-first-century Britain, no matter how awkward the journey down had been.

From London Paddington it was possible to catch a GWR *Night Riviera* sleeper train that ran six days a week, departing at 11.45 p.m. from Monday to Friday (11.50 p.m. on Sundays), arriving at just after 7.50 a.m. in Penzance. In the other direction, the trains left earlier in the evening, arriving just after 5 a.m. at Paddington, where customers could stay snoozing in their couchettes until being turfed out at 6.45 a.m. Aside from the *Caledonian Sleeper*, which I would be taking later, the *Night Riviera* was the only such public night train service in Britain, although an upmarket private travel company named Belmond had just announced – at the time of my rail adventures – that it was about to introduce a trio of "Britannic Explorer" three-night sleeper rides covering loops from London to Wales, the Lake District and Cornwall. Thirty-six guests would be accommodated guests in eighteen "luxury" suites said to be inspired by British stately homes and promising a "lavish yet laidback" experience with "personal butler service" for the best suites (as opposed to "impersonal"), massages in a "wellness suite", yoga classes, "on-board curated" meals by "renowned" three-Michelin-starred chef Simon Rogan and "carefully curated" (as opposed to "haphazardly curated") excursions promising to reveal "a kaleidoscopic narrative of the past". The price for all this? From £5,800 per person for three nights in one of the cheapest suites – or 17 per cent of the average annual salary for a full-time worker in the UK (£34,963 in 2023). This was nothing. For one of the three "grand suites", the price per person was £14,100 – 40 per cent of the average annual salary. For a couple, this would, of course, be doubled to £28,200 – more than 80 per cent.

A far cry from how I had made my way to Cornwall.

Maybe next time. Or perhaps not given the cheap suite alone was more than the cost of my entire trip round Britain.

Penzance, way down in Cornwall's south-west tip, had almost Zen-like quality for the embryonic Train Nut. This was especially so if you walked along the coast, past the huge shed of the station and back down the lines, watching the chrome-green trains gliding back and forth.

In the drizzle of the early morning, with a heavy fog on the Atlantic Ocean, it was a pleasure to inspect GWR trains purring by with locomotive names such as *Lincoln Callaghan*, *Flying Carolean* and *Henry Cleary*. Like a true old-school trainspotter – why not? – I jotted these names down while admiring the red-brick Penzance Signal Box, a train-washing facility and a strange little locomotive named *St Piran* (after the patron saint of Cornwall) resting on a siding and painted black with a white cross on it: the colours of the Cornish flag. Curious and unable to resist, I looked this up: *St Piran* was made at the Horwich Works near Bolton in 1959 and had served for many years in South Wales. It was a famous loco and even had its own Hornby model.

The "train world" was full of such rabbit holes of knowledge, I was finding.

Along the misty path passing such train delights you went, coming to the disused station of Marazion, where the old station sign had been nailed to the side of an old shed. Waves slapped and fizzed on the shore. The air was heavy with the smell of salt and seaweed. Gulls cried plaintively. Ahead, the pyramid of St Michael's Mount poked up through the sea haze, looking like a ghostly galleon.

I took to the beach for a stretch, then cut inland to avoid a river channel before returning to the path and soon finding myself in the comfortable lounge of The Godolphin pub/hotel facing St Michael's Mount, across a rough stone causeway more than half covered in seawater. I ordered a coffee and sat in a comfortable chair, with a copy of *The Cornishman* newspaper, watching an amphibious boat from the island arrive on the shore and drive across the sand. The island was managed by the National Trust and the St Aubyn family and was home to a medieval church and castle, still used by the St Aubyn family, as well as a handful of occupied houses. At certain times of the year, boats ran across, but not when I went, although you could walk if the causeway was clear.

The Cornishman was reporting on a visit to Cornwall by the then Prime Minister Rishi Sunak. This had taken place just a few days earlier. The reporter, Lee Trewhela, however, was unhappy about the experience, as the opportunity to ask questions had been extremely limited. He had hoped, for example, to quiz Sunak on whether he had flown to the county or taken the "perfectly good (arguably) rail link". Sunak was, famously, a fan of helicopter rides.

"So what did we get from our twelve-minute audience?" Trewhela asked before answering his own question: "A party political broadcast, basically, with interruptions ignored or replied to with 'I respectfully

disagree with your characterization of what we've been doing.'"
Problems with housing that meant 800 families were homeless, living in temporary accommodation in the county, were not given a look-in. Nothing on HS2, of course, as it was miles away from Cornwall (Sunak had, notoriously in train circles, been the one to sound the death knell for the Birmingham to Manchester route for what were believed to be party political reasons based on his own survival… which was not to be for much longer anyway).

A melodic song, *Summer Wine* by Nancy Sinatra and Lee Hazlewood, played on the stereo, while outside all was grey. A waitress joined me for a while, no other customer was about, and we watched the manoeuvrings of the amphibious vehicle in the un-summery conditions while she told me what she thought of trains in Cornwall.

"Recently, they've been on strike a lot," she said. "We live in Hayle. In the summer we would never dream of driving to St Ives because of the traffic and because there's nowhere to park. It's just the volume of people."

But with strikes on she had no choice. Similarly, worries about hold-ups had meant her driving for 9 hours to Stansted airport for a flight to the Czech Republic; taking trains would have been less than 7 hours of which 5 would have been to London Paddington.

"It was only a couple of hours to Brno," she said of the flight to the Czech Republic's second city.

I returned to Penzance past the station and up Chapel Street by the ferry port (with services to the Isles of Scilly), past a house where the Brontë sisters' mother, Maria, had lived before moving to Yorkshire and meeting Patrick Brontë, and located Penlee House Gallery, which was down an alley from The Globe.

This was a treat for two reasons.

The first: the art. Evocative old paintings of St Michael's Mount, ships gathering in St Michael's harbour, old tin mines, beaches, the Penzance promenade and an original "PENZANCE: TRAVEL BY TRAIN" poster by the artist Jack Merriott (1901–1968) lined the walls. But one picture stood out. It was by the artist Stanhope Forbes (1857–1947) of a sunny view of Penzance, with a farmer leading a horse and cart in the foreground, children playing in a lane and a steam train rolling along the coastline.

A friendly, knowledgeable and kindly museum assistant named Jenny saw me looking and came over.

Jenny was the second reason I liked Penlee House Gallery.

"Yes," she said. "Isn't it wonderful? Stanhope Forbes was probably the best known of the Newlyn School."

This was a school of art based in Newlyn, the fishing village that ran into Penzance, close to Penlee House Gallery.

"He painted this in 1922. It is a painting of hope and optimism, farmers coming in from the fields, steam from a train going along the line, kids coming home from school. The war memorial [shown in the picture] has just been erected. Forbes had lost his only son in the war, in the Duke of Cornwall's Light Infantry. His son died in the first days of the Battle of the Somme. Of course, the children in the picture were to get caught up in the next war, sadly. But it's a beautiful landscape and a statement that life goes on." The steam train being part of that "message".

Jenny, who was in her sixties, was brought up in Penzance. As I had with the waitress at The Godolphin, I asked her about the train service to the town.

She said, "The railway is very important to Cornwall, of course. Thank God Brunel built his railway! It was not only for passengers. It could also take goods to London, fish from the fishermen, stuff from the mines. When they built the line, the Bolithos, who owned mines and a bank, lived at Trengwainton House with land needed for the line. The family still lives there." The story went that it was agreed that the required strip of land for the railway would only be made available if it was promised that "no trains would run during cocktail hour, though I don't think they keep the promise to this day."

Given that landowners in the early days of trains could be a tricky lot (demanding personal stations as well as great sums in compensation), a little bit of quiet during "cocktail hour" sounded fair enough.

Jenny turned to how they ran these days: "The state of trains in the south-west is an absolute disgrace. If it's raining in Dawlish there are no trains at all. I'm being unfair. They've fortified the seawall. At least they've done that. But there can be no trains from London. You can be cut off. And strikes. It's not funny. People have been campaigning for years for the old line over Dartmoor to be reinstated. We're trainless from Truro to Newquay. You can feel quite cut off down here, which is actually part of its charm. When I was a teenager, I wanted to go where more was going on. Now I'm retired I'm delighted."

Unreliable trains could have their upsides too.

We spent the best part of an hour talking. Then I returned to Penzance station and caught the 13:15 to St Erth.

The 6-mile connection from St Erth to St Ives had to be along one of the most beautiful little branch lines in Britain.

It was known as the St Ives Bay Line, skirting an estuary and rising above cliffs and tumbling grassy dunes overlooking the sweeping sands and foaming breaking waves of Carbis Bay and Porthminster Beach. For the best views, you sat on the right going out and the left coming back – and you peered out and could not help thinking, *Just keep on going like this, keep on going forever along the cliffs above the foaming breaking waves.*

But six miles was six miles, and the train drew to a creaky halt at a station by a car park a short walk from the maze of narrow cobbled lanes at the centre of the popular seaside town of St Ives – such a holidaymaking draw that some locals would not dream of driving to it during the summer.

This train line was completed in 1877, when it immediately became a tourist destination and a haunt for artists seeking its renowned soft light (why the Tate eventually opened a local gallery in 1993). It was the last track anywhere to be built to Brunel's impractical broad gauge (and, like the Heart of Wales Line, was another narrow survivor of Dr Beeching's cuts).

Popularity for the tiny railway had grown further still from 1904 onwards when the twelve-carriage *Cornish Riviera Express* began direct services from London Paddington to Penzance, with a stop at St Erth for passengers to travel onwards to St Ives, and a journey time more than half an hour quicker than the previous 9 hours from London Paddington. In the mid-2020s, the Cornish Riviera Express name was still given to two daily trains that stopped at multiple stations in Cornwall: the 10:06 from London Paddington and the 08:44 from Penzance.

Cornish tourism and trains were inextricably linked.

On the platform, gulls wheeling above making a racket, I asked the train guard what type of train we had been on.

The guard, a young man, said quick as a shot, "A Class 150 DMU."

How old was it?

"I'm not that much of a train buff," he said. "I'm a trainee guard. The only traction I really know is pushing the trolley. I was a host before."

What was a "host"?

"Trolleys," he said, as in wheeling food-and-drink trolleys and "hosting", as though passengers had been invited to a dinner party (except they were just taking a train).

What was it like being a guard?

"Less physical, mate. Just need to know the doors and that," he said, and he returned to the train for the journey back to St Erth.

It was a short walk down a pleasant little lane, listening to the gentle swish of waves on the shore, to the St Ives Arts Club, down by the waterfront. On the exterior was a sign saying "THE PLACE WHERE IT ALL BEGAN – FOUNDED IN 1890." This was just about the first place that was not a holiday home or a B&B that you came to.

Inside, an artist was sitting at a table in a corner painting art amid a gallery of walls covered in his beautiful, intricate, abstract works. His name was Peter Giles, aged 64, and he had lived in St Ives for fourteen years but was originally from Milton Keynes (he was more than happy to answer my usual nosy journalistic-style enquiries). Peter was busy completing a drawing, wearing an old green woolly hat and heavy-framed glasses. I complimented him on his art and asked him whether he used the local trains much.

"Trains," he said, in an artistic, musing manner. "Trains," he repeated, even more musingly. "The trains brought the artists here in 1877. The day they came, artists came." He paused and added, with a dose of healthy scepticism, "That's the legend." He had known the date straight away; obviously an important one for the previously sleepy fishing village.

Peter returned to my question.

"We gave up our car here six years ago and use public transport, the bus and the train. We go at their speed," he said, as though he had surrendered himself to public transport, buses and trains: *wherever they go, however they go, that's the way I go.* A good train attitude, I felt, in keeping with my own thoughts on the method of transport.

"Driving is not what it used to be," Peter said. "Not having a car, that's put me in a very rail-glamour mode."

By this he meant that he might splash out on better classes of travel from time to time.

"Even for European travel. We go into London. We go to Paris. We go south."

Definitely a train-loving artist.

I left him to it, musing away at his easel… and spent a pleasant afternoon in St Ives.

You do not have to do much to enjoy yourself immensely in the place: a stroll around the small harbour; a wander to an uncrowded beach; a drink at the sea-doggy Sloop Inn; some oysters, chowder and chips from a stall (where you may be asked, "Do you want salt and vinegar with that, my lovely?"); a stop by the avant-garde Tate; a visit to the tucked-away Barbara Hepworth Museum and Sculpture Garden. The latter, where Hepworth (1903–1975) had lived, was my favourite spot: a secretive glen of smoothed bronze sculptures in abstract shapes cut with circular holes and looking like sacred artefacts belonging to a long-lost ancient tribe. All in a sloping garden on a hilly terraced street; you would never have guessed from the outside.

Jenny back at Penlee House Gallery, a source of much local information, had tipped me off about Hepworth: "When she was old and a bit of a lush, they would call ahead from each pub and say, 'She's coming'. She didn't have a good reputation. She had a bit of a temper. She wasn't well liked."

Maybe. But her art had more than stood the test of time.

Trains could transport coal from collieries, immigrants to New Worlds, fish from docks, tourists to beauty spots, and artists to little havens with perfect light.

What a great invention.

But what a pity the Cornish Riviera Express did not run quite as often as it did in its heyday – no longer so famous and hyped. With so many dirt-cheap flights to Europe, maybe that was unsurprising. Still, it was a shame. Why did we not all, like Peter, give up our cars and take to the rails? Life would, probably, be a whole lot easier (and nicer too).

The real "father" of the railways
St Ives to Torquay

In the breakfast room of the Western Hotel in St Ives there was a chance to indulge in a bout of vintage railway poster appreciation.

Prints of posters from bygone days covered just about every wall space. On one, issued by GWR in 1939, a steaming green locomotive flew across the tracks above the heading: "CORNISH RIVIERA EXPRESS DRAWN BY LOCOMOTIVE '*KING GEORGE VI*' NO. 6028: GREAT WESTERN RAILWAY OF ENGLAND" (produced, it seemed, for the American market, as enquiries were invited to be made at 9 Rockefeller Plaza, New York City). Another, also from GWR, was headed simply "CORNWALL", depicting two fishermen attending to a lobster pot on a lane running down to the Sloop Inn. And on yet another from 1955, two more fishermen (looking suspiciously like the same two fishermen) were smoking pipes by the harbour wall, with a beach in the background, and two children were petting a cat, part of a British Railways campaign entitled, "ST IVES GLORIOUS SANDS, TRAVEL BY TRAIN, CORNWALL IDEAL BATHING".

Then there was the most peculiar poster by far, which showed men with shields, spears and helmets filing up dunes from a beach where two longboats were anchored. It had been produced in 1926 by the artist Percy Spence and the headline read, "GREAT WESTERN RAILWAY. CORNISH RIVIERA, THE VIKING LANDING ON ST IVES BEACH." The historical accuracy of the event depicted, I could not quite ascertain. The Vikings had certainly got around just about everywhere on the British coast. Something to consider as you ate your cereal.

I strolled back up to the station, past the Arts Club, and while waiting for the 09:02 to St Erth, inspected a modern-day railway poster.

The latest GWR offering featured a train curving round a viaduct, with the sea and bobbing boats in the background at what seemed to be sunset. One window of the train was lit up and inside, parents, a daughter, son and dog gazed out across the countryside where a road was clogged with traffic. It was in the pictorial style of Enid Blyton's *Famous Five* books and the message read: "FIVE SPEED OFF TO THEIR NEXT ADVENTURE. GET TO YOUR NEXT ADVENTURE QUICKER WITH GWR."

A nice message, when it worked in practice.

I boarded the 09:02 to St Erth, followed shortly after by the 09:20 to Newton Abbot in Devon, watching through the carriage window as tumbling green hills flashed by.

Soon after, however, the train slowed near warehouses, forklift hire depots and what looked like smokestacks from old tin mines. This was Redruth, where the train stopped for a while before an announcement was made by a guard: "We will all be held here until further notice as a lorry has hit a bridge in Par."

Oh, I thought to myself, *here we go again*.

As with the pause back in Taunton, though, at least it offered the opportunity to remember another Very Important Rail Person, one of the key figures in the history of steam trains: the person who many consider to have invented them. And Redruth was a suitable spot to have been held up, as that key figure came from the very parts in which the 09:20 to Newton Abbot had just drawn to an involuntary halt.

It would be remiss to visit Cornwall on railway investigations without mentioning Richard Trevithick (1771–1833). For if anyone can be said to have come up with the idea for locomotives, it is Trevithick, the son of a mining captain, brought up close to Redruth.

He was by no means a straightforward character. After completing his education, Trevithick had found a job at the local tin mine where his father worked. So much so normal. On the job, however, he quickly became fascinated with the early steam engines used to pump water out of the mines and – having a maverick give-it-a-go streak – decided to adapt an engine to create a lightweight version to power a prototype "road carriage". This he did, naming it the *Puffing Devil*, which managed in 1801 to transport some of his friends up a hill, except it broke down, got stuck in a ditch and, after being abandoned as Trevithick and his friends went to a nearby pub, caught fire and exploded. No one was hurt.

This did not stop his continued messing about with movable engines and in 1803, after various other trials and tribulations, his simple steam high-pressure locomotive, adapted to rails at a Welsh iron works in Pen-y-Darren, Mid Glamorgan, was able to pull a ten-tonne load at up to 5 mph over nine miles. This was done to win a bet, with crowds coming to watch. Afterwards, the locomotive was used as a stationary engine, with horses pulling wagons on the track rather than his curious invention, which had not been deemed up to speed for use in day-to-day production.

So, in theory, Trevithick could lay claim to being the "father" of railways, just ahead of George Stephenson's exploits on the Stockton and Darlington Railway (Stephenson had been very aware of Trevithick's work and picked up key elements). Jenny back in Penzance had said to me, "Look up Trevithick in the record office in Redruth. He really invented the steam locomotive engine, not Stephenson." Yet Trevithick – after failing to capture the public's imagination with another locomotive named *Catch Me Who Can,* which had run on a circular track at a site in Bloomsbury, with passengers charged a shilling a ride – gave up and disappeared to South America to work on pumps in silver mines in Peru, Colombia, Mexico and Costa Rica before returning almost penniless in 1827… two years after everything was all up and running in the north-east.

Yet you could say that from *Puffing Devil* came *Locomotion No 1* and from *Locomotion No 1* came *Rocket* – and onwards.

A Cornishman had started it all off.

But I did not have time to go to public record offices in Redruth and, anyway, the bridge at Par had been passed fit for use.

The train zipped off across the landscape I had seen two days' earlier, arriving around noon at Newton Abbot in Devon, where I boarded another train, in the company of some hooded teenaged youths, heading for Torquay.

Torquay was a complete whim. I only intended to be there an hour or so to go and see the hotel that had inspired the 1970s comedy series *Fawlty Towers,* starring John Cleese, Connie Booth, Prunella Scales, Andrew Sachs and others, about a chaotic English seaside hotel. It was probably my favourite television comedy. I had always been curious to see the hotel (I couldn't really say why). This was to be a drop-by on the way to Okehampton, further north in Devon, where I had a room booked.

At the ticket office at Torquay station, I asked for directions and the GWR assistant regarded me: a backpacker who seemed to have come to Torquay just to look at a building from an old television show.

"It's been knocked down, mate," he said. "Save yourself the walk."

He smiled faintly – he must get all sorts coming by.

Anyway, I looked online, and he was of course right.

I had come to Torquay for no good reason.

I thanked the GWR assistant, who smiled faintly once more. A nice enough chap, even if he did think I was some kind of backpacking loon.

Rather than simply return along the line I had just taken to Exeter for the connection to Okehampton, however, I followed a sign that said, "ENGLISH RIVIERA" and arrived at a thin shingly-sand beach strewn with wads of seaweed and some wooden structures that looked like the bases of former beach huts.

A run of kiosks was on one side with red Wall's ice-cream flags. The wooden shutters of one of these was open with no customers outside. On the beach, a solitary dog walker crunched across the foreshore. Apartment blocks rose on a hill on the other side of a bay while waves slapped against mossy steps leading to a deserted promenade. It was the off-season, admittedly, but I had expected slightly more of this "riviera".

At the kiosk, I tried to buy a cup of tea. Attempting to do so, however, was quickly to unravel, precipitating the third confrontation of my journey (so far): after the youths in the car and the friendly station employees in Liverpool.

The problem was that the owner noticed me taking a picture of his kiosk using my phone. Various items, including fridge magnets, mugs and slate coasters, were being sold as "English Riviera" souvenirs; I had been considering buying one of these to remember this English Riviera by, though I did not really fancy carrying whatever it might be on trains around Britain. The kiosk employee took offence at this picture-taking and told me the kiosk was "private". I said I simply liked what was for sale and might come back and buy something, and then – rather foolishly in retrospect – asked him whether there was a law against taking pictures of his booth. This question acted as a trigger for the kiosk employee, just as a similar comment had at Liverpool Street station. Taking great offence, and saying I was "being disrespectful", the employee refused to serve me a cup of tea.

I was his only customer. There was no one else apart from the dog walker as far as the eye could see.

I was not getting on so well in Torquay.

The beach was next to The Grand Hotel, a large white Victorian building with turrets and high windows that was built in 1881 after an upgraded rebuild of Torquay station in 1878 (the station originally opened in 1859). You entered up steps via a modern section at the back that looked like a municipal pool, thinking, *John Betjeman would probably not have liked this addition all that much*.

Inside, though, I sat before a grand fireplace in a comfortable gold-and-red-striped armchair, next to some marble columns and figurines holding lamps, and ordered a cup of tea that was actually delivered by a kindly waitress with tattoos, who also fetched me a history of The Grand Hotel, printed on a piece of A4. This explained that the great railway-loving writer Agatha Christie, who had lived nearby, had been on her honeymoon (for her first marriage) at the hotel in 1914; the hotel had an Agatha Christie–themed suite, complete with a desk with a manual typewriter, in the room where she is believed to have stayed. The piece of A4 also said that "rock royalty" the Rolling Stones, the singer Mel C, the magician Derren Brown and the comedians Jim Davidson, Alan Carr and Jack Dee were all former guests.

This was an excellent spot to wait for a train from Torquay station, so close it was effectively the station bar and lounge.

Torquay and the "English Riviera", despite the *Fawlty Towers* mistake and another altercation, had finally come good.

"Completely changed the whole dynamic of the town"
Torquay to Okehampton via Exeter

It was just under an hour, on a direct train along tracks previously taken, to Exeter St David's station.

On arrival, I had about half an hour to wait for the Okehampton service.

Nosing about Exeter St David's station, I admired its potted daffodils and purple tulips, some old-fashioned tiles with raised platform numbers, and murals on a footbridge depicting passengers on GWR trains gazing through carriage windows at St Michael's Mount and other south-west landmarks. A faded sign from another era said "REFRESHMENT ROOM, SNACK BAR & DINING ROOM" in silver lettering above the ticket hall. It was a well-maintained station – one of the better ones.

Inside the ticket hall, I pottered about and soon found myself standing before an orange-and-white vending machine selling Penguin books (only Penguin books). Works by authors as varied as Gabriel García Márquez, Richard Osman, Haruki Murakami, Bill Bryson and Lee Child were for sale. Having never seen a machine like this before, I wondered what it was doing there and, helpfully, a little information panel to one side explained that in 1934 the founder of Penguin Books, Allen Lane, was waiting for a train at this station and wanted something to read but had been disappointed by the cost of books offered at the station bookstall. So, the story goes, he decided to publish his own books – hence Penguin Books, launched the following year, "kickstarting a paperback revolution that would sweep the world".

Apparently, Lane, who was managing editor of Bodley Head publishers at the time, and who had pushed for the publication of James Joyce's groundbreaking novel *Ulysses* against the instincts of many of his colleagues, had been returning from visiting Agatha Christie and happened to be changing trains at Exeter when he had this eureka moment. Instead of costly hardbacks, which were prevalent at the time, Penguin Books would sell "quality books at a reasonable price" in paperback. One of his first selling points was a vending machine, similar to the one at the station, on Charing Cross Road in London, nicknamed the "Penguincubator".

All inspired by Exeter St David's station.

I went to platform 3B and caught the train to Okehampton.

Day one: Colas Rail Freight locomotive at platform two of Darlington station

Locomotion No 1, *from 1825, at Locomotion museum in Shildon, County Durham*

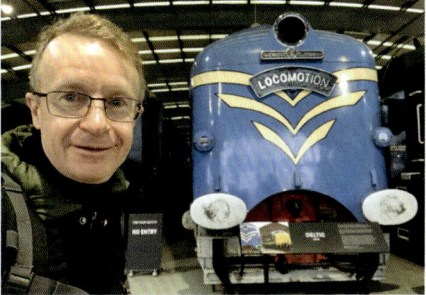

Author with "Deltic" diesel-electric locomotive built in 1955, Locomotion museum, Shildon

Robert Stephenson's Rocket, *built in 1829, at Locomotion museum, Shildon*

Royal Scot locomotive at Grosmont station on the fantastic North Yorkshire Moors Railway

A peaceful ride on a grey day: the North Yorkshire Moors Railway

Author shovelling coal into furnace of Royal Scot *at North Yorkshire Moors Railway*

Mallard *locomotive at National Railway Museum in York – holder of the world speed record for steam locos at 126 mph, set in 1938*

Graceful curve of York station

Locomotive 41241 on the Keighley and Worth Railway

Bleak beauty: Ribblehead viaduct on the Settle–Carlisle line in the Yorkshire Dales

Liverpool Crown Street park

The Quarryman service, Blaenau Ffestiniog station, Gwynedd

First-class carriage on Ffestiniog & Welsh Highlands Railway, Porthmadog station

Manchester Liverpool Road station

The Snowdonia Star service at Caernarfon station, Gwynedd

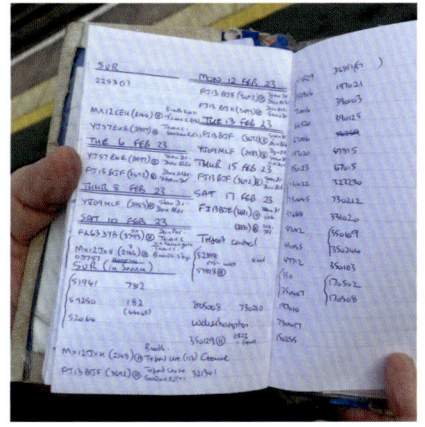

Trainspotter's notebook, Crewe station

Beach seen from St Ives Bay Line, Cornwall

Exeter station, Penguin books machine

Sign at Okehampton station, Devon

"Victorian day" at Swanage Railway, Dorset

Swanage Railway furnace

Corfe Castle station

Island Line train, Isle of Wight

Isle of Wight Steam Railway

Bognor Regis station, opened in 1864

Dog on bus to New Romney, Kent

"Tony Amos" c2c train

View from Victoria Railway Bridge over the River Thames, London

Southend Pier Railway, Essex

Locomotive on North Norfolk Railway

The Whistle Stop pub, Grantham station, Lincolnshire

Southend "Cliff Lift", opened in 1912

Norwich station, dating from 1886

"Jolly Fisherman" statue, Skegness, Lincs

Britannia Grand Hotel Scarborough

World's longest station bench, Scarborough station, North Yorkshire

Viaducts near Chinley, Peak District

Old railway station sign at bus stop in Adlestrop, Gloucestershire

Caledonian Sleeper, London Euston station

View of coast on way to Aberdeen

The magnificent Forth Bridge, opened for trains in 1890, seen from South Queensferry

Edinburgh Waverley station

The replica Rocket, *Shildon*

Author on replica Rocket, *Shildon*

Where it all began in 1825: Masons Arms Crossing, Shildon, County Durham

It moved slowly away, passing apartments on a hill and swiftly entering a rolling pine-tree-covered landscape, followed by fields with shire horses. The track made a clickety-clack sound. A guard with long scarlet-coloured nails checked my ticket. Nothing much else happened at all and 36 minutes later the passengers all disembarked at a red-brick station with more flowers in pots, some resting on an old, red porter's cart.

Okehampton station had an endearingly traditional look, with glossy green paint, yet more vintage railway posters, including one depicting a young blonde woman in a bikini along with the slogan "EXMOUTH: GO BY TRAIN" that reminded me of Larkin's curious poem back in Prestatyn (though it had not been vandalized). There was a café and a bookshop, both just closed for the day, and an unmissable large sign that said, "258,479 DARTMOOR LINE JOURNEYS IN ONE YEAR."

This was why I had come. Three years earlier the Dartmoor Line, as it was known, had reopened, covering the fifteen miles between Exeter and Okehampton, reversing Dr Beeching's edict to close the railway, put into effect in 1972. Previously, the line had gone further than Okehampton, continuing to Plymouth in the south and with branch lines to the seaside towns of Bude and Padstow in North Devon. This connection to Plymouth, operated by London and South Western Railway, had been important as it offered an alternative to the GWR route, providing competition and attracting passengers landing by boat in Plymouth. Services had begun in 1876.

The reopening had been a big deal as it was part of a politically prominent plan called "Restoring Your Railway", launched by the Conservative Party government of ex-Prime Minister Boris Johnson. A total of £500 million of public money had been earmarked to reverse Dr Beeching's cuts and 44 bids had been swiftly accepted, with the Dartmoor Line to Okehampton being the first to see tracks reopen to passenger services – others in the pipeline included the five-mile Camp Hill Line between Birmingham New Street and Kings Norton and the eighteen-mile Northumberland Line between Newcastle and Ashington.

Which all sounded great. The only problem was that some were questioning what would happen to this "Restoring Your Railway" project due to a coming change in government and recognition by the Labour Party that the Conservative Party had created a large hole in public expenditure by making declarations to throw cash at projects such as "Restoring Your Railway" but not balancing the books, i.e. making bold promises that sounded great to voters, but simply being unable to afford them.

All of which was more than murky, and whether any of the money that had been allotted to the dramatically ditched high-speed (HS2) line between Birmingham and Manchester would really filter through to alternative rail initiatives, such as "Restoring Your Railway", as proposed by the Conservative Party before the Labour Party took over, was unclear. Some cash seemed to be being spent improving current stations, such as Middlesbrough and York, but what about the lofty plans to reverse Dr Beeching on branch lines?

You did not need to be a political expert to come to the conclusion that it was all a bit of a mess.

Or you might say, shambles, farce, national embarrassment, humiliation, abject failure.

Call it what you will.

However, at least the Dartmoor Line, where the tracks had never been ripped away after 1972, and where the occasional privately owned heritage train or "murder mystery" service had been operating for some time, was back up and running properly. That was all that mattered for the moment, and the proudly announced "258,479" annual figure sounded as though things were going well.

During my short stay in Okehampton, I asked a few locals what they thought about the reopened 15-mile line.

I started at my comfortable little B&B called the Meadowlea Guest House, a short walk from the station down a quiet hill, past Victorian mansions (including one that had belonged to one of the first local railway chairmen). Wearing a black Okehampton Social Club polo shirt, Mark, co-owner of the seven-room guest house with his wife Lesley, was a dapper man with a grey beard. "It's certainly done the town some good," he said. "Hopefully it will pave the way to open more across the country. The next step is to continue to Tavistock and then the idea would be to go to Bude. It seems madness that the whole of the south-west relies on a railway line exposed to the sea."

He was referring to the tracks down by Dawlish on the other line to Plymouth.

Lesley, stripy top and glasses, agreed: "We fought for many years to reopen the line here. More people come on the trains. Business is up 10 to 20 per cent. People used to come to Exeter and have to hang about for the bus to get here on public transport."

Money spent on reopening branch lines could reinvigorate local economies, breathing life into the regions, she said. And far less was required for such common-sense projects, compared to multibillion-pound, headline-grabbing high-speed schemes. Lesley made a comparison with the plans for fast trains to Birmingham and beyond: "You hear all about HS2, but from London to Leamington in an hour?" The current journey time was about 1 hour 20 minutes. "Actually, that's not bad."

She had a point. Why blow cash on faster trains between the Midlands and London – the part that was continuing despite the Manchester link seeming no longer to have any hope of happening – when they were quite quick anyway? Though it did not quite address the point many were making about a new railway taking freight off motorways and not just being about passenger journey times.

I walked further down the hill into Okehampton.

Birds trilled in treetops. The smell of coal fires wafted from chimneys. A crisp, clean feeling hung in the air as though the calm that must have existed deep on the moorland of the adjoining Dartmoor National Park had floated across and settled on the small town, newly re-established on the railway map. I arrived at a corner with an old inn, The White Hart

Hotel, where William Pitt the Elder often came in the 1750s when he was a local MP and which had been the fifth stop for a change of horses on the 271-mile "Trafalgar Way" from Falmouth to London, delivering news of the defeat of the Spanish and the death of Lord Nelson in the Battle of Trafalgar in October 1805. Back then, Okehampton had been an important stagecoach town, and that important journey with famous news had taken 38 hours and cost £46 – the equivalent of £10,817 in mid-2020s money.

As well as an Immersion Virtual Reality Arcade, Okehampton (population 5,800) was home to an Indian restaurant, a small Victorian arcade with a vinyl record shop, a jewellery shop and an inviting-looking café. Around the corner was Dogberry & Finch Books (where the owner Kate said the reopening of the railway has been "brilliant" for Okehampton), as well as the Chapel of St James, a prominent, narrow-shaped fifteenth-century church with a tower and a barn-like interior with rafters. While on the outskirts of town, close to the station, were the jagged ruins of Okehampton Castle, built by the Norman conquerors.

I talked to John Elson, owner of the Granite Way Cycles Hub, a bike-hire shop/café right by the station with easy access to Dartmoor National Park, which began on Okehampton's southern edge. Did he like the railway? "Absolutely," he replied – his business would not have been there without it. "We built this café and the bike shop a year ago. We have six staff." Jobs that would not have existed without the railway.

John himself took the train for work purposes. "I just went to Bristol for insurance for the property." To talk to building-insurance brokers face to face. "You can work on the train." Which meant he did not waste time driving. "We would like the line here to go all the way to Plymouth."

John rushed off to deal with a call and one of the bike shop staff, whose name I did not catch, said, "The railway has completely changed the whole dynamic of the town. It's taken pressure off parents." He had three teenage children. "Now they are able to come and go to Exeter. It's made life so much easier."

There was another effect. "Okehampton's growing now, there's rapidly expanding housing." People could more easily commute to work in Exeter and the town was particularly spreading to the north-west, towards Sampford Courtenay. "They're getting closer and closer," he said: Okehampton and Sampford Courtenay. "They've almost merged into each other."

Railways had totally transformed many places in Britain, and they were still clearly doing so – 200 years after Stephenson fired up *Locomotion No 1* and sent it chugging down the line.

A Dartmoor discussion
Okehampton to Exeter

More voices of train approval were to be heard on the 11:27 back to Exeter St David's, where an impromptu forum about trains in general soon began.

A man sitting at a table across the aisle was drinking a can of cider. He had noticed me struggling to repack my bursting backpack with its overflowing train books. After a while of watching me doing so and – seemingly feeling he was on safe ground and that I probably liked trains based on my reading material – he began to tell me about his own fondness for them.

"My old man," he said, taking a sip of cider. "My old man, oh yes, he loved trains." Sip of cider. "Passed that love to me." Sip of cider. "Arrrgh," he said, as though expressing pleasure from his drink, being on a train and simply talking about this and that to a stranger (me).

My new friend had a broad, flushed face and seemed in a confiding mood. "GWR," he said. "GWR."

What about GWR, I asked.

"The first company to have a pension," he said, beaming and pleased I did not know this but he did. "Oh yes, I think you'll find that."

He tapped his nose. And I thanked him for this (though maybe "one of the first" was more accurate).

"People fought long and hard for this railway," he said, referring to the Dartmoor Line – which was, I knew by then, the general consensus in Okehampton.

As he did so, a skinny, elderly man with grey hair and a scar on his face poked his head over the seat from the row behind and cut in.

"It's a super success," he said. "What Brunel did one hundred years ago, it's amazing."

He looked over at the man drinking the cider. "My old man was a massive train enthusiast too."

Everyone's father on the 11:27 to Exeter St David's seemed to have been a rail enthusiast.

The elderly man with the scarred face continued. "When I was younger, I was a trainspotter. I had all the books and underlined the trains. Names and locos – castle and kings. The famous *King George* locomotive with the bell on the top."

He was referring to the legendary *King George V* locomotive (not the locomotive pictured in the breakfast room in Penzance, the *King George VI*).

The good trainspotting rail enthusiast knew such stuff and would never dream of confusing the two.

"I used to go all over the place spotting trains. Cornwall to Swindon. Back in those days, there were rackety old trains. When I began."

Yet another man, another train lover, had come over to listen to us, though he did not say anything. He was perhaps in his seventies and had a hunched, shaky posture. He simply sat down at a seat close to the three of us – with a look of acknowledgement that seemed to suggest *yes, I'm one too* (a train lover) – knitted his hands together and listened.

The cider-drinker started talking about Dr Beeching, looking as though he did not approve of him. Not many "train people" did.

"Why would you downgrade the trains?" he said, as though this had been sheer lunacy. "Smaller lines should be subsidized."

The man with the scarred face said, "Dr Beeching and Ernest Marples." Marples had been the minister of transport who had given the green light to Dr Beeching's railway cuts in the 1960s. "The whole thing was corrupt. Beeching had shares in haulage. Marples was building the M1 at the time and he wanted to get people onto motorways. He also happened to have his own road-construction business." This had been a great controversy back then, with people calling out this obvious conflict of interest.

The man with the cider said, "Arrrgh."

The man with clasped hands said nothing.

The guard arrived and asked us for our tickets.

Her name was Stephanie and she was younger than us by quite some distance and worked us out at a glance: *some rail enthusiasts talking all sorts of nonsense about trains.*

"It's a very friendly line this one," she said, after looking at my ticket.

Which evidently was true. She hung around with us for a while until the train pulled into Exeter. "It feels like we're part of the history of it," she said, referring to staff working on the "new" Dartmoor Line.

A *good news* train story… for once.

CHAPTER SIX

EXETER TO HYTHE VIA TAUNTON, MINEHEAD, POOLE, SWANAGE, THE ISLE OF WIGHT, BOGNOR REGIS, NEW ROMNEY AND DUNGENESS

STEAMY IN THE SOUTH

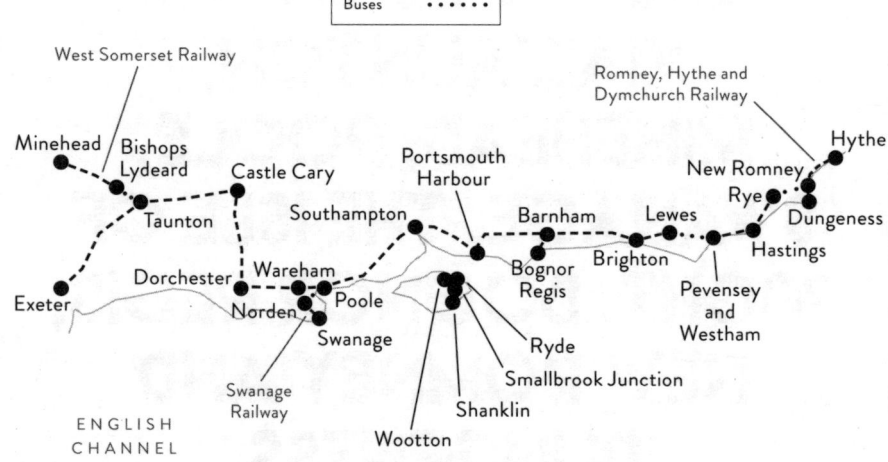

On the 12:15 from Exeter to Taunton a couple across the aisle was having a little party. Small bottles of pink champagne and cans of Thatcher's Gold cider were placed on their table along with what looked like hummus accompanied by nachos. Opposite me, at my table, a woman was talking on a turquoise-and-gold phone about a "bloody cocky solicitor" who was dealing with her daughter's separation from a former partner. With nothing better to do (and little option) I listened to the travails of her daughter during her messy split and what the "bloody cocky solicitor" had been doing wrong. The woman changed subject to her high cholesterol and how she had "another bloody hospital appointment on Monday", which I found less interesting and switched off to after a while. It was amazing what people would talk about quite openly on their phones on trains.

The 12:15 flew past ploughed, russet-hued fields. The sun was out and there was a hopeful mood. Shafts of light illuminated water left over from the floods of a few days earlier, creating little heavenly streaks of silver across the countryside.

I was about to re-embark, had I ever indeed disembarked, on some further train education. Three heritage lines in quick succession lay ahead (the West Somerset Railway, the Swanage Railway and the Isle of Wight Steam Railway) before I would traverse the south coast, joining yet another vintage track for a short ride (the Romney, Hythe and Dymchurch Railway).

These old lines would mark my way to Kent. Then, as previously mentioned, the intention – coming to fruition so far – was to weave up England's east coast to Scarborough, very close to Darlington, and slip down though the Midlands to London to catch the *Caledonian Sleeper* north for the circle round Scotland, and back to Darlington. The "wobbly treble clef" journey of Britain by train complete, I would return, reluctantly and with some trepidation, to the real world once again. To life where trains and their histories were not the be-all and end-all and you had to worry about mortgages, energy bills, booking MOTs, remembering family responsibilities and holding down a job (where my boss had kindly and tolerantly allowed me time off for "your trains", as he had put it, raising an eyebrow and casting a benevolent yet somewhat concerned look in my direction before turning his gaze to another colleague and saying nothing yet seeming to communicate much with his expression).

Frankly, I found the prospect of re-entering this trainless "civilization" quite worrying.

"The sound of the industrial revolution"
Taunton to Minehead and Poole

To reach the West Somerset Railway from Taunton's rather bleak station on an incline on the edge of town required a bus to the village of Bishops Lydeard. There you got off and walked past a roundabout and a brewery before arriving at a platform with a large train steaming away and occasionally hooting and whistling.

It was, after an absence of some days since a proper big steam train (the Ffestiniog & Welsh Highland Railways being the last), strangely uplifting to see this old loco, which was being admired by a small squadron of passengers about to board for the 22-mile journey to Minehead on the Bristol Channel.

I got straight down to Train Nut business, ascertaining that the locomotive was built in 1934 and had first operated out of Stourbridge in Worcestershire.

Then I asked a patient man working for the West Somerset Railway, dressed in oily overalls, about the loco, which had no name, just a number: 9351.

"It's a bit of a mongrel," he said. "Nine three five one was originally a tank engine."

What's a tank engine, I asked.

"One without a tender," he said.

What's a tender, I asked.

"It has water in it," he said.

The water for the steam?

"Yes," he replied, looking at me.

"When BR got rid of steam locos, many went to Barry's scrapyard and this was one of them," he continued.

What was Barry's scrapyard?

The man explained that Barry was the name of a town in South Wales, rather than a person, where around 300 defunct steam locomotives were sent by British Railways in the 1960s, with more than 200 of them saved by railway preservation societies and restored. It was a key place, almost legendary, in rail enthusiast circles. Back in the 1960s, train lovers who had descended on the scrapyard simply to ogle the locomotives as they awaited their fate – the scrapyard having become a tourist sight of sorts – had come up with the idea to buy them from the owners, Woodham Brothers Ltd. Had these rescues not been made from Barry, the steam train world might have been almost completely wiped out.

"This one was there, and it was in a pretty bad state," said the man in the oily overalls. "Before it was restored, it was decided to remove the tanks and attach a tender to it. All that work was done at this railway."

The man in the oily overalls was named Martyn. He had been a volunteer on the West Somerset Railway for 20 years and was previously a court usher at Taunton Crown Court. He pointed across a platform and told me to go over and talk to Kerry Noble, the railway's general manager, adding, "She's a very busy person, she might not have time to speak to you."

Kerry did, however, have time and was equally patient. She wore hipster glasses and had a quizzical manner, perhaps wondering, *Who the hell is this guy?* "This guy" being me.

I asked her how many passengers a year travelled on the West Somerset Railway.

"One hundred and fifty thousand. Last year was in line with the year before. Twenty-five per cent up on 2019. This seems to be a trend across heritage railways," she said.

How did she know about the others?

"There's a general managers' group that meets every six months," she said. "The Heritage Railway Association has spring and autumn conferences. People are exploring more with experiential options." By this, I took it that she meant murder mystery rides, upmarket dining services with live music, beer trains and Victorian day-style events. "Heritage railways are getting better at selling product. There's a general want for 'vintage' right now. Vintage clothing, vintage records."

Vintage trains fit into all of that, she implied. Old steam trains were, apparently, becoming "cool".

She thought about this and added, "It's just nostalgia, isn't it?"

The railway had reopened fully in 1979 after closing in 1971, and the journey to Minehead was "about one and a half hours, it's the longest standard-gauge heritage railway in Great Britain."

What about narrow gauge, I asked.

"That's the Ffestiniog and Welsh Highland Railway," she said, making me feel ashamed (I really ought to have known that).

I thanked her and boarded the train to Minehead.

Steam was soon wafting past the windows as we moved away in a juddery motion, passing thatched cottages, banks of wildflowers and remote countryside with gorse, bracken and brambles. For a while I fell into a trance, watching water flowing in a meandering trackside stream. A deer darted from a hedge and hopped across a field. Rapeseed fields blazed in golden yellow. Sheep scattered at the sight of the puffing and panting 9351. Pheasants stood dead still and stared. Frothy waves broke on the Bristol Channel. In the distance, across the way, large buildings rose in Wales, maybe in Port Talbot. The inside of the retro carriage had wood panels and natty, comfortable lilac, aquamarine, pink and black-speckled seats. It was a lovely, peaceful ride.

We came to Watchet station. A woman in the row ahead said, "There's something about that sound, isn't there?"

The train had begun to make a slow churning noise as it gathered speed, moving on after the station stop.

The man she was with said, "It's power, raw power."

The woman replied, "The sound of the industrial revolution."

We arrived at Minehead, which was a hive of activity and also in the midst of a weird, sudden, unseasonal hailstorm.

On the waterfront, I helped a woman who owned an ice-cream kiosk rescue a sign for her business that had been blowing away. "Thanks," she said. "It's not normally like this."

It was too cold and windy to look about. I returned to the train and went back to Bishops Lydeard and caught the bus to Taunton station. Then, having just missed a train, I sat for a while in a Starbucks in which two sets of tinny pop music were playing simultaneously. One was for staff in the kitchen, on so loud it emanated into the café. The other was for customers. The result was a strange cacophonous combination of Cyndi Lauper, Red Hot Chili Peppers, Rolling Stones and Taylor Swift hits. When I pointed this out to the staff, one of them said "Oh yeah" and turned down the kitchen music – and I proceeded to read an obscure (heavy) second-hand book entitled *Brunel's Britain* by Derrick Beckett that I'd picked up somewhere or other before taking a 20-minute train across some soggy fields to Castle Cary, where I sat for a while in a small (quiet) station waiting room before catching a 40-minute train to Dorchester West.

The latter ride was memorable for its sunset. On boarding and setting forth, the last of the late afternoon sunshine was bathing the skeletal trees, hedgerows and fields of disconsolate-looking cows in a warm amber glow in this out-of-the-way corner of the West Country. It was a glorious sight after the grey swirling hailstorm of earlier, heightened by an almost full moon that had risen to the east and hung low and mysteriously on the horizon towards London. Meanwhile, to the west, ethereal clouds had billowed upwards in a bonfire of crimson and pink sunset colours, while directly above the train the sky was a perfect lilac that was slowly darkening as we moved down the tracks. Nature was putting on a show.

Then I stood for a while at a platform at Dorchester South station (having walked for ten minutes from Dorchester West station), waiting for the half-hour train to Poole. This duly arrived, a South Western Railway service with grimy blue seats. It proceeded to cross low, dark fields, followed by a bay, before arriving bang on time at Poole.

In a few hours, on a few little snaking trains, I had swapped the Bristol Channel for the English Channel.

The south coast of England, and its railways, awaited.

Best ride yet
Poole to Swanage and Shanklin, Isle of Wight

In Poole, accommodation offerings in my self-selected price bracket had been somewhat limited. In the end, after some online browsing, I had found a cheap B&B where I had been allocated a "premium single room with a 4-foot bed" (I had been sent a text about being upgraded from "standard", with a less wide bed, to "premium"). The bathroom in "premium" with the 4-foot bed would still be down the hall, but it would be slightly better than "standard". Why I had been chosen for such preferential treatment, I did not know. The B&B, which had a punch-code system so there was no receptionist, was conveniently close to Poole's desolate main bus depot, from where I would be taking a bus in the morning, as well as the town's dreary central mall, a short walk from the train station via a passage beneath a flyover.

Now, on the one hand, you may well be of the opinion that it was my own fault, if I booked such cheap places, that I "suffered" them. In the punch-code B&B, for example, I was awoken in the depths of the night by creaking and rhythmic thumping from the floor above during what might have been described delicately as a passionate amorous tryst – a particularly rigorous, lengthy, passionate amorous tryst. There appeared to have been little soundproofing at the punch-code B&B.

On the other hand, such "digs" helped save on the cost of the journey and were clean and not that bad really (usually). There was also the added plus that you usually slept quite well, passionate amorous trysts in rooms above aside, and tended to be raring to move onwards (and get out) in the morning to continue one's train investigations. A silver lining of sorts.

However, I had begun to feel that it might be time to start splashing a little more cash on this front. While not made of money, I could afford a little bit better: to up the ante accommodation-wise. My attempts at what I took to be sensible economizing were beginning to push me into the realms of the downright dire.

From Poole's desolate bus station, I caught a Breezer bus for the fifteen-mile journey to Norden station, where I went to the platform and assessed my second steam train in as many days.

Things were going on that I had not expected to be going on at Norden station. I had unwittingly booked to travel on a "Victorian day". I was about to enjoy an "experiential option", as Kerry Noble back on the West Somerset Railway had said. This "experiential" occasion would come in the form of most people working on the Swanage Railway that day being dressed in Victorian clothing and speaking and behaving in a perceived Victorian manner.

On the platform, a woman dressed in a lace bonnet and a black-and-white dress – I believe she may have been a ticket inspector, although she did not ask to see my ticket as I had not yet boarded – curtseyed and asked me, somewhat coquettishly, "Hello, sir, what might I do for you today, sir?"

I replied that I was *fine thank you* and would be boarding in a bit. I had not known that Victorian ticket inspectors could be so pleasant.

Then I went to the front of the train where a large black locomotive with a number not a name again (number 31806) was being attended to by a man dressed like Isambard Kingdom Brunel.

He wore a top hat and a flowing jacket, had similar sideburns to Brunel's and was short and stocky, just like Brunel too. He was inspecting the wheels and some piping beneath the loco and from a distance, and even quite close up, was a dead ringer for the famous engineer.

I asked Brunel's ghost when locomotive 31806 had been built and how fast it went, as a rail enthusiast icebreaker.

"1926. The top speed? I dread to think. Ninety miles an hour back in the day, here the speed limit's twenty-five miles an hour max," the ghost said. Twenty-five miles an hour was the maximum speed by law on all heritage lines, he added. I really ought to have known that: a common experience, and sensation, in the presence of true "train people". I was getting used to it.

Then I enquired what 31806 was like to drive.

"Every loco has its own feel. They're just so 'alive' and have such character and you engage with them. It's a two-way conversation with the engine. You listen to it and feel it and you're not just looking at the dials. Even if two locos are mechanically the same, each behaves differently. This one just wants to go and keep powering on," he replied, sounding a little as though he was talking about a new second-hand car he had just picked up, a Ford Focus or Hyundai SUV, perhaps.

Another Swanage railway employee had been listening to us. His name was Steve, and he would be driving the train to Swanage, about six miles away on the coast by the English Channel, unlike the ghost of Brunel, who seemed to be a supervisor.

"This used to be a river tank engine; now it's a U-class," said Steve, who was also dressed in "Victorian style", though he lacked a top hat and side whiskers.

A feeling of hopelessness filled me. I had no idea what he was talking about. I would never, I realized there and then, ever truly understand all this steam train stuff. What made it a U-class, I ventured.

"Why 'U'? That's just a letter. You have U-class, S-class, N-class freight or wheel configuration. The only difference between this and an 'N' is the size of the wheels," he said.

"Oh," I replied.

I tried to ask a less technical question: "Can you say why you love trains so much in a single sentence?"

Steve looked at me squarely and replied, "I'm sorry, no."

He paused, then he relented: "My father was a driver of steam trains. He helped re-lay the tracks here in 1995. Preservation had begun in 1976."

This was not, obviously, a single sentence.

Will, a trustee of the Swanage railway, who had been listening to us, and who was going to be the "fireman", putting in the coal for the journey to Swanage, said, "My dad was a fireman too. Our fathers [his and Steve's father] went to school together in the 1970s. They went by train to school. So I think for me, to answer your question, it's family history. I have a strong, emotional connection – friends and family. It's also just nice to see other people enjoy the ride."

Then Steve, who had been mulling over the "one sentence" request, said in response, finally, "It's romantic, isn't it?"

All three – Will, Steve and Brunel's ghost – were in their twenties. The Swanage Railway, after being closed in 1972, when seven miles of tracks had been immediately ripped up and removed, reopened in stages to cover its current six miles (after a major local dispute to prevent parts of the railway being turned into a bypass for vehicles), with an extension of about three miles to the town of Wareham to the north possible. All of this was the work of volunteers, with cash coming from donations and ticket sales.

Will and Steve then invited me to ride on the footplate, the driver's cab where the coal was placed in the locomotive's furnace, for the 10:30 ride down to Swanage – which was both completely unexpected and extremely kind of them.

Which was how I found myself shovelling coal into the fire of an old loco as the rolling Dorset countryside passed by and the dramatic outline of the ruins of Corfe Castle arose, built by William the Conqueror after 1066, and where it is said King Edward the Martyr was assassinated at a Saxon stronghold in 978 aged sixteen (the result of a family dispute that saw his twelve-year-old half-brother Ethelred the Unready take to the throne). There it sat on a hill: gaunt and tragic, jagged and spectral, beautiful and blood-soaked, concealing a thousand secrets and more.

All I could say was *what a great ride*. The train shunted along in a rat-a-tat, clip-clop rhythm, heat from the furnace rising in fierce waves, and the smell of coal and soot engulfing the three of us in the cab. The engine felt somehow alive as it pulsed and throbbed and spat and hissed. We were moving across a historic landscape on a large, strange, monstrous machine.

People lining the tracks took pictures and waved. Steve let me pull a chord to blow the whistle and, as we moved along, Will, who worked as a "performance improvement specialist" for South Western Railway when not volunteering for the Swanage Railway, said, "It takes two years' training to be a fireman and eight years' to be a driver. The main danger is the water level. You've got to watch it." He pointed at a gauge that showed a "psi" level. If this "psi" level was not watched, the whole locomotive could explode "like a balloon", but, due to "a lot of safety in place", this was "unlikely to happen". Which was pleasing to hear.

One of the biggest problems for the railway was the price of coal.

Will said, "It's the war in Ukraine, Russia's invasion of Ukraine. We used to get a lot of coal from Russia. It was one hundred and seventy pounds a tonne. Now it's about four hundred pounds a tonne. It's our biggest variable cost. Combine that with inflation and the cost-of-living crisis and it's a very hard time for heritage railways at the moment."

I was gradually, thanks to Osian back in Porthmadog, Kerry in Bishops Lydeard and Will on the way to Swanage, learning a great deal about the nuts-and-bolts operations of British heritage railways. Visitor numbers seemed to be doing pretty well – Will had confirmed this – but there were hidden pressures, no thanks to Russia's President Putin. Global affairs touched all corners of life, even heritage railway lines.

We were crossing the Purbeck Hills beyond the castle. It was a gentle, peaceful landscape, no matter the bloodshed of centuries past.

Will said, "Basically, it's an unchanged view for hundreds of years. It's always lovely coming down here. You can see wild garlic and sloe, buzzards and deer – it's a real natural conservation corridor, you know."

Then Will told me a little about his job for South Western Railway. It was an important one. "My work is focused on digging into data. Conflicts between two trains – one is late running, what do you do? At London Waterloo, if two trains need the same infrastructure, the same platform, and one is delayed by 30 seconds, it will delay the other. So you put them apart from each other, move them to different platforms. It's exciting. As you can probably tell, I quite like trains. It's a real privilege to do something you love."

The train arrived at Swanage and I hopped out of the cab and thanked Steve and Will. It had been, hands down, the best journey yet.

The turnaround at Swanage was quick… no time to see the town as I had a ferry to catch, after a few trains, later in the day.

Through a carriage window on the return journey, the elegant English countryside unfurled as the train retraced its tracks. Instead of continuing to Norden, though, I disembarked at Corfe Castle station, where I soon found myself in a superb old-fashioned train station with a superb old-fashioned ticket office with a superb old-fashioned roaring coal fire with a shiny brass fender, a "SUNNY WORTHING, GO BY TRAIN" railway poster featuring a blonde woman wearing a bikini (of course), and a superb old-fashioned painting by the artist Terence Cuneo entitled *Signal Success*: a scene at Norwood Junction in the London Borough of Croydon, with a steam train and swirling smoke and figures in a signal box beneath a pink and grey dusk sky. This was quite brilliant and, while staring at this atmospheric scene, I looked up Cuneo (1907–1996), who turned out to have been a veritable Monet of railways, except that instead of waterlilies, he had concentrated on trains and tracks.

The station also had a superb old-fashioned bookstall on one side, where I picked up some superb old-fashioned books about Scottish trains and the superb old-fashioned bookstall attendant said "Oh, don't worry" when I was a pound short in cash to buy them.

Then I posted these, and a few other accumulated train books, back home from the post office at Corfe Castle, admired the castle up close, caught a bus to Wareham, a train to Poole, another train to Southampton Central (initially delayed slightly "because of a problem currently under investigation") and another to Portsmouth Harbour station, where – at the end of the platform – a ferry was purring, ready to depart across the Solent to the next railway down the line.

Ticket to Ryde
The Isle of Wight to Bognor Regis

The *Wight Ryder 1* ferry took 22 minutes to cross the bumpy sea to Ryde Pier Head, where you were deposited at a station with a Costa Coffee café, the sound of sloshing waves on the pier below and a little "history corner" with information on how the half-mile-long pier was built in 1814 to allow ferries to drop off passengers at low tide and that, following the introduction of horse-drawn trams in 1864, a steam train service began along the pier in 1880 to be replaced six years later by pioneering electric trams.

Good "train knowledge".

There was not much else, however… including trains.

A little digital display by the platform at Ryde Pier Head station informed that 15:45 had been cancelled. Assuming another one would come along soon enough, I bought a coffee from the Costa Coffee and waited. It was then I noticed that the next train and the one after were also cancelled. In the absence of a ticket office or any train staff, I went to the Costa Coffee to ask the woman working there what was going on.

She said, "You need to get the number two or three bus at the end of the pier. At least, I think so. I've only been here a few months."

I thanked her for this.

"No bother," she replied.

A ticket office existed at the other end of the pier at Ryde Esplanade station, where a man was in a dispute with the ticket attendant in the booth.

He had been waiting for trains at Ryde Pier Head too. "You need to keep people informed, you know," he was saying. "One hour I was waiting."

The woman in the booth replied, "But trains are running from Ryde St Johns Road station. There should be a minibus coming down the pier, taking people there."

To this the man replied, "How are we to know this?"

This was a reasonable enough question: there had been nothing to say this was the system.

The woman in the booth did not reply to the man, who was in a state of some agitation.

"It's absolutely ridiculous," said the man, who wore a blue bow tie, a blue waistcoat and flat cap; I took him to be a musician, or someone involved in "entertainment", on his way to an event.

He departed in a fury.

I asked the woman in the booth when the minibus would arrive to go to Ryde St Johns Road station; the seaside town of Ryde seemed to have a lot of stations.

"Yes, but I'm just not sure where it is at the minute," she replied. Then she made a phone call.

"Keith. Hello, Keith?" she said into her phone. She paused, then she said, "Keith's not answering."

I left her to it for a minute, looking around the small station and listening to a recorded announcement: "Trains have been cancelled, this is because of the sea flooding the railway."

The waves had apparently been dangerously splashing across the tracks of the railway on the pier.

Then the woman called me over. "It's coming, just go out there," she said, pointing to the door.

So I did, and there was Keith in his minivan, who drove me to Ryde St Johns Road station, where a train awaited with former London Underground carriages painted shiny navy blue and yellow. "ISLAND LINE" was written on the side.

I boarded. The train promptly departed, rattling and swaying with the familiar movement of a London Tube train, yet passing small Lego-like houses and entering countryside with woodland thick with ivy-clad trees, followed by lumpy fields featuring clumps of reeds and horses eating feed poured into old tractor tyres. There was something completely bizarre about the ride, as though we ought to be calling at Piccadilly Circus or Charing Cross but had become terribly lost.

The overall sensation was of somehow having broken free from the shackles of modern life, of being on a plucky train with shiny-blue-and-yellow carriages that had escaped the big bad smoke and gone for a canter in the countryside combined with a spell of sea air. We, myself and a handful of passengers who appeared to be locals rather than tourists, were on an Isle of Wight rebel ride.

It lasted nine minutes, passing four stations – Smallbrook Junction, Brading, Sandown and Lake – before arriving at my destination, the curious seaside resort of Shanklin. At this small station, where we all disembarked, an old map in the tiny ticket hall was worth stopping at for a good look.

This map, dating from 1914, showed a spider's web of railways that back then covered most corners of the island's 23 miles from east to west and thirteen miles from north to south. In all, there had once been 55 miles of railways on the Isle of Wight. At the time of my visit, there were eight miles. Once, you could catch a train from Freshwater and Yarmouth in the far west, not far from the island's famous Needles rock stacks, putter along to Newport, the island's capital town, close to the geographical centre, slip down to Ventnor on the south coast, once frequented by Queen Victoria and Charles Dickens (who described the seaside resort as "the prettiest place I ever saw in my life, at home or abroad"), rattle up to Ryde via Shanklin, or go halfway up to Smallbrook Junction and cut across to Newport again and go to the northern port of Cowes.

It had been a veritable feast of Isle of Wight train opportunities. A service called *The Tourist* had once wiggled around the lines, stopping at most of them. In 1901 there had even been grand plans to dig a 2½-mile railway tunnel beneath the Solent to link the island to southern England's main line, crossing from near Lymington in Hampshire to close to Yarmouth. An act of Parliament was signed, giving the green light, and there were talks of a Ventnor–Waterloo Express, but the idea was a slow burner (partly because the railway companies had interests in ferry services that they realized, after working out the sums, would lose revenue from new competition) and, despite construction beginning in 1914, the outbreak of the First World War got in the way and afterwards the idea was shelved. In the mid-2020s, any discussions for a tunnel to the mainland, including a project known as the Solent Freedom Tunnel, were focused on vehicles. Trains did not get much of a look-in.

By the 1950s, with the railway tunnel long forgotten, and accelerating in the 1960s after Dr Beeching's report, railways on the Isle of Wight began to close. The economics did not add up. Usage was high during the summer, but extremely low at other times. The trains were not paying their way. One of the former railway tunnels was, for a while, turned into a mushroom farm. At the time I was going, the only main line train ran from Ryde Head Pier to Shanklin, with a small heritage line, the aforementioned Isle of Wight Steam Railway, twisting for five miles inland from Smallbrook Junction.

In a way, what had happened on the Isle of Wight was a microcosm of what had happened to trains in Britain on a wider scale. The good little map on the wall of the tiny ticket office transported you into another Isle of Wight train world – and told a story.

Shanklin grew on you.

Part of that was due to its isolation. It felt like, and literally was, the end of the line. You strode out of the station, and down a short hill along the road was the sea. If you left London Waterloo at 9 a.m., you could be there by noon, in a sleepy English seaside town with amusement arcades, mini-golf, a sand and shingle beach, some collectibles shops and pubs decorated with nautical paraphernalia serving (decent) seafood chowder. Sure, this was achievable in a quicker time in Brighton, but in Shanklin it felt like you had taken a train to a different country, one step removed, thanks to having crossed on the ferry. If not quite the "prettiest place I ever saw in my life", as Dickens had said of Ventnor, there was a certain charm, the way the cliffs curved round the golden bay and the town clung to its hill.

Like the Island Line at Ryde Head Pier, it had its quirks. I was staying near the station at a hotel called the Channel View Hotel. My small single room was a cut above the punch-code B&B – it had its very own bathroom – but to see the Channel required craning your neck at the window and gazing at a small triangle of sea across a car park. Meanwhile, the heater, a plug-in electric device, was not working.

I went to the reception to ask if there was a replacement heater, or even a room with a working plug-in heater and a full sea view.

"You're in the room the coach drivers usually have. Easy to get in and out, isn't it?" said the receptionist when I requested a different one. This was said as though it was a special, in some way superior, room. It was indeed easy to get in and out; the door to the car park was right beside my door.

"Do most of the rooms have better Channel views?" I asked.

"Yes," the receptionist replied.

"Are you full?"

"No," he said.

"Oh," I replied.

I was given a new electric plug-in heater that worked.

The man said, "Any other issues, just let us know."

It was a good evening in Shanklin, down at a pub by the beach.

In the morning, I caught the 10:14 from Shanklin station to Smallbrook Junction, accompanied by a group of women, part of a local society called Gal Pals, who were travelling to Heathrow to catch a flight to South Africa for a safari holiday.

They were, unsurprisingly, in an ebullient mood. They hoped, they told me, to be spotting lions, water buffalo, white rhinos and zebras.

"Giraffes in Swaziland, the Big Five. We'll be staying for two nights in round huts with paraffin lights," said Mandy, originally from Nottinghamshire and who worked in "front of house" at a hotel (not my hotel). Tourism accounted for about 30 per cent of the Isle of Wight's economy.

They were all fans of the Island Line, though Mandy said, "It used to have these really old 1960s carriages – the old ones were really bumpy. Personally, I preferred them, but I've got no complaints with these."

The four of them were all originally from outside the Isle of Wight. Mo, a retired nurse from County Durham, said, "We're Grockles. That means *not from the island*. People from the island are Caulkheads, but you've got to be here three generations to be a Caulkhead."

The word "caulkhead" came from a job for which locals used to be renowned: caulking up the hulls of boats, filling gaps so they were leakproof. Mo could not explain the origin of Grockle but added that mainlanders were also referred to as Overners, especially people who had recently moved over.

There was a bit of "them and us" of this sort that went on among the population of 141,000. Mo said, "I was talking to someone in a pub who was in their fifties and who had never left the island. In the west of Wight, it's very rural. The man said to me 'I've never left the island, and I don't want to go.'"

I wished them well on safari, hopped off the 10:14 at Smallbrook Junction and was shortly chugging along in a third-class carriage built in 1916, with slam doors and seating for six (with a red-and-black floral moquette) in each self-contained compartment. Although third class, it was really quite comfortable. Outside, fields and hedgerows passed by. Inside, a man wearing a woolly hat and thick glasses, perhaps aged 80, was the only other passenger. He began to talk. Having nowhere to escape and, anyway, finding his talk interesting given how close I had (by this stage) inched towards full Train Nut status, I listened.

This is what he said: "Third-class carriages originally came courtesy of parliamentary trains. An 1844 act of Parliament. Cheaper trains for the masses. That's what we're in." He was fondly admiring the polished wood of the carriage and tapping a leather strap with holes in it that could be adjusted to set the window at different heights to allow air in.

"Britain really is lucky, you know," he continued. "In the past I've travelled all the way round the world. New Zealand, sixteen thousand miles. Five Concorde trips. But nowhere else on Earth has so many heritage lines as here. People are willing to put their hands in their pockets to pay for them. There are five hundred steam locomotives altogether working. It's extraordinary."

The man was facing forwards, staring at the red-and-black floral moquette of the carriage seats, not looking my way at all. Steam was floating by the window. I kept quiet and listened some more.

He began to talk about the Didcot Railway Centre, a museum in Oxfordshire: "You can turn up there by train and there's an underground passage from the station to the ticket office. It's in twenty acres. If you go there, you'll see a recreation of Brunel's old track, seven feet and a quarter of an inch. Two locomotives have been recreated with three or four wagons. When you see that seven-foot gauge in front of you, you think, *Oh my God, that's amazing, Concorde on rails*. From the late 1840s to the 1890s there was broad gauge. Then in 1892 – that was an extraordinary occurrence, when you think how long it takes to do things now – they changed it all in one weekend, three hundred miles, roughly, of track. Gangs of workmen came to carry it all out, four thousand people. A monumental task. They could not fail. It had to work. And they did it."

All of Brunel's ill-advised broad gauge was altered to standard gauge over a Saturday and Sunday in May, ready for the week ahead: George Stephenson's 4-foot-8½-inch track had won out.

The man began to compare the speed and efficiency of that changeover to work on the railways today: "It's tragic what's happened… that it won't go all the way to Manchester and Leeds. It won't even go properly from London. HS2 will go from Old Oak Common to Birmingham. But Old Oak Common is a station that's not where it should be. It's in west London, in Uxbridge, not in the centre of London."

He was referring to the London terminus of the much-discussed major project to build a high-speed line from the capital to the north of England.

"Yes, I know Old Oak's adjacent to the Elizabeth line and trains will take ten minutes to get to the centre. But it's not where it should be."

He was exasperated. He slapped the seat beside him. "Brexit was an enormous mistake. We don't have Brussels rules, et cetera, any more –

well, OK. We can buy from British factories – *well, OK*. But by dithering about HS2 – *well, factories can't live on thin air*. The factories that built the rolling stock, what can they do now? There's nothing more to build here. In Europe it's cheaper to build their own stock, we can't build for Europe. All that skilled labour? What is it going to do? We don't have any Brussels rules. We don't have anyone telling us what to do any more. And then we do nothing. We dither. If we do that, factories will close down. And then, if we do want anything made in the future, we'll have to buy it from Europe and pay import duties and all of that. Would France let its engineering skills and factories go? I don't think it would. It's ridiculous."

He was impassioned. He was still staring forwards. Then he turned to me. We had travelled from Smallbrook Junction to Wootton station and had returned down the line to Havenstreet station while he had been talking. "Might see you later," he said, shaking my hand, looking quite defeated and upset as he exited the carriage. Though I never did.

I got off at Havenstreet, too.

This station acted as the Isle of Wight Steam Railway's hub, with a museum on Isle of Wight trains, a restaurant and a bookstall. At the latter, I had a look at the old railway books, refraining from buying any (I had enough), and examined an extraordinary collection of old vinyl records that were of old recordings of the sounds of steam trains, with titles such as *Trains in the Hills*, *Memories of Steam* and *Steam Railroading Under Thundering Skies*.

"Do you really sell any of these?" I asked a man named Mike working at the stall.

"Oh yes, a few. Back in the sixties and seventies everyone used to buy them," he said.

"So they were especially popular fifty to sixty years earlier?"

"Oh yes," he said.

The bookstall had recently received three or four "major bequests" of books, as rail enthusiasts who had begun as trainspotters in the 1940s and 1950s had passed away. These trainspotters had, of course, begun during a fantastic time for spotting steam locomotives, which had kept on going into the early 1960s despite advancements in diesel and electric trains. Back then, many would set forth to the tracks clutching books published by a company called Ian Allan Publishing, which had produced the famous, must-have *ABC of British Railway Locomotives*. Ian Allan, who had worked in the publicity department for Southern Railway, had spotted the trainspotter trend and also a gap in the trainspotter market. By listing the names of locomotives, and there were around 20,000 at the time of nationalization in 1948, he gave rail enthusiasts a focus for their enthusiasm and sold thousands of copies, taking the hobby into the mainstream and acting as a catalyst for many other train guidebooks, which trainspotters as boys (for they were almost always boys) bought and then moved on to other weightier train tomes when they stopped hanging around by tracks, preferring armchair trainspotting in later years. The result of the bequeathments was a glut of old second-hand railway books in the 2020s.

"You get a generation that passes away and this is what happens," Mike said. He held up a book entitled *Bagnalls of Stafford* with a picture of a red locomotive on the front. "This one here was a hundred pounds originally, we're doing it now for sixty pounds. The book market has gone way down."

The subject turned to the Beatles.

Among the vinyl records for sale, I had just noticed out of the corner of my eye, was one album called *Last Train to "Ryde": Recordings made on the Isle of Wight of the now extinct ex-LSWR Adams 02 Class 0-4-4 Tanks* with a picture of an old steam train on the front – probably an extremely rare recording; I could not imagine too many of them knocking about in dusty attic boxes. "LSWR" stood for London and South Western Railway.

Seeing this reminded me that I had in my pocket a ticket to Ryde… and of a story about the phrase "ticket to ride".

Some believed that John Lennon and Paul McCartney came up with the title for their catchy pop song "Ticket to Ride", released by the Beatles in 1965, after visiting the Isle of Wight and taking a train to Ryde. Paul McCartney once said that the title was in reference to "a British Rail ticket to the town of Ryde on the Isle of Wight", although he was also on record admitting Lennon came up with "sixty per cent" of the lyrics for the song (and Lennon is said to have claimed later that he basically wrote the whole thing). So it appeared that one of the Beatles' most famous tracks was quite possibly inspired by Ryde – if McCartney was recalling matters correctly about the song mainly written by Lennon.

All this said, the alternative theory about the song's title, which threw a spanner in the "Ryde" theory, involved prostitutes in Germany and "tickets to ride" required for sex workers, the "tickets" of those "tickets to ride" (with a whole different connotation attached to the word "ride") being all about proving that the prostitutes had a clean bill of health. Lennon is said to have mentioned this version of the song's title in an interview that had been noted by prominent Beatles scholars. The band had stayed in Hamburg, where such health cards had existed, for some time while performing live at clubs. Given that Lennon allegedly said this, and he was more seemingly involved in the writing of the lyrics, then perhaps the song was not about Ryde at all.

"Yes, it was meant to be *Ticket to Ryde*. It was from when they came here. That's what I heard," said Mike.

This was good enough "evidence" for me.

With that I took the train, using my "ticket to Ryde", all the way to Ryde Pier Head station (which was open again) then got the ferry to Portsmouth Harbour and a train to Barnham via a large number of playing fields and warehouses on the outskirts of Portsmouth, a section of countryside criss-crossed with rapeseed fields and the small cathedral city of Chichester. At Barnham station, I joined the train to Bognor Regis, accompanied by a group of rowdy teenagers, who were to be stopped by a guard at Bognor's ticket barrier. "You've got one ticket," he said. "There are four of you." The youths looked a bit perplexed as to what to do next and it appeared they might have to return to Barnham.

I left this mini drama to unfold.

It was 4.20 p.m. and a bright afternoon by the British seaside. I was a train traveller. I was looking forward to exploring sunny Bognor.

On the beach
Bognor Regis

I was not the first – far from it. Trains had been coming to Bognor Regis, then known simply as Bognor, since 1 June 1864. For long before that, however, well-to-do travellers had been visiting the purpose-built resort, or "watering place", for the medical value believed to derive from sea-bathing and drinking seawater. In the eighteenth century a Member of Parliament named Sir Richard Hotham (1722–1799), a convert to the health benefits of the seaside, who had made his money in the East India Company, had begun buying up parts of the coast around an old fishing village and building terraced houses. His hope had been to entice the wealthy to rent his new properties by the coast, ideally "for the season", rather than stick to Brighton and Weymouth, already established resorts attracting the likes of the Prince Regent, later George IV, when he was in his early twenties in 1783. The king-to-be was so taken by Brighton that he built an Indian-palace-style home there: the Royal Pavilion.

Bognor did well enough, though not quite hitting the jackpot of a royal visitor, and after Hotham had passed away, it continued as a place for the nobility to rest and recuperate by the sea. But it was to be the railway that changed the small town forever.

It took a while coming. Although 39 years after the Stockton and Darlington Railway does not seem long, the first trains to Brighton from London had arrived in 1841, while Weymouth in Dorset was connected to the railway in 1857 – and a train service from Brighton to nearby Chichester had been in place since 1846. Confusingly, this line to Chichester had stopped at a station known as "Woodgate for Bognor", the location of the current Barnham station, about 3 miles from Bognor, from where horse-drawn carriages would take genteel visitors the final short distance before the proper station for the town opened.

By the 1860s, Bognor had some catching up to do, yet very soon the tourist hordes were piling into carriages, many having "done" other seaside resorts and looking for somewhere new. The journey from London Victoria was a mere 54 miles, with trains taking around 2 hours and 15 minutes and getting quicker and quicker. More people came and by the time of the Bank Holidays Act of 1871, Bognor, as with other British seaside resorts up and down the country that had just acquired their own stations, was ripe for "discovery". Cheap tickets to Bognor from London Victoria were snapped up, and by 1877, day trips allowing Londoners to leave at 7 a.m. and return at 6 p.m. were hugely popular.

The trains kept on coming in the years to follow, to such an extent that by 1907 almost 6,000 visitors were arriving on bank holidays, prompting local councillors to vote on requesting railway companies to limit numbers (narrowly failing to pass an edict to do so). This could just have been Britain's first official recorded backlash against "overtourism".

Bognor's refined qualities must not have been completely wiped out by the arrival of mass tourism on trains, though, as in 1929 the most famous thing ever to happen in Bognor was to play out. King George V visited a house just outside the seaside town on the advice of doctors to get some sea air. After he left, local councillors, who seemed a busybody lot, quickly wrote to the king, requesting that they change the town's name from Bognor to Bognor Regis. The story goes that the king, possibly in a state of irritation or just scatty humour, said to an adviser, "Oh, bugger Bognor!" This adviser then wrote a message to the councillors of Bognor saying, "The king has been graciously pleased to grant your request."

The truth of this story, of which there were various versions (and local tourist officials seemed coy to discuss, if absence of any mention of the affair on visitor information panels was anything to go by) was about as tricky to establish as the origin of the Beatles' song title "Ticket to Ride".

Anyway, Bognor Regis became the new official name; Sir Richard Hotham, somewhere up in the sky, must have been extremely pleased. Bognor finally had a royal money-spinner, though no Indian palaces were subsequently constructed. Instead, amusement arcades came. It was not long before the flamboyant entrepreneur Billy Butlin had opened his first amusement park, in 1932, with funfair rides, fruit machines, a zoo with leopards, polar bears and kangaroos and – intriguingly – a shooting range featuring targets including Adolf Hitler and Joseph Goebbels. With the establishment of the 1938 Holidays With Pay Act making time off from work (a week a year) part of law, the resort was to become one of the most popular in southern England, and after the Second World War, Bognor really boomed as Butlin extended his offerings to include a holiday park with places to stay for the night.

So when you went to Bognor Regis, or just about any place on Britain's coastline with a railway station, although the West Sussex seaside resort was an extreme example, you were almost always visiting somewhere that was once *completely changed by trains*. The entity known as the "Great British seaside" was, effectively, invented by the railways. From Grange-over-Sands to Prestatyn, St Ives, Torquay (and the English Riviera), Minehead, Shanklin, Bognor Regis and beyond, the railways had come, and life had changed beyond recognition.

Those were just the spots I had happened to drop by at, not to mention biggies like Blackpool, Weston-super-Mare and Bournemouth, along the route I had just taken.

The more you messed about on trains in Britain, the more you realized how closely industrialization and "leisure" were entwined.

Which made sense really: machines, such as trains, saved time.

What were you going to do with it?

Past a Railway Social Club ("members only"), a Polish grocery shop and a Samaritans office, you walked down a row of pastel-coloured terraced houses beyond the Bognor Regis Museum – stopping, possibly, to admire an old fly poster on the front wall advertising gigs by David Bowie and Jimi Hendrix in Bognor in 1966 – soon arriving at Bognor's pier.

This was built a year after the railway came to Bognor Regis. Amusement arcade lights flashed beneath a sign that said "NEPTUNES FAMILY ENTERTAINMENT CENTRE", and a security man stood at the door, eyeing my bulging backpack. Somewhere inside, perhaps with a side entrance, was a sports bar called Legends and a nightclub called Sheiks that was said to be "the biggest and busiest nightclub in West Sussex", according to Bognor Today's website. One of the pier's claims to fame, you learned from an information panel, was that a former impresario had turned down work by a teenage comedian named Charlie Chaplin, who soon after emigrated to the United States to see if there was more interest in a place called Hollywood. The seaward end of the pier, which poked out 107 metres, was in a poor state and much was closed; large parts of the pier, which had once been 350 metres, had been lost to storms over the years. Campaigns to raise Heritage Lottery cash for repairs had failed.

The pier was a good place to gaze across the pebble beach, listening to the wash of waves on the shore. A gentle pink sky had descended, mingling with the soft-grey water of the Channel. Despite the razzle-dazzle of the seaside amusements and the proximity of West Sussex's biggest and busiest nightclub (yet to get started, it being so early, of course), this was a peaceful spot.

I wandered down the promenade watching people try the bumper cars, the Twister rides, the Waltzer rides, the Fun Wheel, the 'ook-a-duck and the Runaway Train, which I resisted. I discovered that to enter Butlins holiday park would cost £18 for a day visitor pass, so did not enter. I walked past an empty octagonal bandstand. I ate a *nasi goreng* Korean chicken dinner from a place called the Bonito Lounge (not bad).

Afterwards, I watched a souped-up electric-blue Range Rover rev down the main street and walked past a grocery shop offering Polish, Lithuanian, Latvian, Romanian, Slovakian, Hungarian and Turkish food, and another called Sofia Market: Traditional Bulgarian Food. Many of those who came to the UK when it was still a member of the European Union appeared to have found their way to Bognor Regis.

I returned to my accommodation, a small, cold room above a pub, and planned the next day's rides.

Rolling, rolling, rolling

Bognor Regis to Hythe via New Romney and Dungeness

Bognor Station was adorned with Southern Railway posters that were not about the delights of rail travel. They were about the non-delights of rail travellers. "CYBER FLASHING. UPSKIRTING. EXPOSING. CATCALLING. STARING. TOUCHING. PRESSING. IT'S ALL SEXUAL HARASSMENT AND IT WON'T BE TOLERATED ON OUR NETWORK. BE SAFE. FEEL SAFE. TRAVEL SAFE," said one. Another, accompanied by a picture of a cactus, said, "THERE'S NO EXCUSE FOR PRICKLY BEHAVIOUR. OUR COLLEAGUES WEAR BODYCAMS FOR EVERYONE'S SECURITY. ABUSIVE BEHAVIOUR WILL NOT BE TOLERATED UNDER ANY CIRCUMSTANCES. OUR COLLEAGUES ARE HERE TO HELP YOU, SO PLEASE TREAT THEM WITH RESPECT. WE WILL ALWAYS PUSH FOR THE STRONGEST PENALTIES FOR ANYONE FOUND GUILTY OF ANTISOCIAL BEHAVIOUR. BE SAFE. FEEL SAFE. TRAVEL SAFE."

Southern clearly ran a tight train line.

At the Express Café and Sandwich Bar, I bought a black Americano and complimented the charming owner of the independent business on an intriguing picture of Bognor from Victorian times, which showed bathing machines with wheels by the shore and folk with straw hats and rolled-up trousers on the beach. The owner was Polish, with slicked-back hair and a startlingly un-British entrepreneurial can-do attitude. He stared dreamily at the photograph and commented, "Everything was nice back in the day."

As we stood there staring at the picture, he began to tell me about some of the Express Café's sales strategies, about which he was passionate.

"Water!" he exclaimed. "People want water! I give them water! That is why I have the cheapest water in the south of England!"

A bottle, he told me, was 69 pence.

"People want chicken!" he said, moving on from water. "So I give them chicken! Chicken leg tastes better! I give them chicken leg!"

He patted his leg as though to indicate chicken leg.

"I want to feed the people in the morning!" he said. "And I want to feed them when they come back in the evening!"

He paused, thinking about these statements.

"And in the day too!" he said, not wanting to miss out on the market between morning and evening.

We chatted for a while about his menu and his plans for a newsagents/shop in a vacant space across the concourse.

Then I went to catch a train – the first of many on what was to be a long day on the railways of southern England.

I was about to take a succession of trains, mixed with buses, from Bognor Regis in West Sussex to New Romney in Kent via Brighton and Lewes in East Sussex: four trains, two rail replacement buses and a regular bus. This journey would take almost five hours, all going to plan. It was an experiment of sorts: *would this mad journey really work*? It was disappointing, frankly, that there wasn't a lovely train ride that hugged the south coast and went all the way, but you couldn't always get what you wanted with British trains. You just had to live with it.

And that was just the start. From New Romney, once I had taken four trains and three buses, I would take *a further two trains*. New Romney was a station on the Romney, Hythe and Dymchurch Railway, a heritage line on a narrow-gauge track (1 foot 1 inch wide). The two additional trains, bringing the day's total to five, a record for the trip, would be steam trains to and from a place that had always intrigued me: Dungeness, home to a lighthouse, a nuclear power station and a pub on a desolate stretch of out-of-the-way land comprising mainly pebbles and sand.

There you had it: I had finally lost the train plot.

Like a railway hors d'oeuvre, the 08:05 from Bognor Regis to Barnham rolled off, beginning the feast of train to come. It puttered along on the short ride, past damp fields beneath a pearl grey sky, arriving at

Barnham, whereupon I joined the 08:31 to Brighton, accompanied by a hen party ("I think I'm still pissed from last night") and we continued rolling along. The train crossed a flatland of dykes and egrets, passing a farm with a large greenhouse and the distant outline of Arundel Castle, a long way off on a hill – where Queen Victoria once stayed in 1846, perhaps having dropped by on a train on the way to her country getaway, Osborne House on the Isle of Wight.

The great monarch of the rail age – admittedly aged six when the Stockton and Darlington Railway had begun – had taken a while to join in the burgeoning "railway mania". Her first train journey, at the age of 23, was on a GWR service from Slough, conveniently close to another of her homes in Windsor, to London Paddington, in June 1842. For that ride, a "royal saloon" carriage had been fitted out with silk curtains, plush velvet sofas and mahogany tables. Up front, Isambard Kingdom Brunel himself had overseen the locomotive.

Her verdict? "Delightful and so quick." She had also been "quite charmed by this new way of travelling", although she and her husband Albert were nervous train travellers, requesting a top speed of 40 mph, and Albert had sometimes been heard to say, "Not quite so fast, Mr Conductor, if you please." Although the duo evidently did very much take to the tracks, allowing Queen Victoria to buy yet another country home in Balmoral, up near Aberdeen – which would have been impossible to visit quite as regularly as she did without the new invention.

The 08:31 rattled onwards.

Electricity pylons came and went... holiday home parks... long ploughed fields... Goring-by-Sea station... Durrington-on-Sea... West Worthing... bungalows... a Lidl... a harbour... great piles of sacks by a dock... Hove station... a tunnel.

We arrived at a large greenhouse-like station, Brighton station, where I switched platforms for the 09:26 to Lewes.

The train rolled on past roofs of terraced houses, and I listened to a large muscular man on the seat ahead. He was wearing a tracksuit and box-fresh Nike trainers. He might have been a heavyweight boxer off to go training.

"I'm buzzing that I've got this," he was saying on his phone. "My probation officer came to me and said, 'You've just got to wait a few weeks.' Then they just let me out. Just like that."

He paused, listening to the other end of the line.

"Yeah, I know. Yeah. It's a joke," he said. "Really, I should have been out in August last year. At least I've got it now. Yeah. I'm buzzing."

He paused to listen again.

"Oh bless," he said. "Yeah. Wicked. Yeah, see you soon. Yeah, bruv. Yeah sweet. Bye, bye, bye."

The train curved by the Amex Stadium, where Brighton and Hove Albion were playing Liverpool the next day, into a pillowy landscape of hills, soon after arriving at Lewes station, where the just-released prisoner and I disembarked.

Mass confusion reigned outside Lewes station, where crowds of passengers affected by the engineering works floated around like small schools of fish, being told by an elderly man in a hi-vis jacket "Polegate? Polegate is over there!" And we all went over there, where a younger woman in a hi-vis jacket said, "No, no, no. Only Polegate? Over there!" We all went "over there" and the elderly man seemed aggrieved that the younger woman had sent us all back, but we boarded the 10:00 rail replacement bus, and it took us to Polegate via some twisty roads between chalky hills.

At Polegate, we swirled around like small fish for a while once again, near some people from a church playing guitars and saying to passers-by "Jesus is alive today and has been changing people's lives for two thousand years… Come and join us!" Instead, we boarded the 10:32 rail replacement bus to Pevensey and Westham, where I sat next to a roofer who said he had a "roof to do" in Hastings, and an interior designer who said, "I'm going to Hastings as well to view a vintage property – my speciality is giving some TLC to restore former glory, it's only two rooms and a hallway."

We all sat there cramped in the bus. Our driver engaged in some light road rage. "There's nothing going to move, mate!" he yelled at a car driver in a lane during a stand-off. Then we arrived in Pevensey and Westham and all piled onto the 10:55 train to Hastings: the roofer and the interior designer still with me.

The interior designer wore a striped scarf and had curly hair. Her name was Laila. We sat down at a table together and she said, "I treat life as an adventure. On trains, I listen to music. I also talk to people. Most people think I'm a nutter. In the times we're in, I think it's really important." She meant talking to people. "Challenging times, community is important. I'm a Brightonian. But Brighton is getting a Londoner aspect. In London, it's quite blinkered. People think you've stepped out of a mental asylum if you talk to anyone. Like it's really strange. It's like *you're talking to me*? But when you break down the scared coldness people have, it's fantastic."

The roofer, John, who was in his thirties, and who had a neat side-parting and the air of a no-nonsense lower-division football manager, was infected by Laila's soliloquy. He said, referring to our buses and trains, "To be honest I've had quite a few long journeys, worse than this. I was going to London to Charing Cross one time and the train made this shudder. There was an announcement that we'd just hit a tree. We were stuck there four hours. They said we might have to get off onto the track. A few months ago, that was. My sister and children were on that too. We got rolled back and we got a taxi to London. South Eastern [the railway operator] had an account [with a local taxi firm]. To be fair to them, they paid for it." The whole journey had taken from 1 p.m. to 9 p.m.

Through the window we got a glimpse of sea then we arrived at Hastings, and my new friends left to do their jobs and I caught the 11:25 to Rye, sitting close to a thirtysomething man with a hipster beard and lots of yellow sticker-notes on a book. He seemed in a general state of agitation. "Oh f***ing bollocks. F*** it," he said after a while – he had hurt himself and was addressing me and anyone else listening. "Smacked my elbow. Excuse my language." He began a phone call: "For f***'s sake.... Just wait... where does the bad stuff start?" He continued in this vein. He was flicking through the book. We exited the terraced houses of Hastings and slid into woodlands blanketed with snowdrops and primroses. Fields of sheep opened up after Winchelsea station, and a child nearby, who must have heard the hipster's various tirades, said, "There's a thousand! A thousand!" He was referring to the sheep and was delighted by the sight of them.

And then a bus from outside the Cinque Ports pub by Rye station left at noon and arrived 40 minutes later at a little train station with little railway tracks and a little locomotive puffing away at a platform.

I had traversed a large swathe of southern England, come across a few characters along the way and located some more old trains: train job done for the day... almost.

The Romney, Hythe and Dymchurch Railway was opened in 1927 by an eccentric millionaire racing driver and former army officer Captain John Edwards Presgrave Howey, who had inherited much of his wealth from his great uncle Henry Howey, a landowner who had settled in Melbourne, Australia. With his friend Count Louis Zborowski, another millionaire racing driver, who famously drove "Chitty-Bang-Bang" Mercedes cars, which provided the inspiration for the car in Ian Fleming's children's book *Chitty Chitty Bang Bang*, Captain Howey set about indulging a passion for steam trains by creating a miniature line, finally selecting the remote and mysterious Romney Marsh after attempting to purchase the Ravenglass and Eskdale Railway. Sadly, Count Zborowski, whose Polish title was of somewhat dubious origin though he was a society figure married into the prominent Astor family, died in a racing accident at Monza in Italy.

Captain Howey, however, pushed on and with the help of a leading miniature locomotive engineer named Henry Greenly, a legend in the miniature locomotive engineering world, completed a line from the seaside town of Hythe to Romney, extending it a year later across the shingly headland, referred to by some as "England's desert", to the isolated hamlet of Dungeness. The 13½-mile public railway proved extremely popular with the public, especially after the 1938 Holidays

With Pay Act, with crowds descending, and then after the war a grand reopening attended by the comedians Stan Laurel and Oliver Hardy. Since soon after Captain Howey's death in 1963 it had been run by the Romney Hythe and Dymchurch Railway Association, supported by volunteers.

Those were the basics. Yet there was a mystique about the line due to its peculiar geographical location and that it took you to the edge of two nuclear power stations, Dungeness A and Dungeness B, both no longer operative, where an artistic community had sprung up amid the pebbles of the tiny former fishing hamlet, where the prominent filmmaker and gay rights activist Derek Jarman (1942–1994) had lived before dying early of an AIDS-related illness.

At New Romney station I bought a ticket to Dungeness and back to Hythe from a ticket office attendant named Olie, who said, "I'm nearly sixty years old. This railway has been a part of my life for sixty years. I live in New Romney. If the trains weren't here, they would be sadly missed. Dungeness is incredible. Doesn't matter what day you go on. It always looks different."

Another ticket attendant, named David, who had been listening to Olie, cut in: "It's beautiful, absolutely stunning. It's mad to think there's a nuclear power station there. You almost don't notice it. The power station provides a lot of employment. My parents worked there. They began decommissioning 'A' a few years ago. 'B' will happen soon. My mother was involved in catering, my father in 'health physics radiation checking'. It's beautiful out there. So beautiful."

David gazed almost adoringly in the direction of the power stations, as though he could see their beauty emanating through the walls of the New Romney station ticket office.

Then Julie, who had been listening to David, cut in. Julie was one of the trustees of the Romney, Hythe and Dymchurch Railway and was a big steam train fan. "They call me the puffer nutter," she said, by way of introduction. "I help raise money for maintaining the locomotives. We've got two diesels and the rest are steam. We have galas, people come from all over the world, Germany and America. There's one hundred and twenty staff. It's expensive. We've got a huge fleet."

Julie had a full-time job on Bexhill Council – her work as a trustee for the line was in her spare time – but had come to New Romney station just to see the trains on her day off.

The railway was not just loved (seemingly adored) locally, it was also clearly an important part of the community.

Ticket in hand, a feeling of "train love" in the air, I left Olie, David and Puffer Nutter and went to find out why.

The 13:21 to Dungeness, puffing by the platform, was pulled by a diminutive, olive-green locomotive named *Green Goddess*.

It worked like this. You oohed and aahed at this diminutive, olive-green locomotive for a while. Then you took a stiff, nylon-covered seat, any stiff, nylon-covered seat (no ticketed seats). Then, sitting in your tiny compartment with a wooden-plank floor and the doors left open, if you so wanted, *you just let it happen.*

Into a tunnel, out of a tunnel the *Green Goddess* went. Into fields of spiky low crops, out of fields of spiky low crops. Into little settlements with conservatories, satellite dishes, garden gnomes and sheds, out of the little settlements. Past banks of primroses, brambles, daffodils, thistles and clumps of tall, coarse grass – a semi-wilderness zone – before bending round into a weird, wide shingle-land with almost no vegetation at all, just a handful of clapboard houses down by the shoreline in pastel pinks, pastel blues, rusty reds and bright yellows. Not a soul in sight.

Great looming buildings arose ahead: the power stations. Then a striped tower: a lighthouse. A solitary building just before you came to the station was the pub (the Britannia Inn). Such strange beauty all around: bleak, pared-down, empty. Pebbles everywhere, millions of them.

What a wonderful ride. No connections required (only one line). No announcements telling you how sorry anyone is to announce anything. No delays. No replacement buses. Just a rattle. Just a clatter. Just a waft of smoke, a smell of soot, a hoot every now and then across the strange, sun-baked stones.

You may well enjoy the Romney, Hythe and Dymchurch Railway.

You may also stroll beside the barbed-wire walls by the power stations down to the sloping pebble beach. You may ask the fishermen what they caught that day and they may show their buckets and say, "Sharks... well actually dogfish. They look like sharks, don't they?" You may drop by a clapboard art shop. You may eat prawns and drink a pint at the jolly, well-run Britannia Inn. You may catch the train to Hythe and arrive at a small market town with a high street, a church and Martello towers beside a Ministry of Defence firing range by a beach. You may check into a pub in Hythe after eating a good Nepalese curry for dinner and be woken in the night by another passionate amorous couple (several times).

But never mind that.

One way or another, you will have had an excellent day on the trains of southern England.

CHAPTER SEVEN

HYTHE TO GRIMSBY VIA DOVER, SHEERNESS-ON-SEA, SOUTHEND, WALTON-ON-THE-NAZE, SHERINGHAM AND SKEGNESS

DREAMING UP THE EAST

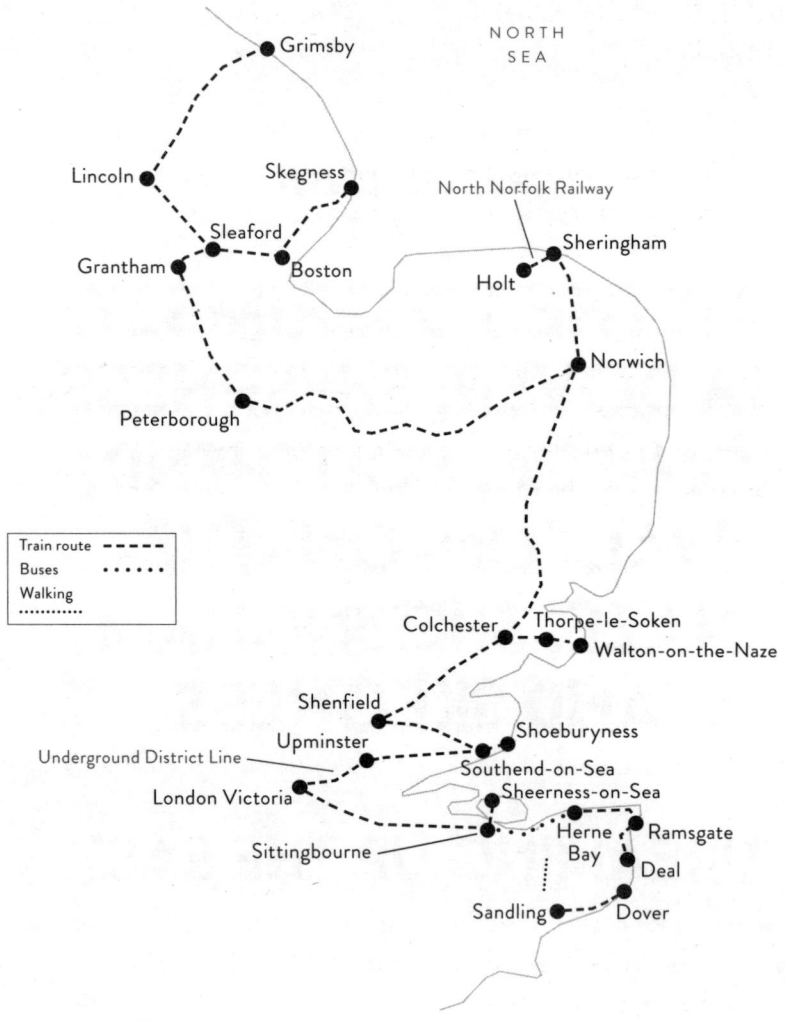

Travelling along the Romney, Hythe and Dymchurch Railway had felt like drifting along in another world. And it had reminded me of Charles Dickens's take on trains, which he wrote about in an essay titled "RAILWAY DREAMING" in his *Household Words* weekly journal in 1856:

> I am never sure of time or place upon a Railroad. I can't read, I can't think, I can't sleep – I can only dream. Rattling along in this railway carriage in a state of luxurious confusion, I take it for granted I am coming from somewhere, and going somewhere else. I seek to know no more. Why things come into my head and fly out again, whence they come and why they come, where they go and why they go, I am incapable of considering. It may be the guard's business, or the railway company's; I only know it is not mine. I know nothing about myself – for anything I know, I may be coming from the Moon.

Sometimes trains could leave you feeling that way (especially around Dungeness).

Getting an early start, I walked up the hill from Hythe to its nearest mainline station, Sandling. This required trekking two miles via the mock-Tudor mansions, Porsches and Audis of the village of Saltwood. The unmanned station was tucked away beyond these splendid abodes, where I was 20 minutes early.

I sat at Sandling station, thinking of Charles Dickens.

Going to Kent always prompted thoughts of the author, who had made the county his home at Gad's Hill Place in the village of Higham near Rochester and the wild marshes of the Hoo Peninsula. Travelling by train through Kent had the added dimension of his relationship with railways, which had been a rocky one – for he had almost died on one. On 9 June 1865, Dickens had been returning on the 14:38 "tidal train" from Folkestone to London after a trip to France with Ellen "Nelly"

Ternan, his mistress (27 years his junior), and her mother, when their train derailed at Staplehurst in Kent, about 30 miles north-west of Sandling station, which Dickens's train must have passed through.

At Staplehurst, workers who had lifted the rails to conduct repairs by a bridge over the river Beult had misread the timetable to disastrous effect. Other first-class carriages plunged into the riverbed, but Dickens's carriage had luckily hung above the abyss. He, Nelly and her mother managed to escape – Nelly with minor injuries to her arm and neck. After clambering clear, Dickens made sure Nelly was alright and that she and her mother left so no one would see the famous novelist with them and he could avoid tittle-tattle. Then Dickens, reputation intact, filled up his top hat with water, took his brandy flask and went to attend the injured; ten people had died. At one point in the midst of all this, however, he remembered something: part of the manuscript for *Our Mutual Friend* was still in his jacket in the carriage. So the story goes that he went back to the carriage and retrieved it, putting himself in some danger.

Later, Dickens admitted he was "quite shattered" by what had happened, and his daughter Mamie was to say his "nerves were never really the same again". By extraordinary coincidence, he died precisely five years to the day later, aged 58, having used railways extensively throughout his short life: touring large tracts of America and visiting Switzerland and Italy as well as much of Britain on reading tours. Dickens had been the impressionable age of thirteen when the Stockton and Darlington Railway had begun, and they were to have a huge impact, one way or another, on his life and works.

Plenty to consider on the platform at Sandling.

Though it was not long before the 08:30 to Dover arrived.

This Southeastern train with purple seats hurtled along, stopping once at Folkestone Central then moving high above houses, dropping into a tunnel and exiting to a view of the Channel before pacing below a high white cliff above a calm sea and entering a succession of further tunnels to reach Dover Priory station.

At Dover Priory, I met my brother, Ed, who lived in the port. As planned, we proceeded to walk a dozen miles along the rolling cliffs to the neighbouring town of Deal, enjoying the views, catching up and getting a bit of exercise.

No trains were involved whatsoever.

This did not, however, stop me quietly casting my newly attuned railway-oriented eyes in the direction of the Dover docks.

Down there somewhere, a long time ago, the Southern Railway and Compagnie Internationale des Wagons-Lits Night Ferry sleeper train, seen way back at the Locomotion museum in Shildon, used to be rolled onto tracks fitted on a waiting ferry and taken to Dunkirk. This service, begun in 1936 and discontinued in 1980, must have been quite a way to travel: depart London Victoria at 9 p.m., from platform two, and arrive in Paris Gare du Nord at 9 a.m., after docking at Dunkirk at 5.34 a.m. On the return, the Night Ferry left Paris at 9.45 p.m. and arrived at London Victoria at 9.10 a.m. There was also a daytime service on the *Golden Arrow* for the London–Dover leg and on the *Flèche d'Or* for the Dunkirk–Paris section, with passengers disembarking to take the ferry while the trains stayed on land and caught corresponding rides on the other side.

Trains, it seemed, had really seeped into me over the past few weeks.

I was beginning to look at old dockyards and wonder, *Very nice, but did any trains ever go there?*

We arrived at the seaside town of Deal, having passed the place on the coast path where Julius Caesar was said to have landed when conquering Britain in 55 BCE, and went straight to the Queen Street Tap pub by the local station.

From Deal, I had booked a series of trains and one rail replacement bus to Sheerness-on-Sea on the Isle of Sheppey on Kent's north coast, a journey of 3 hours and 14 minutes, including a half-hour wait at Ramsgate and 40 minutes in Sittingbourne. It was a somewhat mad journey, even I admitted that, but I had always wondered what happened in Sheerness-on-Sea and this was my big opportunity.

Ed flat out refused to join me.

As we drank pints of Moretti lager in the sunshine on a table outside the Queen Street Tap, he elaborated on why.

"So," he began, clicking on his phone, making a calculation, "it is, as the crow flies, forty-one point eight miles to Sheerness."

He paused and clicked some more.

"So your train journey will be averaging fourteen miles an hour," he said.

He paused and took a sip of Moretti.

"That is why I'm not joining you," he said.

He would be returning by train to Dover, a journey of eighteen minutes.

"I'm tempted to pay for a cab for you," he added, his beer-drinking seeming to unleash a sudden outpouring of largesse (though I knew there was not the slightest chance he actually would).

Then he said thoughtfully of his own journey "Eighteen minutes to cover ten miles, not bad. Just goes to show how good the trains are. It was three hours to walk here."

Then, editorializing on my behalf, he said, "You can put, *When I got to Sheerness, I realized I could have flown to Croatia.* I'm guessing that's about right, somewhere better than Sheerness. *I could have been in Gran Canaria in the same time. Instead, I'm in Sheer-hell.*"

He took another sip of Moretti and chuckled to himself.

"It could be quite nice," he said, referring to Sheerness. He seemed to have his doubts about the place despite never having been there.

"I don't really know," he said, and with that we both went to catch our respective trains.

Perhaps he was right. In fact, I knew he was right, about the journey. But he was not, unlike me, in the "train zone".

He was clearly not even close to it.

I, meanwhile, had become, by this stage, deeply ensconced, saturated, flooded and immersed in *all things train*.

So I continued, brother-less, onwards. And so began a strange series of rides to Sheerness-on-Sea, best captured in a series of snapshots from the carriage (and replacement bus) windows.

On the 14:31 from Deal to Ramsgate: a stop at Sandwich, some paddocks with small chestnut horses, a marshland of dykes, more small chestnut horses, followed by a series of bleached-yellow wheat fields.

On the 15:22 from Ramsgate to Herne Bay: man on board saying "Oh ah eh, oh ah eh" and clutching a can of Baltic lager, who seemed to want to make my acquaintance or considered me an old, long-lost friend; followed by stops at Broadstairs and Margate, and a stretch along some golf courses before Herne Bay.

On the 15:57 from Herne Bay to Sittingbourne rail replacement bus: a woman sitting near me discussing her weekend and how she "fell over and smashed my face, oh my God, you know what I'm like, super-super scatty, and I threw the suitcase and I thought I'd done his Captain Morgan and he looked a bit bewildered, and like, we was walking and we got drunk, really drunk, smashed proper, and when he woke up, he said, 'You can't smoke and drink proper', then we had a long chat, talking all day, there's a few issues…"; followed by a stop at Whitstable station and a drive along the M2 before arriving at Faversham station, where a man was angry at not being able to board with his bicycle.

On the 17:34 from Sittingbourne to Sheerness (pronounced *cher-ness* by railway announcements): industrial scenery, warehouses, factories then a bridge (the Sheppey Crossing over the river Swale) and a silver-grey flatland, dykes, more factories and a wasteland of yards, spiky metal fences, wind farms, scaffolding depots and timber yards.

Arrival at Sheerness-on-Sea station.

No wonder my brother had not been so keen – what a journey! Though it was a curious sensation moving onto the Isle of Sheppey, yet another Kentish "edgeland", a bit like down in Dungeness, just without the bleak, haunting, oddly beautiful scenery.

As with the rides over from Deal, however, I found that Sheerness-on-Sea seemed to lend itself to snapshots.

1) A walk from the station down a path leading to a shingle beach facing the Thames Estuary, where a wall mural featured a mermaid with her hand on a TNT detonator. Accompanying this mermaid was a message in the style of an old-fashioned railway poster: "WELCOME TO SHEERNESS: YOU'LL HAVE A BLAST". This referred to an American ship, the *SS Richard Montgomery*, which sank close by in 1944 with an unexploded cargo of bombs that if detonated would probably have caused the largest non-nuclear explosion in history. It still lay out there somewhere, untouched.

2) Locating my hotel above a bar where Sunday afternoon revellers were belting out "Sweet Caroline" at a karaoke event, next door to the Sheerness Conservative Club.

3) The consumption of a large chicken kebab at a restaurant called Arizona near an old-fashioned clock tower, where a trail of dried blood marked the pavements by a bookies, a Poundstretcher and an off-licence advertising whiskies with giant pictures of bottles on the outside.

4) A decision not to go to the Wetherspoons for a drink.

5) Avoiding eye contact with a gang of youths near the Wetherspoons on the way back from Arizona.

6) Returning to my room after buying a copy of the *Sheerness Times Guardian* – motto "Your Island, Your Voice, Your Paper" – and reading about a local historian who was reported to have plans to turn the nearby town of Queenborough into a "tax-free haven like Monaco" using a fourteenth-century law that would exclude residents from paying legal tariffs, such as duty on wine. These hopes, however, had seemingly been dashed as "legal experts at Swale Council have poured cold water on the idea".

7) Venturing out no more in Sheerness-on-Sea.

Perhaps my brother's instincts had been right.

Clackety-clack on a river
Sheerness-on-Sea to Southend-on-Sea

It was a peculiar corner of Britain, for sure – and interesting to note that Dr Beeching was born in Sheerness-on-Sea in 1913.

Train-wise, Sheerness had a lot to answer for that.

In the morning, I passed the Wetherspoons pub, where elderly men were drinking Guinness and white wine at 8.30 a.m. Then I took a Southeastern train back to Sittingbourne and another to London Victoria, past Priestfield Stadium (home of Gillingham FC) and rows of *Coronation Street*-style houses to Chatham and Rochester (and its prominent castle), across ploughed fields to Bromley South and semi-detached suburbs and a tower on a hill that looked like a mini-Eiffel Tower: the Crystal Palace transmitter.

The Shard and the cluster of skyscrapers of the City rose to the north, and the train turned into a corridor of high apartment blocks at Vauxhall station and another of yet more glass flats by Battersea Power Station. To the right across the olive-green Thames, a graceful cascade of pink and grey seemed to float above the water: Chelsea Bridge. I felt at home. I was at home – well almost, it was 6 miles west down the river to that.

But I was not going home.

Across a chaotic wide concourse of people walking every which way, I descended an escalator and joined the District line in the direction of Upminster. London Victoria station was no beauty and the instinct for me had always been to *get out as quickly as possible*. Perhaps this was to do with its strange layout in two halves due to the fact that when it was built in 1850, it acted as the London terminus of both the London, Brighton and South Coast Railway and the London, Chatham and Dover Railway, the latter following the tracks taken earlier. Something in the old alignment of the station, created so these rivals had their own parts of the concourse, seemed to mean passengers passing through were set on a collision course at a bottleneck near the entrance to the Tube.

The District line was busy too, yet it was not a place to spark up spontaneous conversation: fellow travellers looked too preoccupied and serious for that. Instead, with little better to do, I read the adverts above the seats in the row in front. Was I tired and would I like to buy a product, Floradix, to make me less tired? Did I wish to "be bold, be fearless, be a game changer, the future is YOU" by signing up to a course at the University of Derby? Or to "unlock the power of Korean skincare"? Or "get the sales CRM that keeps you on the road to success"? I had no idea what this meant, but I suddenly found myself wanting this and all those other things anyway: to leave the District line feeling refreshed and bolder, with better Korean-style skin and improved CRM on the road to success and game-changing opportunities that would lead to fearless wealth and a generally happier ever after.

Who in their right mind would not want all of that?

It was 28 stops to Upminster.

I settled in for the 1-hour journey as the carriages passed Canary Wharf. The seat moquette on the District line comprised neat little square shapes coloured pink, purple, yellow and green on a navy background, and the fabric was worn, polished down by the legs of a million commuters. The London Underground had begun in 1863 with the Metropolitan line, the world's first underground passenger railway, covering 3¾ miles between Farringdon and Paddington (just 38 years after the Stockton and Darlington Railway). By the mid-2020s the network had spread across 250 miles of track with 272 stations and 11 lines, including the shiny new Elizabeth line winding 73 miles from Reading in Berkshire to Shenfield in Essex, a rare twenty-first-century British rail success story. The average daily ridership was 3.23 million people, which amounted to 1.81 billion a year. This worked out as the equivalent of five per cent of the British population taking its trains each day. No wonder the District line seats had seen better days.

We rolled on by Barking, Becontree and Dagenham East.

At Upminster, I left the carriage and joined the 11:26 to Shoeburyness in Essex.

This was a c2c train with purple, grey and pink seats and it was soon pacing away across open countryside, stopping at Laindon and then Basildon, where a woman boarded wearing so much fake tan it was almost impossible to age her: 24 or 44? You couldn't easily tell. Beyond Pitsea station, the land became flatter and you could glimpse the tops of cranes at the London Gateway docks on the right. Near Canvey Island, a yacht was perched in mud by a riverbank – not looking as though it was going to set sail anywhere anytime soon – while further on, near Leigh-on-Sea, the Thames opened out and you could see the outline of Isle of Sheppey across the estuary.

The 11:26 spun onwards from Southend Central, past a boarded-up railway hotel, and arrived shortly afterwards at Shoeburyness, the end of the line, where I got out and went to the front of the train out of sheer habit (by this stage) to look at the locomotive, as though this was a heritage line and I had been travelling on a "fancy" train rather than just the 11:26 to Essex. The strange thing was, the locomotive seemed to be quite unexpectedly "fancy" in that it had its own name: the *Tony Amos*.

It was not, I realized upon closer inspection, a traditional locomotive. I decided to *try to work it out*.

This is what I found. The *Tony Amos* was a British Rail Class 357 "Electrostar" Electric Multiple Unit (EMU), built between 1999 and 2002 at the Derby Litchurch Lane Works in Derby by a company called Adtranz. This meant that the engines powering the train were, as with Diesel Multiple Units (DMUs), spread along the train, not just in the front like they were in old-fashioned locos as with *Locomotion No 1*, for example. It had a top speed of 100 mph. The rail operator running the train, c2c, was owned by the Italian rail company Trenitalia, which had taken on the Essex Thameside rail contract from National Express in 2017.

However, I had no idea who Tony Amos was, nor why the train was named after him. Wanting to "crack" this, I asked the c2c driver, who was standing near the front of the front of the train, getting some air.

The driver did not seem to mind this "interview". He had taken one look at me examining various features of his train and had clearly marked me down as a harmless Train Nut.

So who was Tony Amos?

"He must have worked fifty years' service in the industry, mate," said the driver, who wore a black cap and was short in stature with a cockney accent. "Haven't done that much myself. Only six years."

A driver with 50 years' industry service could, apparently, have a train named after them. "Look it up online," the c2c driver suggested – the way people increasingly tended to do (not that I held this against him). There was, however, he definitely knew, another train named after the football team Southend United that he sometimes drove.

It turned out – on railwaypeople.com – that Tony Amos had, in fact, put in 47 years on the railway (with a three-year gap in the middle) having joined aged sixteen. After beginning as an engine cleaner at Plaistow Steam Depot in 1954, he had also worked in depots at Ripple Lane and East Ham. "Tony is one of the great unsung heroes of the railways," commented Leila Frances, the route director for c2c. "He was starting his career long before I was even born, but everyone who knew him speaks highly of his professionalism – always well-dressed, reliable and conscientious." The train operator wished him well in his retirement in which he planned to enjoy his hobbies of fishing and supporting West Ham Football Club. All lovely stuff: the industry recognizing one of its own.

There you had it, something close to the *full train story* on the 11:26 to Shoeburyness. I had done a true Train Nut's duty (or, at least, tried my best to).

Seeing as I had the driver there and we were just hanging around a bit, I asked him if he enjoyed his job.

"Yes, I do, mate. I really do," he replied – echoing the sentiments of Katy on the Northern train up in Middlesbrough. "Previously I worked digging the roads," he said, with an expression that suggested this had not been the greatest period of his life. "It wasn't such regular hours digging roads. Here it's unreal – same hours, same start each day and you get days off. I quite like doing the work when it's quieter." Which it had been on the shift he was doing then; the train had been almost empty.

From Shoeburyness station it was a short walk to a beach with mudflats that stretched out a long way before reaching a soupy grey swell of North Sea that stretched out a long way before meeting a similarly soupy grey sky. A solitary dog walker passed by and nodded. No one else was about.

Shoeburyness appeared to comprise suburban-style housing, a pub, a barber shop, an off-licence and not much else. I strolled along the coast towards Southend, past signs saying, "MoD property: Keep Out" and "STOP! DANGER!", warning of unexploded Second World War bombs that might still be on the shoreline. Cargo ships drifted by on their way to the docks at London Gateway. It was a peaceful walk that came to an abrupt end in Southend, where I left my backpack at a B&B and continued on to Southend Pier, past the brightly coloured Las Vegas, Monte Carlo and New York, New York amusement arcades and the Electric Avenue bowling alley.

Southend Pier was not just any old pier, it was "the longest pleasure pier in the world" at 1.34 miles, opened in 1830, initially with a horse-drawn tramway and then, from 1890, an electric railway; trains had arrived on the main line in from London to Southend in 1856.

I bought a ticket for its train ride to the end from an attendant wearing a Southend City Council jumper, who said, "Two hundred and fifty thousand people a year go on this. Southend Pier is the longest pleasure pier in the world." This fact was repeated regularly in pamphlets and just about everywhere you looked on Southend Pier.

"Really?" I asked.

"Absolutely," he replied, surprised anyone might challenge the statement. "Southend wouldn't exist if it wasn't for the pier. It was the only way for tourism from London to come here, by pleasure boats. We still have pleasure boats. People do still moor up. Jetstream boats come from Kent, from Sheppey. Then there's the *Waverley* in September and October, that's the world's oldest seafaring paddle steamer."

He pointed to a quote on the wall attributed to the poet Sir John Betjeman, who had been charmed by the pier and its tiny railway: "The Pier is Southend. Southend is the Pier." The ticket man said, "It's still an iconic symbol of Southend. Sir John Betjeman had it right when he said that."

He paused and scratched his beard. "What's that Conservative politician called?"

I ventured a guess with Michael Portillo.

"Yeah, that's him. He's been down here too," he said.

Then he told me "We've got the 1986 diesel running today."

"Is that special?" I asked.

He shrugged. "I suppose so," he said.

So I took a journey down Southend Pier and back on a narrow-gauge (3 feet wide) train pulled by a blue diesel locomotive named *Sir William Heygate* after a local politician who had campaigned for the pier to be built in 1830, replacing a much smaller jetty.

The train had hard grey plastic seats and on board I was soon joined by a child and her mother, who had switched from another carriage. The mother said to me on boarding "I don't want to be in that other one. They're speaking a foreign language."

She sniffed and fell into silence, and no one spoke any language of any description for the rest of the clackety-clack ride.

Taking a train out into the Thames Estuary felt bizarre, like you were going somewhere a metal contraption with an engine and wheels simply did not belong. The sun had come out and the Thames was glittering with a languid swell, slapping against the pier. The train came to a stop and we all piled off and had a look around the pier head with its Royal National Lifeboat Institution (RNLI) unit and a handful of fishermen hoping for seabass, said one who had not caught a thing all day.

At a café near the station, the Tea with the Tide, I listened to The Smiths and The Cure and read in an official Southend Pier booklet about how King Charles had visited in 2022, when he had unveiled a new train named after David Amess, a local Member of Parliament who had been tragically murdered by an extremist in 2021.

Then I took the train back. It really was a good one, clattering above the river – and, sticking to Train Nut "business", I went to see another train: the Southend Cliff Lift.

This lift, opened in 1912, replacing a peculiar moving walkway, was billed as Britain's shortest railway, 40 metres in length, rising 17 metres from the shore to a Georgian crescent where Lady Hamilton (Lord Nelson's wife) and Benjamin Disraeli (Britain's prime minister from 1874 to 1880) used to stay on holidays.

Its gauge was 4 feet 6 inches and the gradient 43.4 per cent, said a friendly attendant named Mike. Its single carriage looked like a garden shed, one capable of transporting a dozen passengers up and down for £1 a ride. It was maintained by Southend Borough Council and operated by volunteers.

With little better to do, I took a ride in the garden shed on Britain's shortest railway, also known as a funicular.

Then I asked Mike about this confusion of terms and he replied, "Technically, it's a railway, as it's on rails. But they call it a funicular as it's on a cliff."

There you had it.

You got quite nice views of the pier going up and down.

Eccentric in East Anglia?
Southend to Sheringham via Walton-on-the-Naze

A successful day's train appreciation. I had ticked off two notable ones: along the world's longest pier and up and down England's shortest railway. Train accomplishments complete – and after an enjoyable evening of fish 'n' chips and wandering along the Southend promenade – there was no time to dawdle. The east of England stretched above… and I was about to take quite a few trains up it, of course.

The first was the 10:50 from Southend Victoria station to Shenfield.

This was in a rather spiffing, modern, grey and red Greater Anglia train with free Wi-Fi, USB sockets by every seat and faux wooden panels at the carriage ends (not bad, Greater Anglia). It rolled past Southend Airport into sunny farmland with low green crops: a relaxing ride across quiet countryside.

At Shenfield, I caught the 11:41 to Thorpe-le-Soken, also Greater Anglia, across yet more sunny emerald-green farmland, following the river Colne, a Thames tributary, for a while into a wide flatland, pausing at Chelmsford and Colchester and moving onto Thorpe-le-Soken, where I switched onto the 12:41 to Walton-on-the-Naze. Thereafter, the landscape became steadily more remote, with fewer settlements and larger, wider fields of crops. A highlight of this ride was a stop at Frinton-on-Sea station, which featured a platform mural of a steam train plus another of Winston Churchill. Then we trundled onwards into even more emerald-green farmland – that's all there seemed to be, mile upon mile of emerald-green. It was a tranquil feeling, moving into this corner of England that somehow felt secretive and hidden away down the remote, winding line.

Could I say why I was going to Walton-on-the-Naze? The honest reply was not really. It had simply caught the eye on the National Rail map and seemed about halfway "up" East Anglia.

As good a place as any to stop for the night.

The train soon arrived at a small station: Walton-on-the-Naze. The 12:41 had reached its destination. We all got off as this was another terminus, one of two eastern termini of the Sunshine Coast Line, a branch of the Great Eastern Main Line that went north to Norwich, Norfolk's capital. A little information board by the platform said that trains had first arrived in Walton-on-the-Naze in 1867, which had led to its growth as a seaside resort, bathers attracted by its good sandy beaches.

This "railway pedigree" ascertained, I went to take a look around.

Walton-on-the-Naze was a sleepy spot in mid-March (as it was). I walked to a viewing point above a cliff. Down below was a cluster of multicoloured beach huts in terraces above the sea. Ahead was yet another pleasure pier, built after the railway had come, of course.

I went down the hill to investigate. Inside was a cavernous chamber, a veritable temple of twinkling lights on machines that were blinking, clinking, clicking, flashing, banging, whirring, whooping, thumping and making a gloriously cacophonous racket. At the back, music pounded from the Hardrock Waltzer, which whizzed around playing both hard rock, dance music and hip-hop at great decibels: "Rock… rock… this party… whoa! Let's go! Let's go!" and "What's Up? What's Goin Down? Let's go! Let's go! Let's go!" and "Everybody's freee! To feel good! Feel good!"

Beyond this chamber, the pier was quiet, although the boardwalk was fenced off at a damaged section about halfway where a sign said, "DANGER. NO ENTRY."

As I had on Southend Pier and on Dungeness beach, I fell into conversation with a fisherman.

His name was Malcolm and he was hauling in a dogfish.

"I'm trying for skate, but it's not the best conditions," he said. "The water's too green. It needs to be dark brown. It really does. Fishing's really hit and miss now. Cod used to be the mainstay. [In days gone by] I've come off here with more cod than I could carry."

Malcolm and I had a chat for a while. He was aged 86, a plumber by trade, and had been coming since he was a boy. "Nowadays it's hard as regards cod. The cod go off the Dutch coast and they get hammered there [by Dutch fishing boats], and then there's the water – it's just too warm. That's global warming. It's ten to fifteen years since I caught a cod. I used to get twenty pounders, regular."

When he was growing up, catching cod had been a doddle. "In those days I'd never buy fish," he said. "I'd eat it or sell it. There used to be seventy to a hundred of us here." There were only a handful on my visit. "People would walk past and ask for a fish and I'd say, *Sure*. Then they'd walk to the end of the pier and come back and by that time I'd have caught a cod for them. I'd get half a crown. I'd have been fourteen or fifteen then."

That would have been in the 1950s, just before jet travel took off, when British seaside resorts with railway stations were still enjoying boom times.

"I've seen some lovely fish here. Forty-pound stingrays," Malcolm said.

It was not like that any more.

He looked out at the water. "Not brown enough for skate, not quite brown enough," he said.

I wished him luck. Then I walked back down the pier.

I did not do much else in peaceful, sleepy Walton-on-the-Naze, aside from hike along the coast to the Naze, a headland with a tower that was a former lighthouse and which still acted as a marker for shipping entering the estuary of the Stour and Orwell rivers. The latter had been the inspiration for a certain Eric Blair whose parents lived up the coast in Suffolk, and who wanted a pen name: George Orwell would do.

Another claim to fame of the seaside resort – or cultural reference (this one with a train theme) – was its mention in the 1994 song "Tracy Jacks" by the Britpop group Blur. This song was about a middle-aged, office-trudging civil servant, living in somewhere like Colchester (where members of the band grew up), feeling lost during a midlife crisis and taking a train to Walton early one morning, discarding his clothes and running about naked in the shallows on the beach, being picked up by police and escorted home before, later in the song, bulldozing his house to a pile of rubble, as "being normal", he decides, is "just so overrated".

So it is. Perhaps not so advisable tearing down your home and getting arrested in Walton-on-the-Naze to prove it.

However, a diversion to Walton-on-the-Naze, with its peculiar pier and its beaches and its multicoloured huts and its small high street with its collectible shops and pubs and fish 'n' chip shops, definitely was.

Thank you, little blue line on the National Rail map.

From Walton-on-the-Naze to Sheringham on the northern coast of Norfolk was a journey of 3 hours and 45 minutes, with changes at Colchester and Norwich. I would leave on the 08:58, with three rides of about an hour each, the final one pulling in at 12.43 p.m. – Greater

Anglia trains all the way. Then at Sheringham a further two trains awaited: rides along the 5½-mile North Norfolk Railway on what was known as the Poppy Line, a heritage railway: "proper" old trains pulled by steam locomotives again.

Before then, I seemed to float northwards on a wave of Greater Anglia red-and-grey trains, letting whatever might happen, happen for a while.

The ride to Colchester crossed a succession of ploughed fields with earth that had an unusual tomato-red tint. It was nice just to gaze out at these – yet more relaxing East Anglian landscape.

What was not so relaxing, however, was a succession of announcements. More specifically "See it. Say it. Sorted" security messages.

Having long found these annoying (and doubting they had much real point), I decided to try and find out who was responsible. Why not? No point in pretending I was not travelling with a smartphone. I was. And I was using it often for tickets and places to stay and to find out things, like why trains were called *Tony Amos*. Information was at my fingertips – and this is what I discovered about "See it. Say it. Sorted."

An advertising group named AML, based in Shoreditch in London, had come up with the slogan in 2016, and it said that the message had led to a 365 per cent rise in reports of "suspicious" behaviour to the British Transport Police, even if "some people find it irritating". At least those concerned admitted that. Trying to establish how much AML had been paid for the five words, however, I found that a journalist named Martin Fletcher, working for *The Times*, had tried to do just this in 2020 and even made a Freedom of Information request to the Department for Transport (DfT). But he had come up against a brick wall. The DfT had replied publicly to him, saying this was "commercially sensitive" information and could not be released. Letting the figure be known, the DfT said, might deter bidders for future advertising campaigns or help them "tailor their bids accordingly".

So that was that. We would never know.

The train stopped at Colchester and I got off.

The 10:20 to Norwich arrived and I boarded it.

This train tilted across a wide muddy estuary and I tilted too: leaning back in my seat and reading the *Eastern Daily Press*. Plenty was going on locally. An alpaca "who has brought joy to hundreds of people on treks in Norfolk" had been "retired" after a long career in the tourist industry. A teenager with a BB gun had been arrested while "laughing and joking" on a bus in Norwich. And a roundabout would be closed for five weeks due to the roundabout needing to be "realigned".

A couple of women near me, whom I had already overheard were going to TK Maxx in Norwich to do some shopping, were discussing trains and one of them said, "I love trains. I want to do Prague to Berlin to Vienna – fourteen hundred quid. Gav says that's a lot for a train, but I'd like to go to Vienna for the classical music."

Train travel definitely seemed to be having a resurgence around Europe as new lines opened, many with sleeper services, and people began to plan their holidays around them.

If only the same could be said of the UK (still reeling from its HS2 troubles).

At Norwich station I switched trains yet again onto the 11:45, which was soon passing rowers on the river Yare and rolling down the Bittern Line across more tomato-hued fields, followed by fields of horses and sheep. I closed my eyes for a while and drifted off, awakening with a jolt as the train pulled into Sheringham.

Not long afterwards, I boarded a steam train on the North Norfolk Railway.

What can I say other than it was a very nice steam train.

It hissed. It chugged. It made a piercing and rasping hollow-whistle sound. It was painted burgundy and gold and was built in Leeds in 1956 by the Hunslet Engine Co. The seats were the plushest yet, with a golden leaf pattern on a pale-blue background. The carriages had polished wooden panels. A strong smell of sulphur and coal floated in through the windows. It was a very nice steam train.

We passed a golf course, some coastline and large agricultural fields. The contraption came to a halt in Holt, where a little museum was full of information about the history of the little train lines of North Norfolk. The Poppy Line had fallen to Dr Beeching's cuts of the late 1960s but had been re-established in the mid-1970s, as ever, by an army of rail enthusiasts, before being extended to Holt in the 1980s.

On my return journey, a trainspotter sat down near me and introduced himself.

His name was Anthony and he was in his forties, from Ipswich. He told me, apropos of nothing, how he liked Class 37 locomotives, how he used to be a top-level cyclist (almost having made the Great Britain team), how he found all trains noisy ("these days you can't really get quiet journeys"), that HS2 was a "fiasco", that he had "flunked out of school aged fourteen" and that he was working at a temporary job in a lab that developed lures for bed bugs, which involved cultivating bed bugs so they would "piss and s*** and then this paper turns brown and it becomes a lure… I spent my first day and a half just cutting up that paper, it's not my ideal job, I got it through an agency two weeks ago, soldering is more my kind of thing."

A perfectly charming fellow. You did meet all sorts on British steam trains.

The train returned to its lovely old-fashioned station not far from the dull main-line station of the sloping seaside market town of Sheringham, where a Viking festival was being held, but lots of people were wandering around the high street wondering where the Vikings were. There were no Vikings to be seen, but there was meant to be a Viking parade along the high street at a key moment in the Viking festival commemorating the arrival of the Vikings in East Anglia around the late eighth century. Signs near the railway stations said so. Information on the Viking festival website said so too.

After some enquiries, the people milling about ascertained that the Vikings had already gone to the beach, having assembled at the car park near the stations (where we were) as they were meant to but then having left early to set fire to a Viking longboat on the beach. They had done this because the tide was higher than usual and the Vikings had been worried that the Viking longboat would be doused by waves and not light properly if they had waited till the official parade time.

Those who had arrived early had been informed of this and had followed the Vikings to the beach to watch the lighting of the longboat. Later-arriving Viking festival attendees (us) had not. We all went down to the beach just as the in-the-know Viking crowd was dispersing, along with a few people from Norfolk dressed as Vikings, and we went to look at a few smouldering pieces of wood on the beach: the remains of the Viking longboat.

This, mainly, was how I spent my time in Sheringham.

Jolly Skeggy
Sheringham to Skegness

The truth was I was keen to move on – to Skegness.

This seaside resort, where Billy Butlin had started before branching out to Bognor Regis, held an almost magnetic allure. Perhaps it was the legendary railway poster of a "Jolly Fisherman" that did it. This poster, commissioned in 1908 by Great Northern Railway for a fee of £12 from the artist John Hassall, had famously featured the slogan "Skegness is SO bracing" – and it was, to use the poster designers' style, THE railway poster of all railway posters.

Never mind any of the others mentioned so far – this was the iconic grandaddy of the lot that had run for five years in a publicity campaign that had seen people streaming up from London Kings Cross on three-shilling (fifteen pence) return tickets. I wanted to go to the place that had been put on the tourist map by this iconic grandaddy of railway posters and feel the sand beneath my feet in this legendary British seaside resort where rotund fishermen pranced about waving their arms and looking a bit camp, and donkeys plodded along the shore offering rides.

To get there involved retracing the hour-long journey to Norwich, passing the same gaunt flint church on a hill I had laid eyes on the day before (All Saints Church, Beeston Regis) and a succession of symmetrical fields ploughed so perfectly they looked like raked Japanese gardens. After crossing a canal with an idyllic-looking pub named the Rushcutters, referring to workers employed in this important job in the "flatlands" of Norfolk, I disembarked and walked up a hill, past a shopping centre, to a medieval castle shaped like a giant sugar cube except it was made of limestone imported from France in the twelfth century.

This was Norwich Castle. At a small side entrance, you bought a ticket from someone who repeatedly told you renovation works were going on and that the ticket would have cost more if they had not been going on, and entered a corridor with stuffed pelicans, seagulls and ducks that led to an octagonal atrium connected to chambers containing beautiful works by John Crome (1768–1821), John Sell Cotman (1782–1842) and Edward Seago (1910–1974), important members of the Norwich School of Painters.

I mention these artists as they captured so perfectly the landscapes of East Anglia as could be seen from the train windows of Greater Anglia: the towering clouds and accompanying flat, rural land with its complicated web of hedgerows, dykes, rivers and clusters of busy little villages. The luminous vastness of the skies above somehow threw into focus the landscape below. It was quite unlike anywhere else in Britain.

These observations made, I had a look at the fine old cathedral, had a good cup of tea at Reggie's Tea and Snack Bar in the rambling old marketplace and caught the 14:56 to Grantham in Lincolnshire.

The 14:56 to Grantham was an EMR Regional service. "EMR" stood for East Midlands Railway and its carriages were decorated in smart orange, red and blue lines with swirls at the ends near the doors.

The train had a name, the *Lincoln Castle Explorer*, which I dutifully looked up. It was a British Rail Class 158 Diesel Multiple Unit train made some time between 1989 and 1992 in Derby. Its destination was Liverpool Lime Street, stopping before Grantham at Thetford, Ely and

Peterborough. The seats were cherry red and, surprisingly, had USB sockets. There you had them: the train facts.

The guard wore a tattoo depicting roses and marked with the word "ALWAYS" on one of his arms.

He said "Oh, bless you" when you showed your ticket and then again when you said you quite liked the old-fashioned style of the train.

"Oh, bless you," he said.

And when you thanked him for saying that, he said, "Oh, bless you" again.

Such polite service.

Scenes from the Norwich School of Painters unfolded every which way you looked, interrupted occasionally by muddy pig farms. Great blocks of haystacks rose in fields. A woman wearing a face mask sat down opposite and began carefully to clean the table with an antiseptic wipe.

I continued dipping into *John Betjeman on Trains* by Jonathan Glancey, enjoying Glancey's sideswipes at how railways had been run over the years in Britain: "Despised by one car-mad government, with a finger in the road-lobby pie, after another… gormlessly privatized… executives interested in annual bonuses, personal pension funds, the interests of greedy shareholders." Trains had been designed by "visually illiterate monkeys let loose with boxes of children's crayons" with "passive 'customers' assumed to be morons". Glancey used the word "customers" with quotation marks, as he believed that railway companies had relegated the people who paid their wages from "passengers" to faceless economic units, not human beings who needed to get from A to B, preferably on time.

Although the guard on this EMR train had not seemed that way.

Like Betjeman, Glancey did not approve of Dr Beeching. Did anyone anywhere hold Dr Beeching in high regard? (I was beginning almost to feel sorry for him).

Glancey said that Dr Beeching's plans to push on with even more cuts recommended in a second report in 1965, which would have cut British railways to 7,000 miles of routes, were "barking mad". I tended to agree. Dr Beeching was so comprehensively reviled in rail enthusiast circles he had turned into a kind of pantomime villain. Although it should be noted that, after his more outrageous second report was rejected by the Labour Prime Minister Harold Wilson and Dr Beeching had resigned, lines continued to be axed under Wilson, but just not on such a grand scale.

At Grantham, I disembarked and went to The Whistle Stop, a curious little platform pub with a "TRAVEL BY TRAIN" poster, some old barrels for tables and tinny pop music.

Grantham, you quickly discovered, had a few train claims to fame.

The first was that it was the birthplace of Prime Minister Margaret Thatcher, who had championed privatization of the railways, a task completed by her successor Prime Minister John Major. The second was that it was the scene of a terrible crash in 1906 when the London to Edinburgh Mail Train shot through the station, ignoring signals to stop, and derailed at high speed, killing the driver, fireman and fourteen passengers. The cause of this accident was never absolutely established; it may have been a brake failure, and the tragedy just went to show how dangerous train travel on steam trains could be in the early days before automated safety systems were eventually introduced; the worst-ever train crash in Britain was to occur nine years later in Quintinshill in Scotland in 1915 when a troop train collided with a stationary train due to a signal failure, with 230 deaths and 240 injuries.

The final Grantham railway connection was brighter, though.

It was just south of Grantham on 3 July 1938 that London North Eastern Railway Class A4 locomotive No 4468 *Mallard* set the world speed record for a steam train of 126 mph, a speed never to be beaten, and a far cry from the old Stockton and Darlington Railway chugging about at a top speed of 15 mph, admittedly 113 years earlier. There was a picture of *Mallard* in a corner of The Whistle Stop, a must for any passing Train Nut.

The 17:33 arrived for the 90-minute journey onwards to Skegness.

This was another EMR train. Out beyond the allotments of Thatcher's old hometown, we puttered across flat countryside with cattle. The seats had a lizard-green tint and I settled into mine as the train rolled along the Poacher Line, the afternoon light dimming. So many lines seemed to have these nicknames, when you started looking out for them: the Sunshine Coast Line, the Bittern Line and now the Poacher Line, all in a few days. The train stopped at Ancaster, Rauceby and Sleaford, where a man across the aisle with "LOVE" tattooed on the knuckles of one hand and "HATE" on the other disembarked, and we continued past Heckington to Boston, with its stubby-shaped cathedral.

The train rattled and hummed onwards, following a long curve and arriving at Skegness.

I found my B&B down a suburban road near the station, where a man with gold rings and a weather-worn face showed me to a cold, tiny single room.

"Your toilet's down there," he said.

"The room isn't en suite?" I asked.

"You didn't pay for en suite," he replied. This was true. Mistakenly I hadn't.

Then the man said, "You've got to be out by ten."

Then the man recommended a Wetherspoons for dinner, and I walked into the middle of the rainy, low-season seaside resort, passing blinking amusement arcades and tattoo parlours, to the Red Lion Wetherspoons pub – right by the station, as it happened, and decorated with old railway posters, including one of the "Jolly Fisherman".

The railway had come to Skegness in 1873, attracting a steady stream of tourists, mainly working-class people from the East Midlands, before hitting the big time with its 1908 poster. The seaside resort, like Bognor Regis, had been designed by a local bigwig; in this instance, by the 9th Earl of Scarborough (1813–1884), who saw the potential of railways and created a grid of streets on his land near where a fishing village had been and invited speculators to invest.

In the morning – having left before ten o'clock (after a night in a freezing room) – I began some "Jolly Fisherman" investigations.

These formed a three-step manoeuvre.

First, a visit to the "Jolly Fisherman" statue by the beach, erected in honour of the huge boost to the town's prosperity made by Hassall's artwork. Next up, a visit to the town hall to admire two original paintings of "Jolly", as he was known in "Skeggy", as Skegness was known. The third step was visiting a local historian/photographer named John Byford at his terraced house down the road from the town hall.

John had scruffy blond hair, thick-framed glasses with a slight tint and a couple of days' stubble. He wore jeans and an old polo shirt, and had a down-to-earth, slightly distracted manner. He made me a coffee and we talked Jolly Fisherman and trains for a while in the room by his kitchen.

Or rather he talked a lot. I was just happy to listen.

"Jolly is everything to Skegness," he said. "He's our A1 celebrity, our legend. When a shop opens, the town mascot [a person dressed as Jolly] will be invited to it."

Everyone in Skegness liked Jolly, John said. As they did his creator. "When John Hassall drew the Jolly Fisherman in the poster in 1908, he was already a well-known poster artist," he continued. "He'd done Blackpool, and done book covers and stuff for London Underground. But the Jolly Fisherman is what he'll be remembered for."

Hassall had quickly become a local hero, despite not visiting before creating the poster. "When he eventually did come, and it was only once, he was greeted by Billy Butlin at the station and taken to the County Hotel in the evening and wined and dined," said John. "He was given the freedom of the foreshore and a free deckchair and free entry to the swimming pool forever."

But there was a story behind the poster: "In 1904, you'll find the Jolly Fisherman in a book called *Around the World A/Z* by John Hassall representing the 'P' for Penzance. But he was known as the 'Dancing Boatman' in that."

So the Jolly Fisherman was really a Dancing Boatman and might, if Penzance had picked up on his potential, have created a stampede of tourists on three-shilling rides from London down to Cornwall.

How did John know all this? "The University of Essex did some research," he replied, sipping his coffee.

But why did the poster have such a big effect?

"Because the ones before were posters in a posh, art nouveau–style as though for the south of France, covering places like the English Riviera," John said. "If you're going to attract working-class people, these people, the working class, who suddenly have more money in their pocket thanks to holiday pay, they wanted something else. It's believed a railway employee came up with the 'It's SO bracing' slogan. When the words and the image came together, they were made for each other. These days 'bracing' has images of cold, but back then it was 'invigorating' and associated with good health. Being skinny wasn't a good thing back then, and healthy living in some of the big cities with coal and smoke required getting away on trains. People were coming for clean, fresh air, to clean lungs out and have good food – proper fish and chips. And to feel the sand between their toes. I think Jolly captured all of that. The poster pokes you in the eye. It doesn't just smack you in the face, it pokes you in the eye."

Railways, as ever, were key.

"In the late 1800s the railway came, the Earl of Scarborough was behind it," said John. "Mainly for vegetables – the lines were for transporting vegetables back then. Shifting potatoes."

The web of lines across Lincolnshire was even nicknamed the "potato railways".

"But the earl saw a potential to put more bums on seats," John continued. "The railway is fundamental to Skegness and, to be honest, it would have been very difficult to get here otherwise. Even now we don't have a motorway. But imagine getting to Skegness back then, getting across all the fields from Leicester, Nottingham and Derby. These places are still where visitors come from to this day."

Yes, tourism had fallen from its early twentieth-century heyday: "In the 1970s, British seasides suffered from everyone buggering off to Benidorm, all these Spanish places." But things had been picking up: "During Covid, and then as we came out of the post-Covid world, people have been reluctant to get on a plane." So Skegness had picked up business. "What do people do when they come? They go to the beach. It's our biggest asset."

I was not surprised to learn that John had opinions about Dr Beeching. "Under Beeching even Skegness almost lost its railway. Lincolnshire suffered horribly under Beeching's cuts. It's criminal what happened to Louth," he said. Louth was a nearby market town. "Louth has grown and grown, but it's not on a railway. No one understands the problems of the county… people relying on the car, with petrol getting more and more expensive. In Lincolnshire, if you're without a car, you're lost."

John paused and said, "It's such a rural county. If you mention Lincolnshire to anyone, they'll say it's just a flat county with vegetables. These lines are how the humble fish and chips became popular. Fish from Grimsby and potatoes from Lincolnshire, then they got round the country on trains. It's how the national dish got to Britain."

He returned to Jolly. "Oh, he's been used and abused in tabloid papers, cartoons, books. It's just amazing how used and abused over the years. Most politicians have done the Jolly on the beach – Boris Johnson, all of them."

By "done the Jolly on the beach", he meant imitate the pose.

I thanked John for his time, feeling lucky to have met such a Jolly expert. It was drizzling outside as we parted, and John said, "Well, we do say the sun always shines in Skegness, except when the clouds are in the way." With that truism ringing in my ears, I returned to the station.

An arrest, some potatoes, a cathedral and a Spoons
Skegness to Doncaster via Grimsby

The 12:15 to Sleaford involved unexpected drama at Boston station: a fellow passenger was arrested.

A man wearing shades and a hoodie was apprehended by officers and taken onto the platform directly outside our carriage window.

This had led to some speculation on board. "Maybe he was wanted," said a woman across the aisle. "Probably drugs," said another. "Must have been waiting for him," said the first woman.

No announcement, however, was made and we continued to Sleaford, where I changed onto the 13:16 to Lincoln.

This swept across fields, presumably planted with potatoes, arriving after a while at Lincoln, where I had just enough time to pace up the hill to see its striking cathedral and stop in a bookshop on a twisty lane run by the Society for Lincolnshire History and Archaeology.

This bookshop – remarkably – had an entire shelf of books on Lincolnshire railways. The county and its railways were covered in all sorts of historical angles: was this the most chronicled railway county of all? But one tome stood out: *The Lincolnshire Potato Railways* by Stewart E. Squires.

I had to have it. (Some strange impulse deep inside was making me want to possess such old railway books. I was already, just a few weeks after departing, beyond help when it came to this.) The man named Chris who sold it to me knew all about the book: "This was reviewed in a railway magazine at the time [of publication] and the writer said it was the most esoteric book title he had ever come across."

Glancing at my backpack, Chris asked me where I was heading.

"Doncaster is a big train town," he said, when I told him. "And Scunthorpe is one of the major freight hubs in the country – steel-making is a major customer [of the railways] and of course the future is very uncertain, like it is with many steelmakers. Scunthorpe has the biggest set of industrial sidings in Britain. Coal and iron come in. Steel goes out."

After this unexpected briefing, I thanked Chris and went back to the station to catch the 15:32 to Grimsby, where I was staying before passing through Scunthorpe and seeing Doncaster.

Soon the train pulled away into the potato fields of Lincolnshire, stopping at Market Rasen then passing across more potato fields and turning eastwards around Habrough, where cranes poked up on the horizon by Immingham docks and electricity pylons trailed down to South Humber Bank Power Station.

Shortly afterwards, we came to the edge of a town, Grimsby, with some boarded-up windows on a block of flats and a damp-looking sofa in a garden. A little further on came Grimsby station, where I stepped off the train onto the platform.

Then I stepped off the platform and, down a few steps, into my hotel, the Yarborough Hotel, right by the station. It was a Wetherspoons pub.

After quite a few evening meals in them, I was about to stay the night in a "Spoons".

CHAPTER EIGHT

GRIMSBY TO LONDON EUSTON VIA DONCASTER, HULL, SCARBOROUGH, CHINLEY, STAFFORD AND ADLESTROP

SNAKES AND LADDERS

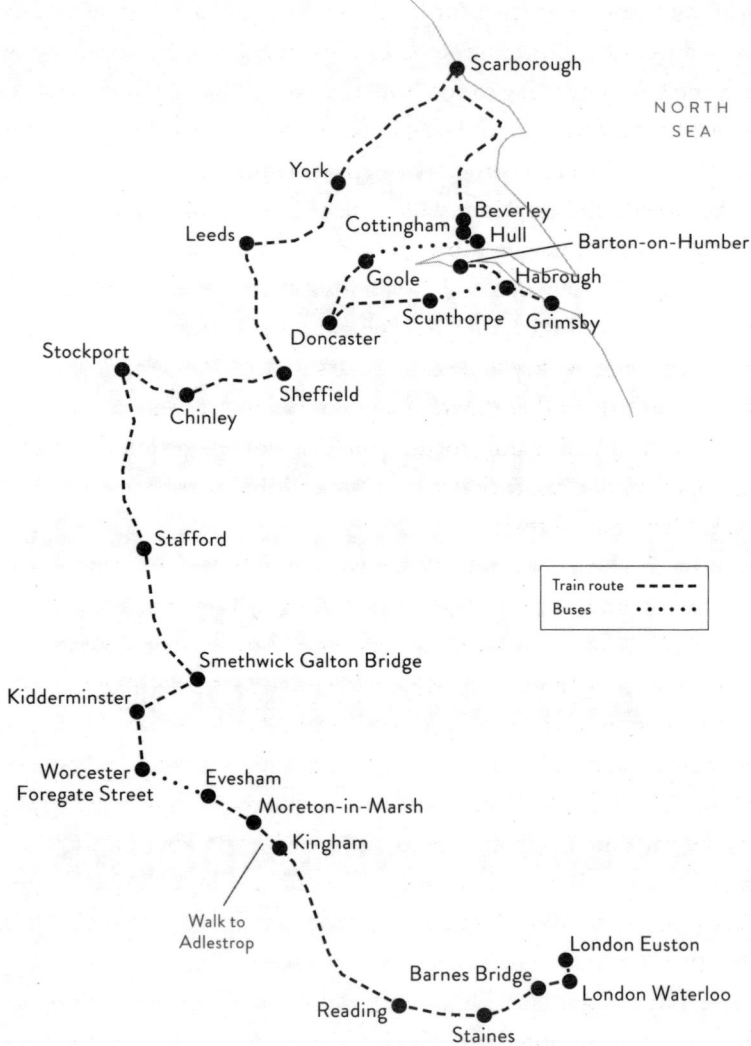

*G*ood Lord, you may be thinking, *he's really sunk to new lows.* Far from it. This was luxury. Of sorts.

OK, the reception at the Yarborough Wetherspoons pub/hotel in Grimsby involved waiting for a lad to be served four lagers, who then decided to order four more so he and his friends would have two lagers each and save time going to and from the bar, and being told by a pleasant barmaid, who had poured the eight lagers, that I needed to go to the far side of the bar round a corner where there was a part of the bar that acted as the hotel/pub reception, which meant squeezing through a crowd of people while carrying a backpack full of train books, including the newly acquired copy of *The Lincolnshire Potato Railways*, and getting to the correct part of the bar, whereupon another pleasant female member of staff gave me my key and said, "That's typical of the council, isn't it?" when I pointed out that the free maps on the counter only covered a tiny bit of Grimsby and mainly focused on Cleethorpes, yet another railway-developed seaside resort that was just round the coast from Grimsby.

OK, there was all that.

However, the room was extremely comfortable: a veritable oasis of calm, a little pocket of perfection above the mayhem of drinkers merrily piling into the cheap booze down below. When I use the word "extremely", it should perhaps be taken along with an appreciation of previous rooms in the run-up to this Wetherspoons room. That said, it was warm, large and had plush carpeting, a big television, a kettle, free biscuits and a decent-sized bathroom with a good shower. The colour scheme was blue, grey and white: inoffensive, nothing particularly to dazzle or wow. But who wanted to be dazzled and wowed, anyway? There was a train to catch to Doncaster past Scunthorpe in the morning. There was no time to be dazzled or wowed.

The Yarborough Hotel had been built by the Earl of Yarborough in 1851 as a station hotel after the railway arrived in Grimsby in 1848, overnight transforming the fortunes of the docks, which could then speedily transport fish across Britain, in particular down to Billingsgate Fish Market in London: hence the rise of fish and chips, as mentioned by John back in Skegness. A boom time followed, with many east Londoners with Thames dock experience and fishermen from Kent and Devon coming to work in the newly made docks, the local population soaring from 8,800 in 1851 to 86,000 in the mid-2020s (the population had been 4,000 in 1831). The quantity of fish exported leapt from 500 tonnes in 1852 to 60,000 in 1878. These glory days continued, with Grimsby rising to become the world's biggest fishing port in terms of volume of catch by the 1950s. But then things began to tail off. European Union laws allowing quotas from fishing fleets from other countries hit local figures. Icelandic fishermen moved in on profitable waters. "Cod Wars" broke out – clashes on the high seas between local fishermen and Icelanders. Yields fell. Trawler captains gave up the ghost. Since then, business had fallen away, resulting in unemployment. "The Fishing", as it was referred to locally, had never been the same after all of that.

Yet again, though, another place in Britain completely transformed by trains.

What did you do with a few hours to spare in Grimsby? Well, you went for a long walk down to the docks. Doing so from the Yarborough Wetherspoons pub/hotel meant entering a desolate-looking shopping precinct past The Vault pub, The Bank pub, The Haven Arms "traditional pub", Walter's Free House pub, The Parity pub (offering "curry and Mexican nights"), Chambers Bar (advertising karaoke), the Tivoli Tavern (more old-fashioned than the others, with Sky Sports), The Pepys pub and The White Hart pub – ten pubs within a couple of hundred metres.

Near the Tivoli Tavern, two people wearing clothing that said "Safer Streets" were walking around, seemingly on patrol. I went over and asked them what they were doing.

"We're here to assist vulnerable people. If someone's hurt from a fight or if young people are shouting out at other people, we try to calm things down," one of them said.

"Teenagers?" I asked.

"Yes, mainly," she replied and was about to say more, but there was some yelling in the distance, and the duo went off to investigate.

A lot of shops had signs on them saying, "Unit Under Development. It's almost time to see the bigger picture. The units have been cleared for the redevelopment scheme." So it looked as though better times were ahead for the city centre near the station, or at least that businesses would be coming soon to the shopping precinct. Down by the docks, a bitter wind blew across the water where a solitary trawler from the glory days, the *Ross Tiger*, was moored by the closed Grimsby Fishing Heritage Centre. No one else was about and I walked to the grand Victorian town hall from where I caught a cab to the main docks, asking the driver, named Dave, if he could take me to Grimsby Dock Tower; this was a 61-metre-high red-brick tower that once had water stored at the top to provide hydraulic power for the docks. It felt like a suitable target and as we went there, Dave told me how his first job had been on the docks when he was seventeen: "I put the fish on the line and then the women packed it in the boxes. Haddock, cod, salmon, monkfish, conga eel, shark, everything, packed in the trays. My shift was 2 p.m. to 10 p.m., or 2 a.m. on overtime. My dad used to be a filleter there."

He was pointing at a dock. "He used to be able to walk from boat to boat all the way across." Though it was just an empty stretch of water when we went. "I stopped working here twenty-five years ago." Dave was in his fifties. "It was a completely different place then. Now you've just got the wind-farm boats." Catamarans that transported repair staff. "And there's still some crab business."

What was it like living in Grimsby, with "The Fishing" so depleted?

"Well, it's not great," he replied as we passed old red-brick depots and a dock with the *Lorna Dean* boat moored, one of the crabbing vessels. "It's gone from a big bustling town with money in it to a benefits town."

He sounded both defeated and matter-of-fact about this, his tone suggesting, *And there's absolutely nothing I can do about that.* Trains took you to and through all parts of Britain, including some spots that had obviously seen better days (Workington in Cumbria, Llanelli, Bognor,

Sheerness), but for the true rail enthusiast this did not matter one jot. It was the train interest that pulled you along. Grimsby had an interesting train history, with its rapid growth on the back of fish trains. Workington, Llanelli, Bognor and Sheerness all had train stories up their sleeves too. As a true Train Nut, you did not pass great judgement on anywhere the wheels rolled. You simply arrived by train and left by train. Life was made more straightforward this way (and generally less controversial).

I thanked Dave for this unexpected "tour", rather than just a ride, and he said, "You got in the right car. A lot of the lads in the rank didn't grow up round here."

Quite what he meant by that, I did not know and did not have time to ask, as Dave was soon dropping me off back at the Yarborough, where I promptly went to one of the pubs nearby. It was Friday night in Grimsby, why not? I bought a pint and looked around. In this long, cavernous pub, male drinkers were displaying their strength at a punchbag machine in a corner. It worked like this. A pugilist, having gathered his composure, stepped forwards, paused, stared at the punchbag as though he really hated it, and with extreme force swung his fist. The punchbag would duly crash against a backboard with an almighty thud. Then a cheer would go up. There would be a brief hiatus before another lad took to the "stage". Another almighty thud would soon come. Another cheer. Simple, really – and entertaining enough in its own way. At least everyone wasn't hitting each other.

As I stood nearby, witnessing these Friday-night proceedings, a man unsteady on his feet brushed into me, swayed a bit, focused his gaze to ascertain whether he recognized me (a visiting Train Nut) and, when he did not, said politely by way of apology "Alright, pal."

The punchbag exploits began to heat up. Whack, thud, cheers… whack, thud, cheers. This was, frankly, a bit repetitive to watch after a while. So I withdrew to closer to the front door, where a woman wearing a T-shirt with the words "FASHIONABLY LATE" answered a phone call and began having a heated argument, flailing her arms around and suddenly screaming what you might describe as an extremely unsavoury character description at whoever it was on the other end of the line.

Then I went back to the Yarborough where I fell into conversation with another woman, who was at the bar waiting for a drink. She asked me what I was up to and I explained I was passing through and had only had a short look about Grimsby. To which she replied, "There used to be a Top Shop and a Sports Direct over there." She was talking about the shopping precinct I had walked through earlier. "But they moved cos rents were too high. House of Fraser, they're gone too. There's not much else to do other than the Heritage Centre. I love Grimsby, I love it, but it's a slowly dying town. Pubs will close down, then they'll reopen with new names. Then they'll close again and reopen again. I probably wouldn't move out of here, unless it was for work. Grimsby has a bad reputation, but that comes from people who've never been here."

Well, I had been, the trains had taken me there, and I liked it, even if it was not (you had to admit) a Skegness "Jolly Fisherman" sort of place.

It was more of a real fishermen and women sort of place, for those who still had work on the docks, that is. And I had to keep reminding myself that all you got on a tour round Britain on its railways was snapshots, little glimpses of places along the way – never, never anything like the full story.

Just impressions.

Just notes from the tracks.

Around the Humber
Grimsby to Hull via Doncaster

The 09:04 to Barton-upon-Humber departed bang on time for its 42-minute journey. Dave in the taxi had recommended this brief side trip on the way to Doncaster, and I was thankful he had on the peaceful walk from its little terminus to where the Humber Bridge spanned the river Humber, from Lincolnshire to the East Riding of Yorkshire.

There it rose across the muddy, grey-brown water, looking spidery, ethereal and magnificent with its long, graceful swoops of suspension cables and calmly curving concrete. Not a train bridge, a vehicle bridge, and a particularly good one, completed in 1981. If rail enthusiasm was not enough, I was beginning to show signs of another affliction: bridge enthusiasm. First Skerne Bridge back in Darlington, then the Tamar Bridge between Devon and Cornwall – plus lovely Ribblehead Viaduct, if that counted, up in the Yorkshire Dales. Where would it all end? What other forms of public infrastructure would begin to tug at the heart strings? B roads and buses? Old canals? Roundabouts?

I returned after this short, but enjoyable, "bridge interlude" to Barton-upon-Humber station and caught a train to Habrough station, where it was necessary to disembark and wait for a rail replacement bus outside a charming little pub with a roaring fire called the Station Inn.

This bus eventually arrived and careered along lanes to Scunthorpe station, where the passengers joined the 14:09 to Doncaster, a TransPennine Express – the second journey on this rail operator (the last had been way back for Middlesbrough to York).

The 14:09, with its lilac seats and tables that were slightly too high, proceeded beneath a mottled grey sky on a raised bank following the route of a canal. The scenery had turned industrial: warehouses, factories, pylons everywhere. We passed close by the ship-funnel-like cooling towers of Keadby Power Stations. Some lads in their late teens or early twenties were sitting nearby.

Lad One: "I woke up and I thought, *I can't drive.*"

Lad Two: "Were you still pissed?"

Lad One: "Probably."

This was why they were taking the train. Good on Lad One for making that decision.

Lad One: "Do you think there will be any scrappin' tonight? I reckon there will be."

Lad Two: "Maybe. I don't think we'll get bothered though."

Lad One: "When we get to Donnie…"

They began planning their night out in Donnie (Doncaster) in more detail.

We arrived in Donnie.

Lad One, Lad Two and I disembarked, and standing on the platform, I found Lad Three – if a sixtysomething trainspotter named John from Nottingham wearing dark shades, a deer-hunter-style cap with the flaps down over his ears and a buttoned-up, two-toned grey and black jacket with a massive Canon camera hanging round his neck counted as a "lad".

John was a phlegmatic man, inscrutable beneath his shades and a complete expert on the subject of trains that might or might not arrive at Doncaster station. He told me that engineering works east of Scunthorpe had caused my diversion by rail replacement bus and that these works had meant that trains that usually went "between Brigg and Gainsborough, not touching Lincoln", heading for the Immingham docks, were making an appearance at Doncaster. Earlier, he had been spotting "Biomass wagons, Class 66. Since coal trains disappeared when they closed the mines at least four years ago, the most interesting trains have been biomass, heading for Drax Power Station."

John said some of his favourite trains were "HST power cars, they're working some new Merseyside units from London to Liverpool" and "Grand Central Class 180s, black with an orange band on them, they're Adelantes, used to be First Great Western". All the time he was speaking, his eyes, concealed by his shades, seemed to be scanning the tracks and noticing things, whereupon he would suddenly say, "Northern. Class 150, I believe." Or make other such observations.

I was lucky to bump into him. John said he didn't often come to Doncaster. His favourite station was Stafford "for freight and passenger trains and a lot of new electric stuff, new units that will be used by Greater Anglia". These new units were being tested out around Stafford and I made a mental note of this.

John explained that some weird-looking locomotives with yellow claws at the front, sitting at a siding across the way, were snowploughs. I really should have guessed that. He also informed me that there was a drivers' strike that day at one of the major train companies "but they've been offering drivers not in the union five hundred pounds per shift". The strike meant that Doncaster was quieter than usual on the tracks too. How he knew all this I did not ask. It all just seemed so obvious to him that it did not occur to me. He just knew. Somehow.

I had an interesting time in Donnie. My apartment required a punch code and was down a narrow hall, facing a pub garden where throughout the day (a Saturday) a DJ was playing dance music, which continued until 11.30 p.m. This music was so loud, with such a booming bass, that the fittings in the tiny bathroom vibrated at especially deep-bass moments, which were frequent.

The apartment was close to a market that was closing down for the day and a Primark next to a shopping mall that snaked towards the station.

On the streets outside the mall, an old man turned to me and said one word: "Drooogs."

Some skittish, skinny youths were yelling at a man: "Come on then, fat b******."

Some street performers had set up a speaker and were rapping about turning their lives around having found God: "Back in the day, when my life was a mess, I was so blind."

With little better to do, I placed £5 on a football game at a bookmakers, of which there were many, and went to eat a very good dinner at the China Palace restaurant, a quiet spot decorated with red lanterns. Then I went back to the apartment, discovered my bet had failed and listened to the vibrating fittings of the bathroom while noticing that the floor was beginning to pulse, too. This was because my room was also above another source of dance music with a heavy bass. Two forms of dance music with heavy basslines had begun competing with one another, and the lyrics of the tracks being played in the garden filtered through the closed windows: "I'm feelin' in the groove…. Oh ah, oh ah, rock ya body." And so forth. I really needed to be more careful where I booked.

So went Donnie. I had breakfast at a Wetherspoons, beneath a picture of the footballer Kevin Keegan, England player and manager, who was from Doncaster but had been rejected by Doncaster Rovers in his early days and signed for Scunthorpe instead. Another local history display explained that a major steam train works had once been in Doncaster. Great Northern Railway's Doncaster Locomotive and Carriage Building Works, nicknamed "The Plant", dating originally from 1853, was where the *Flying Scotsman* (1923) and *Mallard* (1938) were built, designed by the legendary Sir Nigel Gresley, chief mechanical engineer of the London and North Eastern Railway (whose statue you see at Kings Cross station in London). The last of more than 2,000 locos had been completed in 1957, when the works turned to making electric units, and in the mid-2020s it was where carriage refurbishments were undertaken by an American company named Wabtec. Trains had first come to Donnie in 1848 and the city was also home to the Doncaster Carr rail depot, dating from 1876, where Hitachi trains run in Britain were maintained.

Pleasing "rail facts". Thank you, Red Lion Wetherspoons.

What with the Yarborough and the Red Lion (not where I stayed), I had by this stage visited, I believed, if counting right, nine Wetherspoons on this tour of Britain: in Carlisle, Caernarfon, Llanelli, Penzance, Okehampton, Sheerness-on-Sea, Skegness, Grimsby and Doncaster. David and Paul back at Shildon would be quite (but not very) impressed. I offer this information as full disclosure to a growing fondness for the chain I had never previously properly "got". Yes, it was run and founded by someone whose politics did not match mine as regards Britain's place in Europe (arch-Brexiteer Sir Tim Martin), but the pubs offered decent, well-priced food and drink in usually interesting old buildings, and inside you tended to be the beneficiary of at least a few good little snippets of local history along with some old photographs. You could refill your coffee for free and the breakfast porridge with blueberries was not bad, served quickly. Meanwhile, as you were looking about, you could learn about Kevin Keegan, steam train works and how the Red Lion, all low beams and labyrinthine chambers, dated from 1742 and was where the St Leger Stakes, the world's oldest classic horse race, was given its name during a dinner party in 1778. Who would have known?

Chaos reigned at Donnie station – or, at least, quite a lot of confusion.

London North Eastern Railway drivers who were members of the Associated Society of Locomotive Engineers and Firemen (ASLEF) were taking part in a subtle form of industrial action by refusing overtime, part of a long-standing campaign for higher pay. The result, combined with a "signalling failure" somewhere not far from Doncaster, was the cancellation of a large number of trains to Kings Cross. People were milling about looking bewildered, sighing, muttering oaths and making phone calls to explain they would be late. An elderly man wearing a Coventry scarf, who was on his way to Wembley to watch his team play Manchester United in an FA Cup semi-final, was at a complete loss as to what to do.

"I suppose I'll just go home," he said, looking up at the board. But there was a way, taking a Hull Trains service, and I helped show him how, with a man nearby joining in. The Coventry fan thanked us and went off, and the smartly dressed, well-spoken man said, "Yes, I must say the service recently has been c***, all the strikes and disruptions. But I'm not against strikes if they get people what they need to do their job. The government should step in and sort this out. I think empathy for workers is lacking in a lot of businesses."

Not the usual reaction to a departure board full of cancelled trains. It turned out this man was an actor about to go to an audition in London for a role in a play by the German playwright Bertolt Brecht. "I'm auditioning for Brecht," he said, airily. "I'm a great fan of Brecht. It's a piece of his in fragments, *The Swamp*. There are not many of us in Doncaster." He meant lovers of the quite obscure, early twentieth-century German playwright, and off he went in a rush to catch the same train as the Coventry fan.

From Donnie I caught the 09:52 to Goole, halfway to Hull. A rail replacement bus was required from Goole to Hull, due to engineering works, not strikes. The train puttered along via gravel pits, woodlands and Drax Power Station, arriving in Goole, where I joined the bus and sat at the front on the top floor, with the adjoining seat occupied by a man with hunched shoulders and a defeated expression. He looked miserable. I soon found out why. "I'm taking public transport because I lost my driver's licence for a year," he said. He was staring straight ahead, looking out of the front window, wearing a checked shirt and glasses, his hands resting on his lap. It was his first long journey since he had lost his licence. He did not say anything for some time and then, without turning and as the Humber Bridge was coming into view down an embankment (looking just as magnificent as ever), he said, "That accident I mentioned. Unfortunately, my wife died in it, poor lass. She was taken to the Hull Royal and she died there. I was charged with death by careless driving, and I was given a six-month suspended sentence. I'm eighty-one. We had been married fifty-eight years and it was the first accident. I'd had a pretty decent life and then all of a sudden it ends dramatically."

I consoled the man the best I could under the circumstances, having only just met him, and we talked about things for a while, though I mainly listened to how his wife had loved going to the theatre in Hull and London, and how he was on a trip to visit his son to have a pint and talk about going to live closer to him.

We passed Hull Royal Infirmary, where the man turned and said, "poor lass", and parted at Hull Paragon station, where he shuffled off to catch another bus.

You did meet all sorts with all sorts of stories, some sadder than others, on a long journey round the country on trains. Even on rail replacement buses.

Hull was a whirlwind.

Though this was the nature of such an ad hoc journey – in a pleasurable way, I was finding – and for me, Hull's station was the main attraction, one part of it, at least.

Yes, I was looking forward to the prospect of spending some time in Hull Paragon Interchange, as Hull Station was named in full, in conjunction with its bus/coach depot.

I was excited about visiting an "interchange".

Since my last visit, a statue of Philip Larkin (1922–1985), who had lived in Hull and worked as the university's librarian, had been erected in his honour in pride of place on the station concourse. I went straight over. You could hardly miss it, looming by the ticket barriers. Larkin was depicted with wonky glasses, a forward-leaning stance and a mackintosh flowing behind, like a superhero's cape. He was clasping a folder under his right arm and holding a panama hat in his left hand and looked as though he had important documents to deliver to a government department. By his feet, etched into the concourse floor, was the opening line from his captivating poem about taking a train to London from Hull on Whitsun Saturday: "That Whitsun, I was late getting away…" Which helped explain the feeling of urgency expressed in the portrayal by the sculptor Martin Jennings, the same artist behind the sculpture of Sir John Betjeman at St Pancras International station in London.

"The Whitsun Weddings" captured the atmosphere of a trip on a "three-quarters-empty" train as it moved south, stopping at stations where brides and grooms on their honeymoons joined the carriages, with a series of images accumulating in the form of views from the carriage window: "a street of blinding windscreens" in Hull, "short-shadowed cattle" on a farm, "canals with floatings of industrial froth" in the Midlands, and, in the London suburbs, "postal districts packed like squares of wheat".

A bowler on a cricket pitch is described running up to deliver a ball, but before he does the train had passed and you do not learn in the poem what happened next – as you do not about the lives of the wedding couples joining the train with whoops from well-wishers on the platforms (Whitsun Saturday was a popular wedding day). Larkin had nailed the transitory nature of encounters on trains and impressions gathered on them, as well as highlighting the underlying urgency of timetables: *if you don't turn up before the whistle blows, you'll probably miss your ride (probably in Britain, with so many delays)*. Hence the flowing mackintosh. He was dashing to make his train. Yet once on board, "all sense of being in a hurry gone", he could relax and watch the world go by. Larkin had nailed the pleasure of slowing down that trains offered too, no matter – really – how fast or slow the trains went. "The Whitsun Weddings" was my favourite "train poem".

Larkin wrote another quite different poem about Hull Paragon station entitled "Friday Night at the Royal Station Hotel" in which he describes the loneliness and silence of the hotel, which still overlooked the concourse and the statue, on Friday evenings when the "salesmen" from Leeds had returned home. It had changed quite a lot since then, inside at least, which you could not enter any more as a member of the public. The hotel had become a holding point for asylum seekers waiting for applications to be processed. Round the front of the station, I went to have a look at its striking Italianate facade with its columns, arches and balustrades, built when the station opened in 1848. Up and down the steps to the entrance, every now and then, figures wrapped in jackets and scarves slipped in and out, seemingly keen to move away, fearful of dawdling and perhaps being spotted by passers-by. Or so it seemed. The salesmen from Leeds had been replaced by migrants from the Middle East and other countries from afar.

Standing there, I re-read "Friday Night at the Royal Station Hotel" (97 words) and Larkin's penultimate line stood out. As the poem ended, he referred to the hotel's headed paper "made for writing home (if home existed)", for the business folk who checked in during the week. Watching the scurrying figures by the steps, the line – written in 1966 – seemed to take on a quite different meaning.

Something was going on at the main old ticket hall.

This part of the station was built back in 1848 and renovations were underway. The doors were locked but you could look through and see a dusty art nouveau–style ticket office and tiled walls beneath skylights and seats and an original "STATION MASTER'S OFFICE" sign leaning against a wall. Improvements, as they seemed to be at so many northern stations, from Darlington to Middlesbrough and York, were coming soon.

Back by the statue and the locked station entrance to the hotel, I met one of the station security guards, a man named Bobby. He had seen me staring at the statue and we fell into conversation. He said, "The Royal was the best hotel to stay in and there were many parties in there. I don't remember all of them I were that drunk. You'd get some VIPs and some royalty. That's why they call it the Royal Hotel."

Though the name had been around for a while, the hotel was said to have received the "royal" after Queen Victoria visited in 1853.

Bobby was in a chatty mood. "You know that Michael Portillo?" he asked. I said I did. "A few months ago, I was doing a patrol and walking by this statue and standing right there by it was Michael Portillo. He was doing some filming, so I looked after him to make sure it went smoothly."

He paused and a passenger heading for a train walked by.

"Hello, Elvis," the man said.

Bobby greeted the man back.

"Why did that man call you Elvis?" I not unreasonably asked.

"Well, I'm an ETA," Bobby replied.

"What's that?" I again not unreasonably asked.

"An Elvis tribute act. I perform as Elvis." He paused and then said modestly, "I'm locally famous. Not famous famous."

Bobby was late-middle-aged, short, with glasses and spiky hair. "I first heard Elvis when I were five. I heard him do rock 'n' roll and I heard him do ballads. And I thought, 'Amazing. Is that really the same person?'"

We talked about Elvis hits for a while.

Then I walked to the docks, past well-to-do shopping malls, busy pubs and cafés down by the marina, with many more yachts than I could remember from when I last visited in 2008 (city-centre rejuvenation seemed to have kicked in since then) and gazed across the Humber in the direction of Grimsby. Then I took a look in the Streetlife Museum of Transport; plenty of train interest there, including, somewhat bizarrely, a tramcar from Ryde Pier on the Isle of Wight. Then I had a pint in the

Hull Cheese pub on Paragon Street near the station (originally called the Paragon after which both the street and the station were named). Then I went back to my hotel, the Holiday Inn Express right by the station, got an early night, ready to roll north in the morning.

Very grand seagulls
Hull to Scarborough

Waiting by the Larkin statue for the 10:21 to Scarborough, I got chatting to a late-middle-aged woman from Hull. The statue seemed to be a magnet for late-middle-aged chatterboxes.

"So you're going to Scarborough, are you?" she asked.

"Yes," I replied.

"It's not a very nice day, you won't get many up there today. I wouldn't go to Scarborough today," she said. She herself was holding a red plastic bag and was off to Goole.

"Oh," I said. "Well, I'm still going."

"If I were going, I'd be straight in the pub," she said. "That's what I do when I go to Scarborough. I do try to go on a day off."

I thanked her for this travel advice and she asked when I was last in Hull, replying after I told her "It's changed a lot. You've been down to the marina near the fruit market and seen all them boats?"

"Yes," I replied.

"It's changed a lot. We're not as good as Liverpool, but then look at how Liverpool was not so long ago – it were a dump," she said.

We chatted in this vein for a while then I boarded the 10:21, a Northern train with familiar blue-spotted seats, and it was soon spinning beyond Hull Royal Infirmary, the MKM Stadium (home of Hull FC), a large empty concrete yard, a graveyard and neighbourhoods of box-like houses before entering the countryside, passing Cottingham and arriving at Beverley with its towering minster near the station. On a whim, I got off at Beverley and returned to Cottingham, a few miles back, on another train and walked in a drizzle from Cottingham station to Epplewoth Road Cemetery. I wanted to pay my respects to Larkin, at his grave there... which I duly did. How could I, such a fan of his wonderful poems about trains and station hotels (and sharp, dry wit), simply have rolled on by? Sacrilege! I had once even sought out someone who knew him well in Hull, the late Jean Hartley, who had published his first book of poetry, *The Less Deceived* (1955), and who had told me (back in 2009) how she had been saddened that Larkin had been "shamefully shoved in a corner in Hull", overlooked by the city he had chosen to make his home (he was born in Coventry), perhaps due to some seemingly unflattering descriptions, which she felt had been misconstrued.

Not any more. With the statue at Hull Paragon station, that had certainly changed in the years since.

Into the cemetery I went. Larkin's grave was in a corner on the left with no fanfare, no signs nor mentions at the entrance gate (that I noticed). The stone was simply marked "Writer". There lay one of the most popular poets of the twentieth century. Somebody had placed some pink carnations in a flower holder.

Trains could take you to all sorts of places, as long as tracks weaved somewhere close by. Nobody sets any rules where you choose to hop off. That's up to you.

The 12:29 from Cottingham to Scarborough, my third Northern train of the day, spun forth into wide sodden countryside beyond a housing estate on the edge of Beverley before bending into Bridlington via B&Q, Lidl and B&M, and pulsing past folds of ploughed fields and little farms as I read the *Hull Daily Mail*'s front page story: "NEIGHBOURS HELP BUST £150K DRUG FACTORY: POLICE TIPPED OFF AFTER LOCALS NOTICE PUNGENT CANNABIS SMELL" It pulled into Scarborough at 1.43 p.m.

Where there was a temptation.

As the crow flew, Scarborough was 60 miles to the east of Darlington and a mere seventeen miles from Pickering on the North Yorkshire Moors Railway. A few trains and I could be back at the beginning, a grand loop of Britain by railway 200 years after Britain's first public passenger steam train puffed along completed. That was the temptation. Yet there were greater enticements too: a tour "down the middle" of the country – a pit-stop adventure with a purpose: to see some more of the railways down the centre, of course, but also with the ulterior motive of arriving at London Euston in time for an extravagant sweep north from the capital to Aberdeen on the *Caledonian Sleeper* – the longest ride yet, 496 miles (ticket now booked) – ready for a journey round some of the nation's most remote railway landscapes up in the Highlands.

How could you resist that? One temptation was blown away by many others (the way they often can be).

As with Hull, Scarborough was a speedy visit.

I did not go straight to the pub as suggested by my Larkin-statue acquaintance. Instead, I went straight to a little seaside railway, the Scarborough North Bay Railway, begun in 1931 and said to be "Britain's biggest miniature railway", covering one mile in each direction on 20-inch gauge tracks. This was a jolly ride from a park with a pond, up a slope to the coast, with views of a sweep of beach (with nobody on it), and back, pulled by a tiny diesel-hydraulic steam train. Small railways like this had popped up around the country over the years, including at Cleethorpes by Grimsby, but this was *the biggest miniature railway*. You sat in a tiny open-sided red and green carriage and puttered along pleasantly enough at about 8 mph. What can I say other than it was pretty impressive it had been kept running so long and was worth a curious diversion for the (very) train inclined.

Much more curiosity of a train-related nature lay in stall, however, at my hotel: the mad, bad and terribly sad Britannia Grand Hotel Scarborough.

The "mad" came from its dimensions. This enormous hotel opened with four dome-topped towers, 12 floors, 52 chimneys and 365 rooms – to represent the seasons, months, weeks and days of the year – in 1867, making it the biggest brick building in Europe. Comprising six million bricks, it was constructed in a V-shape in honour of Queen Victoria by a syndicate of local business owners who had cottoned onto the tourism potential of the dramatic sandy coastline opened up to visitors by the arrival of railways in 1845. This was how Charlotte Brontë and her ailing sister Anne had arrived in 1849, and their much simpler lodgings on St Nicholas Cliff were to be demolished to make way for the Grand. In the event, Anne had only lasted a few days, enough time to visit the spa and take a donkey ride on the beach, before passing away of her advanced tuberculosis at their accommodation. You can see her grave in a far corner of St Mary's churchyard, near Scarborough Castle on its headland (as I did on the way back from Britain's biggest miniature railway).

The Grand was a Victorian train boom extravaganza, enjoying levels of opulence that made it Europe's premier hotel both in size – 220 feet long, 174 feet wide at one end and 70 feet wide at the other – and opulence. Touches included rose-coloured marble pillars by a Romanesque entrance, a domed entrance hall with a sweeping staircase (possibly inspired by the Berlin Opera House) and balustrades with viewing points of the social "action" below. There was also a ballroom, a coffee room, a drawing room, a billiard room, a smoking room, several bars, a huge restaurant overseen by a renowned French chef, Augustus Fricour, formerly of Hotel Mirabeau in Paris (with a rule that "ladies will not wear bonnets"), an "ascending room for passengers" (aka a lift), "speaking tubes" allowing some guests to make requests to reception, the finest linens on beds, and en-suite bathrooms offering hot or cold fresh water or seawater. All this OTT luxury delivered to the spa town, where "taking the waters" from a freshwater spring with traces of iron had been popular since the seventeenth century (why the Brontës had come), brought a more than doubling of the local population, from 13,000 in 1851 to more than 30,000 in 1900. By 1914, more than half a million people were visiting Scarborough by train, many of the better-off staying at the Grand.

It was a massive hit. But then came the "bad". After the Second World War, despite visits by Winston Churchill (who, fresh from defeating the Nazis, requested a bidet to be installed in his bathroom), its popularity flagged during the austerity years, and then with the arrival of jet planes the attractions of abroad for the type of well-to-do customer required to pay its elevated room rates were simply too strong. The Grand had represented a huge bet on the "railway age" of British seaside tourism – a wager that had paid off handsomely for some time, but no longer. The hotel went into decline and local rumours spread in the 1970s that part of the hotel would be converted into holiday apartments. Butlin's took over and then hotel groups hoping to revive the glamour days.

To little or no avail. This was where the "terribly sad" phase kicked in. A report in *The Yorkshire Post* told of guests with "lurid descriptions" of dead birds on balconies, rats and filthy windows, while a story in *The Sunday Times* was headlined "BLOOD ON THE WALLS AS CHURCHILL'S HOTEL TRIES TO SHED 'FAWLTY TOWERS' TAG". Its TripAdvisor customer rating score, based on more than 10,200 reviews, was 2.5 out of 5, deemed "average" (although 4,227 of the reviews were 1 out of 5 scores with a "terrible" rating), with headlines on six of the ten most recent reviews before my visit declaring, "Shocking", "Disgusting", "The worst stay ever", "Avoid!!!", "Not so Grand!" and "DO NOT BOOK THE NOT SO GRAND", with references to poor service, dirty sheets, "dated and tired" interiors and questionable food.

All that said, this was how my experience of Europe's premier hotel from the late 1860s in the mid-2020s went.

You entered the grand reception after pressing a button on the outside that unlocked the front door. Inside was the decorative hall with the sweeping staircase (still there) plus a fountain (with no water flowing from it). To one side was a bar with fruit machines and televisions showing snooker. To the other was an empty ballroom, although peaceful piano music played over a stereo and on windowsills a great number of seagulls cavorted, sometimes peering down into the ballroom (this was the first time I noticed the gulls).

At a queue-less reception kiosk, about the size of a coat-drop at a theatre, three pleasant receptionists, one being trained, listened to you ask whether you could have a sea view and said, "Let me see, certainly, sir." All very good.

My room, on the fourth floor, did face the sea, through grimy windows with windowsills occupied by three large seagulls frolicking and sometimes gazing imperiously into the interior, just like the ones by the ballroom. A little unnerving. So you banged the windows and they went away. Then you looked round your large room and discovered a double bed and a single bed, a circular coffee table, a fridge, two horseshoe-shaped leather armchairs and a piping hot radiator, all for the price of the B&B in Skegness. Not bad.

You went for a short walk to the harbour, taking another cliff lift – like the one at Southend, this one dating from 1881 – and wandered around by the seawall, looking at the choppy grey North Sea and returned via the cliff lift, noticing for the first time something quite incredible happening on the side of the Britannia Grand Hotel Scarborough. This was the squawking, screeching, scuttling, bickering, brawling and general racket-making of several dozen seagulls that had made their homes on the side of the Britannia Grand Hotel Scarborough. Heaped nests dripping seagull splatter lined windows, cornices, drainpipes and just about anything that was sticking out. Perhaps the birds preferred this sheltered northerly side, although when you walked round looking up at the hotel, many other seagulls had selected berths elsewhere. It seemed extraordinary they were there, free to do as they pleased, and so established and, even, happy-looking, *thriving* (at least they seemed pretty content). The Britannia Grand Hotel Scarborough had been transformed into a grand Victorian seagull colony.

On return at reception, not mentioning this, you may find yourself asking about dinner and being told it was available – three courses for about the price of a couple of drinks in a London pub, and that service had "just started", running from 6 p.m. to 7 p.m.

So you bought a ticket for dinner (that was the system) from the receptionist, who might just have looked startled that you had actually decided to do so.

To reach the dining room, you passed the ballroom, where a live singer may be crooning with hardly anyone about, and soon came to a long, curving art deco restaurant, almost completely empty save for a few tables occupied by mainly elderly guests, who seemed to perform a constant carousel movement to the buffet. At this buffet, dishes, you may find, are lined up neatly in steaming trays and tubs including (on my visit) leek-and-potato soup; meatballs with tomato, garlic and herb sauce; and lemon sponge cake.

Quite decent for the price, although perhaps not Augustus Fricour of Hotel Mirabeau in Paris standard.

Then you may just attempt to play bingo in the ballroom and find that not enough people have signed up, so bingo is (disappointingly) cancelled. You may then return to your room, passing pots of paint and an old picture frame leaning against a wall in the hallway, bang on the window a few times to see off the seagulls and get a very good night's sleep.

Snaking south
Scarborough to London Euston via Chinley, Stafford and Adlestrop

La belle époque of railways, from late Victorian times up to the First World War, embodied by The Grand Hotel, was clearly so far gone its memory was almost an embarrassment – a bad joke. There may have been glory days too between the wars and a glimmer of glamour for a while afterwards, but the newspaper reports and reviews had become so uncompromisingly downbeat, and the reality of a visit so eye-opening, there was no going back. Symbolism of decline wider than the hotel hung heavy in the air on St Nicholas Cliff.

All that said, was it good value for money? Yes. Was the room OK? Yes. Was the food alright? Passable, too. Was it memorable? Definitely.

Would I recommend it for a romantic weekend break to celebrate an anniversary? Absolutely not.

Anyway, I returned to Scarborough station to catch the 09:48 to York. This station was unmemorable aside from a grand domed clock tower by the entrance and, tucked away at the far end of platform one, "the world's longest station seat" (139 metres). This long wooden bench was being painted by two Network Rail workers wearing fluorescent orange jackets, Chris and Richard.

Chris said, "It's a nice job."

Richard said, "We're putting on an undercoat then a gloss."

Chris asked, "Have you been to Appleby station?"

I replied I had.

Chris said, "We did that [painted it]. It's nice at Appleby."

I agreed it was and walked down the platform to catch the 09:48. After the faded splendours of a once-grand old hotel, I was back on the train beat.

Here began a series of snakes-and-ladders-style rides, which I will describe in snakes-and-ladders-style: in fast-forward, focusing first on the "snake" down to London Euston and matters of railway interest while taking that "snake".

The purpose of the journey south was, as previously mentioned, perversely to travel north on the *Caledonian Sleeper* (the "ladder"), and it was a relaxing sensation just jumping on trains, more or less completely at random, after a glance or two at the trusty and somewhat crumpled National Rail map.

First stop would be Chinley, deep in the Peak District, looking lonely on Britain's railway map about halfway between Sheffield and Manchester. The second stop, Stafford, was purely on the recommendation of John, the phlegmatic trainspotter from Doncaster. Then I would travel via the Cotswolds and make a visit to the village of Adlestrop – the subject of Edward Thomas's famous train poem of the same name (my second favourite after "The

Whitsun Weddings") – and continue to London Euston, platform one, for the long overnight journey to Scotland.

Nothing unusual whatsoever in doing all of that.

During these journeys plunging southwards back to London, I had decided to focus strictly on train matters.

These began with the 09:48 to York, a TransPennine Express that departed punctually beneath a pewter sky and scudded across hilly Yorkshire countryside with hawks hovering here and there. A conductor accompanied by a British Transport Police officer checked tickets in a brusque manner as though half-hoping you might have broken a rule and could be fined £100, as announcements kept mentioning you might be. We rattled on for 50 minutes and arrived past rows of two-up two-down terraced houses at platform four in York.

There, I went to the same cosy little Costa Coffee overlooking the concourse as I had a while back and read *The Yorkshire Post*'s front page headline: "ASYLUM SEEKERS MAY BE SENT TO RWANDA IN 10 WEEKS – PM". A big "may be" with that – including whether the PM himself would be around in ten weeks (the way politics was going in Britain generally). Then I waited on the platform in the glorious, huge York station for the 11:44 to Sheffield, in the company of a solitary trainspotter wearing a Manchester City hat, who whistled a tune while rocking on the soles of his feet and watching proceedings on the tracks as though quite happy with his lot. Rail enthusiasts were, usually, pretty content with the world (when not complaining about the shortage of old diesels in operation and so on).

The 11:44 soon arrived: a CrossCountry service with the eventual destination of Plymouth, due on the south coast at 5.47 p.m. via Leeds, Sheffield, Derby, Birmingham, Bristol, Taunton, Exeter and Totnes.

On board, I continued reading *The Yorkshire Post,* looking up from time to time to inspect flat countryside, with sheep and occasional oak and silver birch woodlands, before various hotels, apartment blocks and building sites arose and we pulled into Leeds station with an announcement of "Please take your bags off seats. This is a very busy station."

Quite a few people boarded, and the train continued as we listened to another announcement about needing to have tickets ready, and another about not leaving bags on seats, and yet another on the subject of vaping being banned and that we should not attempt to break this vaping ban by vaping in the toilets as the "detectors in the toilets are very sensitive". Barely ten minutes went by without some official pronouncement of what we ought not to be doing.

Beyond Leeds, a male guard accompanied by a female guard entered and said – again – to have tickets out for inspection. In the row before reaching mine, however, there was a complication. "You're on the 11:44, but this is for the 12:44. You need to pay for a new ticket or get off at Sheffield," the inspector said – no messing around. My fellow passenger, a middle-aged man with slicked back hair, pleaded for the ticket inspector to be flexible, but the inspector said, "Not with revenue management there." He looked across at the female guard. The female guard was "revenue management".

It seemed to be a hot day for rules and regulations on the 11:44 to Sheffield.

The man with the wrong ticket and I disembarked at Sheffield, where there was enough time to visit the much-heralded Sheffield Tap pub. I found this after departing the station entrance into a wide square with a long, curving steel-fountain feature – in honour of the city's most famous product – to the left of the entrance. It was a converted Edwardian first-class waiting room with a big ornate fireplace, rock 'n' roll music and light filtering gently through arched windows. I ordered a pint of lime and soda and was staggered to discover from the barmaid, when attempting to pay, that "there's no charge, it's free. It's just water, just soda." And for a few moments I just stood there flabbergasted and speechless. I had finally, after much searching, found Britain's best lime-and-soda-serving pub.

With more positive feelings about the future of humanity than when arriving in Sheffield, I boarded the 13:14 to Chinley, a Northern train, where students in the carriage were discussing finishing dissertations and mountain climbing. We entered a long tunnel soon after leaving Sheffield, the Totley Tunnel, arriving at Grindleford station, where a sign said it was at 166 metres above sea level. Proper hills began to rise all around, great folds of pale green and khaki. An announcement said, "Next station Hope." And we pulled into Hope, with its simple platforms and surrounding hills. The train was on the Hope Valley Line linking Sheffield and Manchester, completed in 1894. Then we arrived at Chinley, which turned out to be an extremely quiet village with an extremely charming little post office (where I posted back several books) and the extremely charming Old Hall Inn, where I had booked a room for the night – the best room of the trip, with mullioned windows, tasteful decorations, a huge double bed with good quality sheets and a Nespresso machine.

This was pit stop number one on the "snake" south, with excellent nearby walks along a disused tramway for transporting limestone from quarries and an impressive viaduct or two (used solely for freight) nearby. Good train knowledge stuff.

Chinley was wonderful, but the railways kept rolling.

The 09:55 to Stockport the next morning arrived as scheduled and was off beyond glorious sweeping ridges and various tunnels, arriving not long after in Stockport, where I had a short wander into town, bought a coffee from a McDonald's and had a chat with the turquoise-jumper-ed Avanti West Coast customer service assistants, who were sitting at desks behind a counter in a ticket room with "LEAGUE 2 CHAMPIONS 23/24 STOCKPORT COUNTY FC" written on a glass partition. There were no other customers about and they told me about some of the more unusual questions they had received over the years from those passing through. These included *What platform does the bus go from? What time does the 10:04 leave for London? Do you work here?* And best of the lot: *Where's the beach gone?*

"That's true, that is," said Louise, one of the customer service assistants. The member of the public had thought she had arrived at Southport on the coast. "We said she could, if she liked, go to B&Q and buy some sand."

The 10:13 to Stafford was delayed "due to an incident", according to an announcement but which Louise and the others said was due to "trespassers on the line near Birmingham". Eventually, it left at 10.49 a.m., a packed train. I listened to a large man talking about family relations between repeatedly saying, "I can't hear you. I can't hear you. I can't hear a word you are saying. All of what you just said, say it again. I am on a train and the signal is very bad" – as well as some Americans in an evangelical group, talking about how each had turned to God and what God meant to their lives. "What would God have to say about that?" said one of them, possibly (or perhaps not) about the trespassers on the line near Birmingham. They were discussing an aspect of spirituality.

"I wish we had a time machine and could just go back and be there and ask him," said another. "What would Jesus say?"

Maybe he, and only he, could shine a light on the delays and so on that seemed to happen so often on British trains.

The 10:13 passed Stoke-on-Trent and arrived at Stafford.

Where I was a little disappointed. I had expected great Crewe-style hordes of trainspotters at Stafford – based on John's glowing report in Doncaster – but there was just one: Roger, aged 80, from Bury. It turned out, however, that one was plenty for a brief spell of platform chatter, as Roger was good value, a genial sort.

Roger told me he was a member of the Severnside Travel and Railway Society and said that Stafford was "good for freight" – he had seen some Greater Anglia trains being tested earlier: "Newly delivered, they are."

Roger was bespectacled and wore a red jacket. He clutched a notebook and pen, and a camera bag was slung round his neck, protruding at his side, ready for quick access. He was a very well-organised trainspotter: a well-oiled machine, ready for action.

"My forte is Germany," he said in an almost blasé manner.

By this he meant German trains.

"I go two or three times a year to Würzburg, the Cologne area, the Hamburg area, the Lehrte area near Hanover. I could stand here half a day and see ten freights. In the same length of time in Germany, eighty."

And it struck me, as it had with the old boys in Carlisle – and at other times – how rail enthusiasm and ageing seem to make good bedfellows: getting out and about, even travelling overseas, and having an interest to pull you along the way.

At Stafford, I stayed in an apartment facing some garages and rubbish bins, with a door opening onto the road. I walked up and down a high street with all the usual shops and stopped at the Ancient High House museum, an old Tudor-beamed building where King Charles I stayed for three days on the run from the parliamentarians in 1642.

And then I rolled on.

In the morning, the 07:39, a West Midlands Trains service, left via industrial estates and HMP Featherstone, beneath the M54, and beyond warehouses, scrap-metal yards, ugly grey tower blocks, cooling towers of closed factories, crumbling red-brick edifices and under the M5 – somewhere along the way passing Wolverhampton – arriving at Smethwick Galton Bridge, where I disembarked. It was 8.09 a.m. A large "revenue protection" team was in operation at Smethwick Galton Bridge station, looking like a team of bouncers from a nightclub or perhaps an anti-drugs hit squad hoping to take down a Colombian cocaine baron. Or maybe something between the two.

The 08:26 to Kidderminster was a purple-and-honey-coloured train, in a different livery to the previous West Midland Trains service. It spun onwards too, full of teenage schoolkids causing minor mayhem. On arrival at Kidderminster at 8.54 a.m., I went across a car park to see the old-fashioned Severn Valley Railway train station, where a heritage line that was once part of GWR was based, although no trains were running that day. I had known this but wanted to have a look anyway (just for the rail enthusiast/Train Nut hell of it really).

Then at a platform opposite a wall with a mural saying, "WELCOME TO KIDDERMINSTER: FAMOUS FOR WOVEN CARPETS" accompanied by some pictures of woven carpets, I caught yet another

West Midlands Trains ride (with particularly grimy windows), the 09:39 to Worcester Foregate Street station, where I boarded a replacement bus that wound through rolling hills and past asparagus farms to Evesham. It was 11.20 a.m., though I was not done, far from it. From Evesham, I boarded a smooth, fast GWR train to Moreton-in-Marsh, arriving at 11.53 a.m., where I disembarked and went on quite a long walk.

I had taken four trains and one rail replacement bus, and it was not yet noon.

Letting the fact of this sink in, I set off on an extremely pleasant two-hour walk along Cotswolds lanes to the village of Adlestrop.

What a joy (I shall admit) to get away from trains and rail replacement buses for a while. Birds trilled. Horse chestnut trees bloomed. So did daffodils, bluebells and lane-side daisies. Little cottages with neatly trimmed box hedges led to fields with long drystone walls. Tractors passed, pulling sheep in wagons. There were hay barns. There were hedgerows. The smell of turned earth filled the air.

At Adlestrop, the sign from the village's former station, closed in 1966 by British Railways, was on the bus shelter, where Edward Thomas's short poem was etched on a plaque, beginning "Yes, I remember Adlestrop" and recounting a fleeting visit the poet made, stopping by the station on an express train in June 1965 when "no one left and no one came" on or off the train, with a mystery seeming to envelop the station and the place, Adlestrop, deep in the Cotswolds countryside amid birdsong. Again, as with Larkin and "The Whitsun Weddings", you are left with a transitory, fleeting feeling of life passing by – on trains (and generally).

Just occasionally when circumnavigating Britain by trains 200 years after they were invented – and not obsessing about timetables, old locomotives, general railway matters and finding en-suite accommodation that would not leave you bankrupt – you could enjoy the occasional reflective, dare I say, philosophical moment.

Mellower after the madness of the journey earlier, I dropped by the village post office, where the father of Ralph Price, a co-owner, had been Adlestrop's last stationmaster.

Ralph, who was joined by his wife Angela, showed me some grainy old pictures of his grandfather working on the line. "He was a platelayer monitoring the track, an engineer."

Some of the pictures had been turned into gift cards, which sold well enough, he said, with Edward Thomas devotees often passing by: Poetry Train Nuts (or perhaps just Poetry Nuts, to be fair).

Ralph said, sounding nostalgic as he looked at the cards, "You know, you used to be able to take a train from here to Oxford."

Angela said, "It would be nice to just jump on a train and go down to Oxford."

Ralph cut in. "But Dr Beeching didn't think so."

The dastardly Dr Beeching had struck again.

The station had been demolished; all that was left was the bus shelter sign. I thanked the couple for their time and bought a book entitled *Adlestrop Revisited: An Anthology Inspired by Edward Thomas's Poem*, compiled and edited by Anne Harvey, to add to my growing train book library, and walked on to inspect where the station once was then ambled on again to the village of Kingham, which *did* have a station.

Then I caught a train to Reading. Then I caught another to Staines, and another to Barnes Bridge (and stopped by briefly at home). Then onwards once more to Waterloo and London Euston, where a very long, shiny train – the "ladder" – was rumbling… waiting to go a very long way north.

CHAPTER NINE

LONDON EUSTON TO DARLINGTON VIA ABERDEEN, THURSO, KYLE OF LOCHALSH, MALLAIG, GLASGOW, DALMENY AND EDINBURGH

BACK TO THE BEGINNING

ABERDEEN TO SHILDON

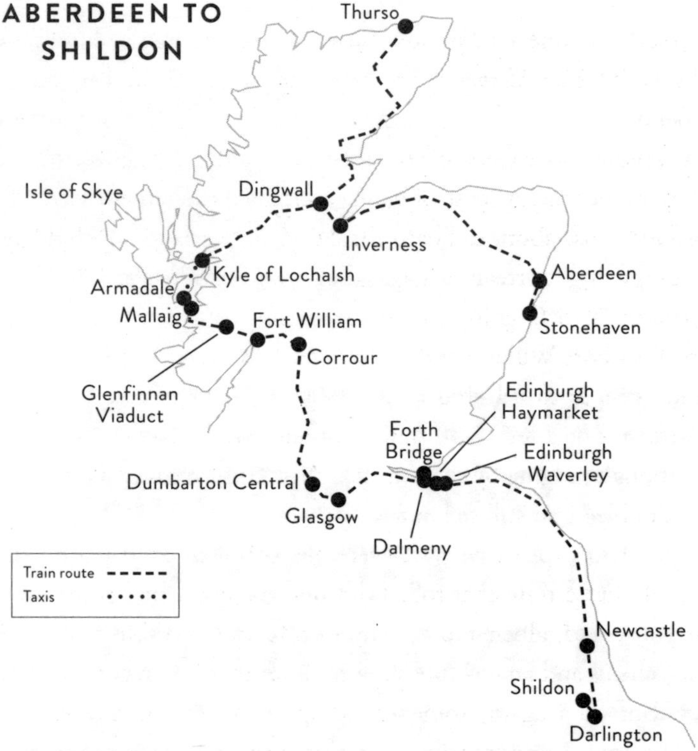

CALEDONIAN SLEEPER

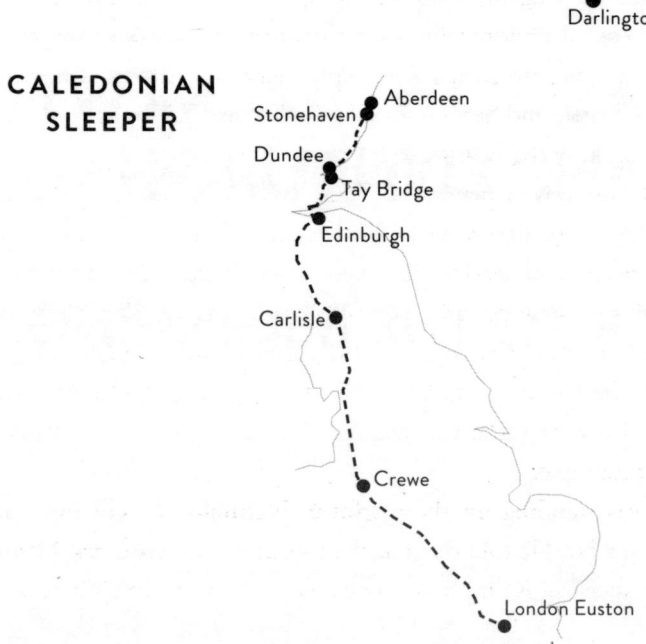

On platform one of London Euston, sodium lights illuminated the *Caledonian Sleeper* as the carriages curled to the left round a station bend.

A few fellow passengers paced forwards, pulling bags across the smooth, worn tarmac. A sense of barely contained excitement seemed to have infected those about to board the 21:15 to Scotland, a "Highland" sleeper comprising fourteen carriages that would divide near Edinburgh, with carriages A to C going to Aberdeen (my Club Car cabin was in C), D to F to Fort William and H to N to Inverness. There was also a "Lowland" sleeper to Edinburgh and Glasgow that departed each day from platform one after 11.30 p.m. Scotland was pretty well-served by sleepers, though judging by ticket availability the services on both routes could be doubled and still sell out.

It was hard to explain why we were all so full of anticipation: this was, after all, just a train that rolled through the night that you slept on the best you could, albeit more easily in a Club Car cabin with a bed with linen sheets and an en-suite shower-room than in one of the seated carriages. But then again, somehow, despite the age of the jet plane and the low-cost airlines revolution, a romance and mystique remained attached to sleeper train travel. We simply could not help ourselves. We had Agatha Christie and her train books, including *Murder on the Orient Express*, to thank, partially at least, for that.

Another factor was at play, too. There were not many sleeper trains in Britain 200 years after they were invented. There was just this one and the *Night Riviera* service that went from London Paddington to Penzance (plus the new, private, eye-wateringly pricey Britannic Explorer trains). So it was a novelty to take a British night train and always had been, really: the country, not being all that big, never had that many. Europe was always better served: the classic Orient Express from Paris to Istanbul, for example.

A guard was standing on the platform. Naturally, I went over and bothered him a bit. He told me that the locomotive was a Class 92 with a maximum speed of 87 mph, so not exactly a "slow train". There were "close to a hundred" passengers travelling, he said. He enjoyed working for the *Caledonian Sleeper*, which was run by the Scottish government under Transport Scotland, as it offered good benefits, free tickets and family discounts. He had a London accent so I asked him what he thought of Scotland and he replied, as though surprised at being put on the spot about the sister nation to the north, "I enjoy it, actually. The culture." He did not elaborate. He had previously worked for Premier Inn, which he said was not as exciting as working for the *Caledonian Sleeper*. Occasionally, the service to Fort William could be affected by "snow and wind and all that", but generally the trains ran on time.

I complimented him on his natty *Caledonian Sleeper* tartan tie and forest-green-and-grey tweed jacket and he looked pleased: "A lot of people compliment us on the tie and the uniform."

I went to the front of the "midnight teal"-coloured train: that was the official description of the colour, or you might just say it was *greyish blue*. I took a picture of the (electric) locomotive.

In the distance, across the platforms, the BT Tower rose, looking like a strange metallic minaret above the rooftops of central London. It was an odd spot down at the narrow end of platform one by a high brick wall as the last lilac light faded and the train growled in preparation for its 496-mile journey north.

Club Car tickets gave you access to a platform lounge. Inside, there was a knees-up party atmosphere, with small knots of walkers discussing routes, and Americans talking about their tartan ancestry. Soul music was playing. I found a tan leather seat by a wall with a red-brick-patterned wallpaper, close to where some Americans were sitting.

"Trump says that one of the first acts when he gets in will be to free them all," said one. He was referring to the Republican Party candidate for president of the United States and those who had caused trouble at Capitol Hill in Washington DC in the aftermath of the 2020 presidential election. They talked about this for a while and then Trump's relationship with the porn star Stormy Daniels and what really happened regarding "hush money" payments.

LONDON EUSTON TO DARLINGTON

Then they returned to tartan-clan talk. The *Caledonian Sleeper* on its Highland branch felt like a tourist train, though there was the odd businessperson and "regular" domestic traveller knocking about.

On board, the Club Car cabin was nothing remarkable: a narrow space with a bunk and a shower room. A couple of chocolate bars, eye masks, earplugs and bars of soap were provided. The walls were clad in tweed. There were plenty of charging sockets. Functional, fairly ordinary and smart enough, but rather superb if you happened to have been travelling for many hundreds of miles on trains, including recently between Stafford and Smethwick Galton Bridge, passing industrial estates and HMP Featherstone under the watchful eyes of hit squads of "revenue protection" officers. The height of luxury, even.

The Club Car dining carriage raised the opulence stakes higher still. Smart rows of tan-and-greyish-blue-coloured seats were arranged in US diner-style booths on the right or at a long zigzag-shaped table by a window to the left. I ordered a good "root veg Thai curry" from a waitress in a natty uniform, watching London slide by as a hazel darkness enveloped the cityscape beyond the carriage window.

I did not do much. I just sat in my seat and talked – to whoever in Club Car class seemed to want to talk.

A solitary passenger across the way said he was going to the Highlands on a 200-mile, two-week walk from Dornie to Montrose. Dornie was closest to Fort William so he was in D to F on the train. He was going alone, wild camping. His name was Jeff, a council administrator from Colchester; in his sixties, tall, lean and steady-eyed, he was wearing water-resistant trousers and olive-coloured sandals and drinking wine.

"I'm probably naturally unsociable," he said of his solo hike, which was in fact part of a great outdoor challenge in which lots of people hiked alone across Scotland.

"Why?" I asked.

"Because we like it," he said, and then added, "Because you make your own way, your own route. Sometimes you see no one all day. I get up at six a.m. and it's thrilling to see the countryside. The deer. The mountain hares. From the north end of Loch Lomond, the views are just…"

His voice tailed off. He could not find the right words to capture the beauty. To be fair, it could be that way; how could you perfectly encapsulate a moment in any landscape: the sounds, the smells, the succession of images and sensations? And then put that into words? Waking up in the Highlands during a long walk or travelling across just about any topography in a train, for that matter. From one instant to the next, it could be quite different. It was all about perspective. It was all about chance, too. I knew that much. Snapshots and impressions from one point of view (your own), taken at one time (not another), were all you could offer really.

Jeff liked the *Caledonian Sleeper*, which he often used as he considered "the journey as part of the holiday" and tried to avoid planes. I mentioned I had been past Colchester on the rides in Essex and talked about Walton-on-the-Naze and the song "Tracy Jacks". To which, Jeff said, "I went to school with the Blur drummer [Dave Rowntree]. He was in my class." "I remember him playing the drums. He was quite nerdy actually."

Jeff departed and Alison came and joined me. She had overheard us talking. She was middle-aged with ginger hair in a bob, a blue-and-white-stripy top and was treasurer of the Aberdeen Bach Choir. "I'm treasurer of the Aberdeen Bach Choir," she said very soon after sitting down, which was how I knew this. The group helped young musicians from deprived areas in Aberdeen. She tipped me off about cafés, said you could spot dolphins in Aberdeen harbour and told me that because of a big new shopping mall called Union Square near the station, other shops in the city were "dying on their feet, really struggling". Hotel rates tended to be high because of visiting executives involved in the North Sea oil and gas industries. "It's not the boom years any more, but it's still going on."

Alison turned serious. "It's really important we get our energy strategy right." By "we" she was referring to Britain. "We're past peak gas. There's a lot of pressure to keep the lights on. But gas is a transition fuel.

We've been moving towards renewables for some time and that's important. I don't want to be beholden to Putin, do you? Don't underestimate the games he's playing with Nord Stream pipes blowing up." These were the gas pipes between Russia and Europe mysteriously damaged by explosions in 2022. "Politicians. Our politicians. Do they care? Sure, they fly in and they fly out [of Aberdeen]. But do they understand the energy sector?"

Alison had been married to a British Petroleum worker for many years and had lived for a spell in Kuwait because of his work. She understood the sector.

Her thoughts returned to Aberdeen. "It's a fantastic place but not everyone likes it. It can be cold and grey and it's a long way. But it's not always grey and the people are fantastic."

On that positive note Alison returned to her couchette. We were the last people "up" in the Club Car dining carriage. Americans near us who had been playing backgammon had turned in some time earlier. The waitress in the natty uniform seemed glad we had finally stopped nattering, and I retreated to my couchette too. It had been a sociable evening on the *Caledonian Sleeper* but it was time to sleep.

"I prefer trains for valid reasons"
Aberdeen to Thurso

In the spirit of (sometimes slipping) brevity, it was maybe best to keep Scotland succinct. The country did not have many train lines marked on the National Rail map; too many lochs and mountains seemingly for that. Anyway, my anticlockwise circular route would not take long. From Aberdeen, I would venture to the very north of Scotland's trains, travelling along the appropriately named Far North Line, to the town of Thurso, home to Britain's most northerly station – meaning I would have visited the most northerly and southerly (the one at Penzance). Then I would take another train to the Kyle of Lochalsh on the west coast, near the Isle of Skye. From there, a ferry would be required to Mallaig to catch the legendary Scottish ride crossing the famous Glenfinnan Viaduct that everyone gushed about – the one that was in the Harry Potter films I had never watched – down to Glasgow.

The idea then was to have a last night overlooking the brilliant Forth Bridge railway bridge spanning the river Forth, having travelled across from Glasgow to Edinburgh. Then a London North Eastern Railway service would take me to Darlington for a Northern train on the last little stretch to Shildon, to the exact spot where *Locomotion No 1* first blew its whistle, with passengers in tow, back on 27 September 1825.

That was the plan.

Although when you looked at the National Rail map, it did appear to be quite an extraordinary thing to attempt.

That said, this had not stopped me yet (and I seemed to have gone quite a long way).

It was not a great night's sleep on the *Caledonian Sleeper*, though this was entirely my own fault principally due to being the last to leave the Club Car dining carriage in the evening and then the first to rejoin the Club Car dining carriage in the morning.

Rail enthusiasm of the Train Nut variety could do this to you.

Having set my alarm to see the sunrise at 5.15 a.m., I was back in the Club Car dining carriage not so long after, swapping stories with Alison and Jeff, somewhat to the surprise of a different waitress with a natty uniform, who brought me a coffee as the *Caledonian Sleeper* swayed, juddered and rocked along, slightly bouncing and gently clattering, occasionally interrupted by the thunder of a service passing south.

The train pulled into Leuchars station, near the town of St Andrews with its university and famous golf course. A few golfers with bags alighted in a spirited manner at Leuchars as though about to head straight for the first tee. You simply had to admire their get-up-and-go. What a way to arrive (in style) for a game.

The sun had risen, but rather than a blaze of glorious light, as anticipated, the sky had promptly turned a leaden grey and stayed that way. Below, emerald fields spread out dotted with gorse, so that if you squinted, all you saw were streaks of grey and green with the odd yellow splotch as you stared out across the east Scottish landscape.

After a while, the *Caledonian Sleeper* arrived at the Tay Bridge, crossing the river Tay for 2¾ miles (precisely) above a leaden-coloured expanse of water that almost identically matched the leaden sky blanketing Scotland's east coast. Sitting at one of the zigzag tables in the Club Car dining carriage, I watched this new, completely leaden-grey vista pass by while eating a bowl of porridge.

The Tay Bridge was an infamous rail bridge, made so by a tragedy in 1879 when all 75 passengers and crew on a train died when the central structure collapsed during a gale. The designer of the bridge, Sir Thomas Bouch, who had been up until then the front runner to mastermind the Forth Bridge, was blamed for not taking into consideration the "wind loading" required in the event of heavy storms. The accident remained the fifth worst in British rail history.

As if this tragedy was not enough, though, along came a Scottish poet named William McGonagall, who in 1880 penned what some have considered the worst poem ever written – on any subject – about the catastrophe, *The Tay Bridge Disaster*. This begins: "Beautiful Railway Bridge of the Silv'ry Tay!/ Alas! I am very sorry to say/ That ninety lives have been taken away/ On the last Sabbath day of 1879/ Which will be remember'd for a very long time…" So it continued – for quite a while. He had even got the number of dead wrong. Not only was this verse deemed the worst poem ever, but McGonagall was, by extension, referred to as the worst poet ever.

Anyway, plenty of food for thought as you tucked into your breakfast while crossing the Tay Bridge.

On the other side, the train pulled into Dundee, where a few more passengers got off. Then we continued to Carnoustie, running alongside another lumpy green landscape that was home to another famous golf course, and onwards to Arbroath, after which the leaden-grey North Sea unfurled to the right once more and a misty cargo ship slid across the horizon. The *Caledonian Sleeper* proceeded to hug the coast for quite some distance, riding high along a cliff before turning inland and pulling into Aberdeen station at 7.30 a.m.

As it did so, I realized something. For sheer movement (almost 500 miles), weirdness (leaving central London and being whisked overnight to a place up by the North Sea, level with Gothenburg in Sweden, as if by magic), comfort (decent bunks in the Club Car couchettes) and sociability, this had to be one of Britain's best rides.

Although there had been so many already… and I was, very shortly, about to experience a few more.

First, however, a little delve into Scottish rail history.

The story of the arrival of trains in Aberdeen tied in with the Railway Queen herself, Queen Victoria, and her leisure habits. She and Albert had leased Balmoral, 50 miles west of Aberdeen, in 1848 and the queen had quickly fallen for its secluded charms, referring to the estate as a "dear paradise". When Aberdeen was connected by railway to the main line in 1850, meaning trains could run through all the way from London, this paradise suddenly became more accessible than ever. Prince Albert, who had been tied up in protracted negotiations to buy the estate, pushed on, no doubt buoyed by this, and Balmoral was to belong to the couple in 1852. All that was required then was a slightly better rail connection, so another railway was built to Ballater, nine miles from her new property, opening in 1866.

"Apparently the Queen did not want the railway to reach any nearer to her estate so that commoners would desist from visiting it," the rail historian Christian Wolmar drily observed in his book *Fire & Steam*. She may not have liked trains travelling at more than 40 mph while she was on them, but she certainly approved of trains in general, especially ones that took her extremely close to her plush Scottish hideaway.

Trains to Scotland spread like wildfires, just as they had everywhere else in Britain. Glasgow and Edinburgh were linked with a 46-mile railway as early as 1842, while the tracks up to Thurso were completed in 1874 (large parts funded by the Duke of Sutherland, who owned an estate along the way), then to Fort William (1894), Mallaig (1901), Inverness (1855) and Kyle of Lochalsh (1897). All places I was soon to stop by down the line.

Meanwhile, the link between England and Scotland had been established via Berwick-upon-Tweed in 1846, under a deal involving a shadowy fixer named George Hudson, a Yorkshire-born early railway Del Boy, nicknamed by some the "Railway King" (a quite different type of royalty to Victoria). Hudson had pushed hard for the extension of the line from Edinburgh to Berwick so it would connect with his own trains, and he got his way. The king of the tracks was at the time flying high. However, it was not to last long as it was soon discovered his business, covering railways from Newcastle to London and many places in between, was a financial house of cards. When it inevitably collapsed, investors lost fortunes, and some were ruined.

Hudson ended up fleeing to Paris to live on the breadline. However, to be fair to him, his ducking and diving and chivvying had at least appeared to have sped up the construction of the railway from Edinburgh to Berwick.

From Aberdeen station, it was a short walk up a hill past a large number of granite buildings, many daubed in colourful street art by permission of the council to brighten up the Granite City (Aberdeen's nickname), to see the statues of Prince Albert and the early Scottish independence fighter William Wallace (1270–1305). These were by Union Terrace, overlooking the railway line. They were also close to the Aberdeen Art Gallery, opened in 1885 and packed with works by masters including Pierre-Auguste Renoir, Francis Bacon and local artist James McBey (1883–1959). A bank clerk in Aberdeen from the age of fifteen, McBey taught himself painting in his spare time, quit his job and then went travelling round the world on many trains and boats, capturing scenes of locations and people in Morocco, America and the Middle East, including a famous portrait of T. E. Lawrence.

Had he been born 100 years earlier, all of that would have been a somewhat stiffer task. A reminder that trains, as well as running late and often being annoyingly overcrowded, could sometimes make dreams come true. Especially back then. Before the railways came in the 1850s it would not have been quite so easy jacking it all in and heading off with an easel to North Africa or moving about too much at all in the Highlands.

I did *tourist things*. I went for a long walk along the coast. I saw the dolphins in the harbour. I took a short ScotRail ride to Stonehaven and back, fifteen miles back along the line the *Caledonian Sleeper* had come, to see the splendid Dunnottar Castle perched on a rocky headland by the sea, said to be where Wallace had defeated the English in a famous battle.

Then I went back to Aberdeen station and caught a train to Inverness.

Beyond Union Terrace and its statues, the line wound past granite-grey housing estates and entered a green hilly landscape. A man with a bushy beard, a crisp white shirt, a Liverpool scarf and a jovial manner sat down across the aisle and stared at me. On an empty seat beside him was a *Caledonian Sleeper* plastic bag. Perhaps he had been on my train.

He had not. His name was Sibtain Rassiwalla of G. J. Rassiwalla Rope Co, Mumbai, India. His company, established by his grandfather (Sibtain was in his thirties), manufactured and exported rope, twine, wicks, tape, packing threads and much else made from cotton, nylon, jute and polyester. He was in charge of "e-marketing, SEO [Search Engine Optimization] and website development", subjects he had studied for an MBA in Phoenix in Arizona, and he had lived and worked for a while in Baltimore, staying in a house near Baltimore Penn station. "It was a very beautiful old station," he said. "I always used to take the train to New York City, two hours it took. By bus it was half the price, but I would happily pay. The buses were not so sanitary. It was a very harrowing experience once – very dirty toilets." He shuddered at the memory. "I prefer trains for valid reasons."

Sibtain was on a month-long work trip/holiday and his trip to Scotland was "holiday", to visit a man named Fergus who had come to his shop in Mumbai and invited him to drop by any time. He was doing just that. Sibtain had an infectious personality and a knack of making friends. "Actually, I was smoking a rollie outside Aberdeen station and an errant seagull sent good luck on me," he said. "Then a cleaner from the station helped me with a towel and sanitizer. Alex, his name was. A gem of a guy. Very helpful. He had worked in Asia for thirty years." Sibtain and the cleaner had chatted about that. He added, "Luckily, nothing had splattered on my baccie."

Before arriving in Aberdeen, he had gone to watch Liverpool play Tottenham in Liverpool. "I was following the prices very closely," he said, referring to the ticket prices. "It was eight hundred pounds for a gold package, the prices had skyrocketed, but then results fell away. I got a gold package for five hundred pounds. I was at the Anfield Road end. I was screaming and everything. I did get a few stares. I knew it was going to be a cracker of a game." And it was, Liverpool winning 4-2. Sibtain had stayed at the Kop End Hotel and Bar by the ground for four nights and gone on a stadium tour. He really loved Liverpool Football Club.

He also really loved Indian trains, preferably when travelling first class. "Mumbai to Calcutta, twenty-four hours. I went first class with butler service. Four-course meal. No alcohol, but I took my own beers. The butlers kept the beers cold and served me. Very good service. There are very many trains in India. You like trains, you must go to India. Many trains."

He recommended the Bori Bunder to Thane line, India's first passenger railway, which opened in 1853 – three years after trains arrived in Aberdeen. It was sometimes easy to forget that the great strides made in Britain from 1825 onwards were picked up quickly across the globe (especially in parts of the extensive British Empire).

After visiting his friend, Sibtain was off to Fort William and then considering a visit to a jute museum in Dundee. He had already been to Stoke-on-Trent and the Peak District for holiday/work fact-finding purposes. After his tour of Great Britain, he would stop in Istanbul to meet a business contact.

The ScotRail train reached Insch station and, after waving his Liverpool scarf, holding it aloft, giving a short rendition of "You'll Never Walk Alone" (the Liverpool song) and advising I read about the travels of "Sir Richard Francis Burton, he was the most legendary British character", Sibtain disembarked. "You must see Indian trains, brother! Have a nice day, brother. Bye!"

For a while I just stared out the window in silence at the green, open scenery with its rolling hills, sheep and occasional distillery. The landscape had a pleasingly tumbledown feel; low, wooded slopes spread out in patchwork blankets between valleys of pastureland. Tea-coloured rivers meandered this way and that. Mini mountains with gently curving summits rose out of nothing as though random additions of some creator. Wooden barrels of Chivas Regal lay in a yard behind a barbed-wire fence on the edge of a place called Keith, piled up and looking like Aztec temples (of the hard stuff).

Then some good-humoured golfing lads, off to play a game, joined the carriage, sat down next to me and we somehow began to discuss the pros and cons of the VAR (video assistant referee) system in football. One of the lads told me that drinking alcohol had been banned on Scottish trains – not that I was drinking alcohol. "It started during Covid," one of them said – the booze rule. "I think it's a bit uncivilized that we're not trusted to have a couple of tinnies on a train. We always used to have a hip flask, port or whisky in it." He gave me a look as though to suggest *Do they think we're really going to give up that?* "Instead of tinnies we take Lucozade bottles with cider in it. The colour's not a million miles away."

With this insider travel briefing, we all got off at Inverness, and I boarded the 10:41 for Thurso, which soon crossed vast swathes of glorious, empty, peaty landscape, skirting estuaries, lochs and the coast, and winding round little towns.

The train clattered and hills rose. This ScotRail train, with its blue seats with little white saltire crosses, had a dream-like quality: an escape from it all. Just keep rolling. Just keep moving. Just keep listening to the wheels on the line. It has been said that if it were not for the Duke of Sutherland and his estate all those years ago, this railway may never have been built. Well, thank you, Duke. Job well done.

Small brown rivers, which looked as though they were probably full of small brown trout, curled by the tracks.

A bald man with a jovial, avuncular manner, a gold watch and a blue-checked shirt sat down opposite me and stared at me as though I was a long-lost friend. I seemed to be attracting good-humoured, jovial types on the ScotRail services of Scotland… a veritable magnet of ScotRail bonhomie.

His name was Holger and he was Danish, retired from development work for the United Nations. He had somehow sensed my interest in trains – by this stage, I must have been emitting strong "train vibes" (God help me) – and Holger wanted to "talk trains". Holger had much to discuss on the subject as he was nearing the end of his own long ride around Britain on trains. I had found a retired Danish rail enthusiast soulmate. I was even wearing a blue-checked shirt myself. We were sartorially matching Train Nuts.

Speaking blue-checked-shirt rail enthusiast to blue-checked-shirt rail enthusiast, Holger said, "Ah, so you are train fanatic?" It was a rhetorical question. "For this journey, thirty-four days. Germany, Belgium, France, London, *Night Riviera* to Penzance, then on to Bournemouth, then to York…" He paused and said as an aside and in a secretive tone, "The railway museum in York? For me it was disappointment. London Transport Museum, much better." From York, he said after this railway museum critique, he had made it up to Scotland. "After Thurso, Glasgow. After Glasgow, Stranraer, ferry, Belfast, Cork, Dublin, ferry, Holyhead, Llandudno, Manchester, London, France, Belgium, Germany, Denmark."

Holger had been on bullet trains in Japan, to Baku in Azerbaijan, across Turkey, Russia, Kazakhstan, Turkmenistan, Vietnam, India, Bangladesh, the United States, Canada and South Africa. "Cape Town to Johannesburg, the *Blue Train*. When it moved a small orchestra played classical music and they served champagne."

I said Holger should not expect such service on ScotRail.

Holger looked at me for a moment. "Ha ha ha," he said, and kept going on his world tour of trains. "In India, Kolkata to Chennai. I chose third class. The people there were so interested to talk about philosophy and religion. They asked me about what I thought about life after death."

His favourite trains were in Japan. "First class, lots of free drinks, lots of space, lots of food, best seats ever, good leather."

Of first class on English trains, Holger said, "You have your fair share of alcoholics here. Two middle-aged women from York to Edinburgh had at least six of these bottles of wine in the middle of the day. On first class you get as much alcohol as you want. Six quite big bottles they had, but you could not see it on them. I think they must be alcoholics."

His main gripe about travel in Britain was breakfast served at hotels. "I am missing cheese. One thing that is missing is cheese. They do not serve cheese for breakfast. Actually, it is more than one thing missing. Also, you do not get good buns. Rolls. In most of Europe you get these buns for breakfast, very good buns. I can eat toast, but I don't like toast. Toast doesn't taste of very much."

It was the company, not just the splendid, remote countryside and the rattle down the tracks that made Inverness to Thurso a memorable ride.

"MAMBA"
Thurso to Dalmeny via Kyle of Lochalsh, Mallaig and Glasgow

Thurso was delightfully remote, with a good little museum touching on the region's Pictish heritage, an old churchyard with twelfth-century ruins and a harbour by the opening of the river Thurso into the North Sea, where you could watch the ferry putter between nearby Scrabster and Stromness on the Orkney Islands.

A lovely spot, in an off-the-beaten-track, down-to-earth way – not a tourist trap, too far "up" for that.

If you ever get the chance, go.

Though I was not there long.

In the morning the 06:50 retraced the journey of the day before, crossing great sweeps of sandy-coloured grass, the occasional hawk soaring above. Landscape like this, I had been informed by a friend who knew about such things, had a name, "MAMBA", which stood for Miles and Miles of Bugger All. Well, plenty of MAMBA was viewed from the Far North Line: many, many miles and miles of bugger all – MMMAMBA.

After quite some time, the train pulled into the pretty little town of Dingwall, where you alighted for the connection to Kyle of Lochalsh on the west coast of Scotland. This came, the 11:32, taking a long bend and crossing some of the most beautiful train scenery in Britain: glistening lochs, empty grasslands, high purple hills, slopes of bracken, tumbling scree, boglands, forests, sparkling rivers, hidden valleys… forgotten worlds waiting down the line. The train horn blew. The sound echoed across the landscape. We pulled into Kyle of Lochalsh and I caught a taxi to Armadale, over a bridge onto the Isle of Skye.

From Armadale a short ferry took you across the Sound of Sleat to Mallaig for an evening in a charming small port with fish 'n' chip shops, pubs and boats bobbing in the harbour.

Another lovely spot, peaceful but plenty going on.

If you ever get the chance, go.

In the morning, I talked to a local woman about *The Jacobite* steam train that regularly ran – or had previously regularly run – along the West Highland Line down to Fort William, operated by West Coast Railways. The problem was that a new government order required trains on main lines to have "Central Door Locking" (CDL), whereas the doors on the old carriages pulled by *The Jacobite* could be opened individually. A stand-off had resulted while West Coast Railways sought a temporary exemption. During this period, some services could occasionally run on a vastly reduced number of carriages that *had* been fitted with CDL. It was all quite complicated and involved.

So far as the woman, who ran a business, was concerned, it just meant one thing: "Footfall is definitely down. We're worried. Listen, this is a tourist town. There's good fishing, but that's declined. We need the tourists."

I caught the 10:06 from Mallaig to Glasgow, due in at 3.26 p.m. This was a mammoth journey of 5 hours and 10 minutes along tracks that had recently been voted the world's best train ride by the travel magazine *Wanderlust*.

I settled back and awaited "train enjoyment". It was soon delivered as the 10:06 slid across west Scotland: little bays, rocky shores, banks of lilac rhododendrons, mirror-topped lochs, darting deer, jagged mountains – wild, wild, wild. And all the while, the train was rasping, juddering, growling, almost grumbling as it slowly rose in elevation. What type of train was this? I had no idea. But you did not need to be on *The Jacobite* to enjoy the journey.

It was not long before the big moment arrived: the famous Glenfinnan Viaduct, all 21 arches of it curving round 381 metres at a height of 30 metres.

When it did, just about everyone in the packed carriage peered through the slightly grimy windows and tried to sneak a glimpse of the legendary viaduct, which was tricky, obviously, as we were on it, although you could catch the arches curving ahead. The train moved slowly as though the driver was allowing time for snaps. A mottled-green valley lay below, with a glimpse of Loch Shiel to the west and a cluster of A-shaped mountains. Everyone who was not a local commuting to work in Fort William (a man wearing a McDonald's shirt ready for a shift was across the aisle with his head in a novel) oohed and aahed and generally seemed to try to savour this *world's best train ride* moment (made even more famous by the Harry Potter films with the Hogwarts Express).

Yet another lovely spot – similar to Ribblehead back on the Settle and Carlisle Railway (with more bend to it).

If you ever get a chance, go.

After this great excitement came Fort William, where a fiddle-player folk musician named Sally sat down next to me and said she was on her way to Kilmarnock to join the *Royal Scotsman*, to play music in the lounge, accompanied by a guitarist.

Even travelling on regular trains, it was tricky to escape the clutches of Britain's heritage train world.

"We play Scottish music, strathspeys, jigs and reels," she said, and I nodded and pretended I knew what a *strathspey* was.

During her time with the *Royal Scotsman*, a luxury train run by a luxury travel company named Belmond, she and the guitarist would also perform on the platform for passengers on the luxury train.

"There's ceilidh dancing," she said, and I nodded and pretended I knew what ceilidh dancing was too, having a vague mental picture of people in kilts prancing in circles.

"It does terrify me, though," she said. "When they get into it and get close to the edge of the platform."

What terrified her was the prospect of an elderly multimillionaire American rail enthusiast dancing off the platform under the spell of a traditional Scottish tune (and potentially suing the fiddle player and guitarist). She was joking about this, really; she didn't really think any multimillionaire American rail enthusiasts would do this, though the thought had clearly occurred.

Sally was tall, softly spoken and had piercing blue eyes and short blond hair. She wore black jeans and was a cool fiddle-player folk musician. Like just about everyone you met on a train in Scotland, she was a train lover too. "I just wish every train was a steam train," she said. "I remember going on a ride on one to Pickering when I was a kid." On the North Yorkshire Moors Railway.

Sally became my (unofficial) train guide. We arrived at Corrour station, Britain's highest main-line station at 410 metres yet famous for less tourist-board-friendly reasons, Sally said, as this was close to where the character Mark Renton, played by the actor Ewan McGregor, yelled to his assembled ragbag of junkie pals in the cult film *Trainspotting*, "It's s***e being Scottish! We're the lowest of the low. The scum of the f****** Earth!"

A rather desolate spot.

If you ever get the chance to go, perhaps think twice about it (though there was a nice-looking small place to stay right by the station).

We rolled on across more miles of very little indeed, just mountains and sandy-coloured grass, real MAMBA land. Then Sally pointed out Loch Treig ("There's a man who lives somewhere down there, in his eighties, he's known as the Hermit of Treig.") as well as where the Glencoe Massacre had occurred in 1692 ("Just over that mountain, the Campbells tricked their way in and the MacDonalds were murdered."). We dropped in altitude. "Over there, that's Loch Lomond," she said, and I looked over as the vast lake spread out to the left. The landscape was elemental, on a scale quite unlike any so far on the rides, and it was great having a folk-musician, fiddle-playing guide (even if she was not actually playing her fiddle) to point out what was what. Sometimes you've just got to be lucky who you sit next to on a train.

Then everything began to go wrong. Something had failed on the 10:06 from Mallaig. Announcements were made: "This train has issues… I'll update you when I can… something's tripping a circuit." And we were stuck for a very long time. During this lull, Sally talked about all sorts.

"Scottish independence? I'm all for it," she said. "With Brexit especially. We felt so let down. Every single area in Scotland voted Remain and then out we went. Scotland has been consistently voting for things it doesn't end up with." Not just Brexit – other issues too. "But I'm just a folk musician, that's just what I think."

Sally recommended some Scottish walks: the West Highland Way from Glasgow to Fort William, and the Great Glen Way from Fort William to Inverness. She told me, "We've probably passed about fifty Munros today." A Munro being a mountain over 3,000 feet, or 914 metres, named after the mountaineer Sir Hugh Munro, who had listed such Scottish peaks. She said she sometimes played at music festivals and was in two bands called Westward the Light, and Heisk. "That's an Orkney word meaning 'excitable'."

All the time, the train did not move an inch. But then finally it did, and we arrived at Dumbarton Central, where we all changed onto the crazily crowded 17:12 to Glasgow Queen Street. This trundled along for half an hour, standing room only. I was in the aisle, with a large bulldog resting against my feet. Its owner was a harassed, fatalistic woman with two young children, who told me that her car, attached to her caravan, had broken down near Mallaig and she had left it somewhere safe after staying a night in the car park of a supermarket and finding she had a £100 parking ticket in the morning. She was returning home and would go back to take the car and caravan to a garage later.

"It's been a disaster, aye," she said.

And we, Sally and I, thought we had been having it pretty bad.

The train arrived at Glasgow Queen Street. We all got off. Sally and I, having formed a partnership in adversity, exited the platform together and on the concourse I looked up the next train to Edinburgh, the 18:16, while she worked out getting to Kilmarnock. We exchanged details and later that evening she sent a picture of the *Royal Scotsman* lounge – all cosy wood panels and tartan – where a bartender had just poured her an espresso martini. "Bit of an upgrade" was her caption. Yes, quite a large one.

The train from Glasgow Queen Street rolled through the darkness down the line to Edinburgh Haymarket, the route of the original 1842 railway. Then the train from Edinburgh Haymarket rolled on to Dalmeny, where I walked down a steep hill to South Queensferry and checked into The Hawes Inn.

My room faced the Forth Bridge, which looped away across the Firth of Forth, all girders and beams, its rust-red outline lit up and looking like a dream disappearing into the fog on the estuary, where several rivers met including the river Forth. It was captivating. Astonishing. The graceful curves and incredible dimensions: 2½ miles across (slightly less than the Tay Bridge) and rising to 110 metres, allowing clearance for the largest ships (the Tay Bridge was a mere 25 metres high). The sheer audacity and vision to have built such a structure 65 years after *Locomotion No 1* chugged over a much smaller first railway bridge (Skerne Bridge in

Darlington with a span of twelve metres) was verging on unbelievable. Yet you had to believe it: the bridge was there.

I definitely seemed to have developed a "thing" about bridges.

It was 8 p.m.

The journey from Mallaig had taken almost ten hours.

Full Train Nut
Dalmeny to Shildon via Edinburgh and Darlington

The Hawes Inn in South Queensferry was right by the pier from where the ferry once crossed the Firth of Forth. This was still used by the RNLI, other official vessels and boats transporting cruise ship passengers for tours of Scotland's capital. The ferry had been superseded by two bridges: the Forth Road Bridge, slightly to the west (a suspension bridge completed in 1964) and the Forth Bridge, which had opened in 1890. The inn was mentioned in Robert Louis Stevenson's captivating adventure novel *Kidnapped*, in which the seventeen-year-old protagonist, David Balfour, is indeed kidnapped after his evil-minded uncle sells him to a disreputable ship's captain who intends in turn to sell him into slavery in the Carolinas. This deal was done over a bottle of rum in an upstairs room with a fireplace at the front of the inn. David is tricked on board the ship when invited for a "tour", taking a boat from the pier and being knocked out and held hostage as the ship sets sail for America.

My room almost exactly matched the one described in the book, with a large fireplace (unlit) and writing desk. It was dominated by a huge double bed and was tastefully decorated in shades of grey with a plush carpet, neat bedside reading lights and original shutters. After so many rooms from the lower echelons of popular online booking websites, I had saved the best for last. There was a kettle with good tea and coffee and ginger snap biscuits. You could hear the gentle lap of waves on shore, while from time to time a ScotRail train would rumble across the Forth Bridge, and out of the window you could even watch it slide away. I mean, *what more could you possibly want?* Such "train luxury" was almost overwhelming.

Downstairs, The Hawes Inn was a semi-shrine to the 1890 bridge, even though the hostelry predated the incredible structure by 200 years. Old black-and-white pictures of the bridge were everywhere, as well as drawings of prototype designs that had been rejected, including that of Sir Thomas Bouch, which looked particularly flimsy and overly fancy. The best, most evocative picture of all showed the iconic bridge – considered Scotland's greatest man-made structure and a UNESCO World Heritage Site, no less – when it was half-built. The cantilevered design was in place by each riverbank and three huge metal structures rose out of the water, looking as though the bridge engineers were about to construct three replica Eiffel Towers in the middle of the Firth of Forth. What they achieved, if I have not already said so (and at risk of waxing lyrical about the bridge), was quite mind-blowing.

It did not come without a cost to human life. Of the 4,600 construction workers, 73 are recorded to have died, or 1.58 per cent. Of every hundred people working on the bridge, at least one would perish, with 38 falling into the estuary to their deaths. Close to the old ferry pier you could pay your respects at a touching memorial to those who passed away.

By the window in the front room, I ate an excellent chicken curry, listening to "Boys Don't Cry" by The Cure, "Smile" by Kate Perry and "Good Times" by Chic. The latter had it about right: plush armchair, pint, decent meal, views of trains passing by an old historic railway bridge. But you had to spare a thought for those who had not made it, who would have come for a drink at the end of shifts at The Hawes Inn, and where bar staff used to line up pints in readiness for their arrival. What a bridge, what a sacrifice.

It was to be a final day full of movement (so little change there). It was time to head back to Darlington and Shildon, to where trains began. My two months were up... reality beckoned. Train Life was about to come to an abrupt end. I was wondering, I had to admit, how I would handle returning into polite, "normal" society where COLAS freight trains, timetables and old stories about Brunel and Stephenson (and the rest of the rail pioneers) were not leading the way, setting the agenda for daily existence.

This might, I realized, be tricky. Challenging. Rapid adjustments required. Was I ready for this? How would I cope after so long down the tracks? Had I been permanently altered by these Train Nut days? Gone railway feral? Was I prepared once again for family responsibilities, re-entering the world of employment and all the rest of it?

To a certain extent, I did not care. There was still a day to go. Why worry too much in advance? But when I thought about everything (jokes aside) it did feel like the moment had come to return home. There was only so long you could potter about along the railways of Great Britain, after all, as enjoyable an experience as that might be.

First, a walk up the hill to Dalmeny station passing a cruise excursion operator who was saying to a colleague, "Have a lucrative day! I imagine it'll be *Ker-ching*!"

The *Regal Princess* cruise ship, a huge object like a floating housing estate, was moored in the Firth; bagpipes had started up on the pier, and boats were beginning to land day-trip tourists. Plenty of *ker-ching* seemed likely.

I waited at Dalmeny station, so close to the Forth Bridge you could see its hump-shaped metal structures along the tracks; it was almost tempting to jump down and walk along the side for a closer look (do not, dear reader, on any account, do this). The 08:22 arrived and an American from the *Regal Princess,* who had shunned the official tours, asked, "Is this the way to Ed-in-bor-ough?"

I said it was and we boarded, moving away on a packed commuter service beneath a pewter sky, a dozen or so minutes later passing beneath the looming fortifications of Edinburgh Castle and humming into a ravine containing Edinburgh Waverley station.

This was a gloomy, cavernous place that seemed to be made of warehouses that had been joined together and fitted with skylights, like a giant, dimly lit commercial greenhouse, though instead of beds of strawberries and tomatoes, passengers were heading in every which direction.

In the centre of the concourse was a pleasant old waiting room with a circular skylight and an old olive tree. Decorations in the skylight featured cherubs holding golden chains of flowers. The walls were adorned with classical columns with hanging baskets of pink flowers attached, as well as a large number of CCTV cameras. This was by far the nicest part of Edinburgh Waverley station.

Adjoining the waiting room was a Bookshop by WHSmith with a lot of local writer Ian Rankin's Inspector Rebus crime novels in the window. (I had just finished an enjoyable one of these entitled *The Black Book*, picked up in Stonehaven, which had included some scenes down in South Queensferry.) But I had a specific request for a book: *Waverley* by Sir Walter Scott. The station makes much of this. A sign I had noticed earlier said, "Waverley is the only station in the world named after a novel… thanking you, Sir Walter Scott", but I could not find *Waverley*, Scott's book about Scotland's Jacobite rising, published in 1814, so I asked an assistant. She looked a little sheepish. "I know it's bad," she replied. "But we don't actually have it in stock." Which was a good sign, I suppose; people must have been buying and reading it.

With half an hour until my connection, I had just enough time to scoot up the hill via a narrow alley to the cobbled Royal Mile leading to the castle to inspect the many haggis, oatcake, shortbread, whisky, cashmere and tweed shops. St Giles' Cathedral with its spiky turrets and high arched windows was closed (too early). A traffic cone had been placed on the head of the bronze statue of the eighteenth-century Scottish philosopher David Hume, but not on that of eighteenth-century economist and philosopher Adam Smith. At a shop close by you could purchase a tartan kilt for £44.99 or tartan trousers for £16.99, as well as tartan neck cushions for travelling, tartan scarves, tartan mugs, tartan ties, tartan picnic blankets, tartan key rings, tartan socks and tartan Tam O'Shanter flat caps with sprouting ginger-haired wigs. A whole lot of tartan. Well, if it sells, why not?

It was a good little walk. No need for waiting rooms at Waverley really.

I returned to the station and boarded the 09:30 to Darlington.

The crazy big circle or "treble clef", or whatever it was, was coming to an end.

The penultimate main-line ride was on a London North Eastern Railway service, running on time, with dirty cherry-red seats and some guys nearby who looked and sounded incredibly hungover.

"How are you feeling?" asked one.

"Aargh," replied another.

"Same here," he said, adding, as if in solidarity, "Aargh."

"Aargh," said his companion once more.

"Remember that barmaid?" asked a third.

"Aargh," replied the second.

"She went through all the cocktails, describing them all, remember that?" he persevered.

The other two failed to respond, even with an "aargh". They looked *poisoned*, which they may well have technically been.

"She took ages going through them all," he continued. "Then we just asked for three beers."

"Aargh," said one of them.

"She looked at us with disdain," he said. "Remember that?"

"Aargh," they replied simultaneously, and all three said nothing further all the way down to Darlington.

The train crawled beneath the castle before plunging into and out of tunnels. We slipped through suburbs and across fields, soon arriving at the North Sea, which was shrouded in a thick, creamy low-hanging cloud. Near the cuboid hulk of Torness Nuclear Power Station, a guard with cropped hair, hipster beard and thick-framed glasses passed by, and I asked which way the dining carriage was. He replied in an upbeat manner, "It's coach 'G' for 'grub', sir." I thanked him and went to get a cup of tea.

You were best off sitting on the left for this ride. That way you were by the cliffs and could gaze out at the occasional little island off the coast and wonder what went on there. We left Scotland. We passed the enticing, pleasant-looking town of Alnmouth. We scudded through Morpeth and beyond the sheds of Heaton Traincare Centre.

We rolled into Newcastle, where student apartments towered by the tracks and you could catch tantalizing glimpses of bridges across the Tyne between buildings (this late-blossoming bridge obsession was steadily getting worse, fuelled perhaps by the Forth Bridge appreciation evening).

Across the Tyne we went, traversing boggy fields of piebald cattle and, not long after, pulling into Darlington station and its massive hall and high, damp red-brick walls.

I was back where I started, minus a "COLAS RAIL FREIGHT" locomotive and a trainspotter named Dave to tell me all about it.

And there was trouble on the tracks. Two trains to Shildon had been cancelled "due to a member of the train crew being unavailable" said the departure board. My last main-line ride – the 142nd of the trip, having covered more than 4,000 miles (I could hardly believe) – would be quite badly delayed.

It did not matter. I was used to it.

I sat in the Pumpkin Café next to its Beat the Banker fruit machine and waited for some time, reading *Kidnapped* (which you could be from time to time on British trains).

Then I caught the 13:55 to Shildon, over Skerne Bridge, Britain's first railway bridge, for a passenger steam train (as I had discovered back at the beginning), and past Heighington station, where, if you looked closely on the right, you could see the crumbling stone slabs of what is believed to be Britain's – and by extension the world's – oldest station platform. There it was, half-covered by weeds, in a collapsed state by a fence near the pile of old railway-crossing barriers I had noticed before. Just a few old slabs slumped by the boarded-up building I had stared out at during the downpour on day one and thought nothing of. Back in the 1820s, Heighington (pronounced high-ing-ton) had been considered the first proper "station" in the direction of Shildon, and it is best to use quotation marks around the word, as "stations" did not really exist in 1825; they were slowly coming into existence. The matter of how passengers actually boarded the strange, steaming contraptions that rolled along the parallel metal tracks that were being slapped down across the country was still being worked out.

Heighington's dilapidated (when I went) former "stationhouse" had been completed in 1826, originally operating as a pub that also fulfilled the functions of a ticket office and waiting room. It had a turbulent past, closing many years back, reopening as a pub in 1984, before shutting once again in 2017 and becoming derelict. However, a group named Friends of Stockton and Darlington Railway was attempting to resurrect the premises. Rail enthusiasts were on the case, doing rail enthusiasm things: as they still were, and had long been, up and down the country. You knew all this, about Heighington, from having spent a long time travelling on trains round Britain reading old train books and whatever else you could get your hands on about such matters.

Which was how I also knew that from Shildon station it was a short walk up to the location of the former Masons Arms pub – the Cape to Cairo restaurant (when I went, though it was closed) – and the spot near a roundabout where *Locomotion No 1* had begun its journey to Darlington on 27 September 1825, with George Stephenson himself directing proceedings. A tourist information board beside some old tracks said, "You are standing at Masons Arms Crossing, a place of importance in world history…" Before the trains came, one of the surveyors for the Stockton and Darlington Railway, John Dixon, had commented that the area was "a wet, swampy field – a likely place to find a snipe, or a flock of peewits". The Masons Arms, being close by, had acted both as an end-of-the-passenger-line drinking hole and the world's first ticket office, and it was a shame Cape to Cairo was shut; I would have liked to have had a poke around.

From Masons Arms Crossing, I took a taxi to a place called the Brusselton Incline at Etherley, a parish three miles to the west of Shildon. This was where coal wagons from a colliery had been loaded to be rolled down hills and pulled back up them by horses with ropes connected to the occasional stationary engine, eventually reaching the flatter land by the Masons Arms in Shildon where Britain's earliest proper locomotives could take over for both the colliery loads and paying passengers. Transporting coal, not humans, had been the primary purpose of the Stockton and Darlington Railway. I asked the taxi driver to pause and got out to take a picture of two parallel lines of stones on the incline. These stones were separated by the space deemed suitable for the width of Stephenson's first tracks: 4 feet, 8½ inches. This unlikely spot on a deserted hill in County Durham was where "standard gauge" had, effectively, begun on a public railway, with wagons and carriages pulled by locomotives – the tracks that were to go on to conquer the globe.

If you were well on your way in the Train Nut direction, Brusselton Incline had, if you like, a Holy of Holies quality. As you gazed upon the old, half-forgotten stones, it was hard not to be struck by the thought *so it all really started… there*. And you might just find yourself staring at the old, half-forgotten stones for a while, thinking, *well, well, well*. Especially if you had just spent quite a large amount of time travelling around on them for 4,000 miles across Britain. It was possible, even, that the hairs on the back of your neck might just stand up for a moment or two as you let the sheer immensity of the significance of the setting, in train terms, sink in.

Forget trainspotting, this was origins-of-train-spotting.

Though the only indication of momentous rail events of the past was a faded sign attached to a stone wall.

No one else was about.

Then we drove back to Shildon – "CRADLE OF THE RAILWAYS", says the road sign on the edge of town – to the Locomotion museum.

Where I was in for a surprise.

Outside the museum, a replica *Rocket* had been stoked up and was offering rides along a short track parallel to the main-line one that went to Darlington. Journey: £4.

Two men in blue jackets, the driver and fireman, were on board the canary-yellow locomotive. Yet there were no other passengers.

Given it was so quiet, would I like a footplate ride, they asked?

Which was how I found myself on *Rocket* as it would have been during its heyday, riding along with Andy, the driver. Smoke billowed from the wooden barrel-shaped body of the loco. Pistons hissed. Then Andy asked, "Would you like to give it a quick drive?"

By drive he meant move a switch that controlled a regulator that powered the engine, while being heavily supervised.

Which was how I found myself "driving" *Rocket* as it was back in 1830 – the locomotive that took all the advancements made by *Locomotion No 1* from the Stockton and Darlington Railway and delivered them to the big time, with the prime minister on board (as well as poor William Huskisson) and thousands lining the tracks on its inaugural service from Liverpool to Manchester. Just five years after the earlier triumph of the Stockton and Darlington Railway, it had been simply spectacular progress.

The pistons pumped. *Rocket* moved faster or slower when I shifted the switch. I could neither believe it nor stop inanely grinning. I was driving Robert Stephenson's dream machine (very closely watched by Andy).

As *Rocket* rolled along, a Northern train passed, heading for Bishop Auckland, and the driver hooted his horn and waved at us from his open cab window. Two hundred years may have separated the technology but the results remained the same: wheels moving down the tracks. What would George Stephenson, and his son Robert, designer of *Rocket*, have had to say? They knew they were on to something big. They knew it would revolutionize movement, that horses could figuratively go back to the stables. But quite so big? So utterly world-transforming? All begun near the Masons Arms pub on a former swamp in County Durham?

I grinned like a madman.

The Northern driver grinned back at me.

I let *Rocket* pick up an mph or two, as though I knew what I was doing.

After a very long journey round Britain's railways, it seemed that I may just have finally (perhaps unalterably) gone full Train Nut.

AFTERWORD

On 19 April 1821 George Stephenson met Edward Pease, the Darlington-based Quaker backer of the Stockton and Darlington Railway. Pease was seeking a quicker way to transport coal from collieries near Darlington to Stockton on the river Tees, to be taken by ship to London. So he invited Stephenson to visit, contrary to a prevalent myth at the time that Stephenson had turned up unannounced and shoeless with a sketchy plan and had managed to convince his gentleman benefactor to adopt his new steam engine (Victorians loved a rags-to-riches story).

The meeting went brilliantly. Unlike others with colliery concerns at the time, Pease was open to the possibility of using locomotives to cover long distances. He had heard of Stephenson's experimentation with locos at Killingworth Colliery, north of Newcastle, and – unlike many who regarded these trials an oddity akin to Richard Trevithick's earlier failures – Pease was impressed.

He was willing to sign up Stephenson, but he had a stipulation. Pease wanted his 26-mile railway to be open to the public, not just for colliery use. His Quaker beliefs prompted this community-oriented altruism. In his commissioning letter, Pease wrote, "In making the survey, it must be borne in mind that this is for a great public way." The company motto for the Stockton and Darlington Railway was to be "*Periculum privatum utilitas publica*" (Private risk for public service).

It was a risky business indeed, requiring a leap of faith. But Pease's hunch was it would probably work for transporting his coal, while better local transport, a "great public way", would pay off for the people of Darlington, also giving Stephenson a chance to shine.

It would be winning all round, and he was, of course, right. The great crowds that turned out to clamber onto wagons and watch on from beside the tracks bore witness to the immediate success. It worked! A whole new way of moving about was feasible, and five years later Stephenson's Liverpool and Manchester Railway was up and running. The "iron horse" wheels of the industrial revolution had begun to spin.

In the run-up to this series of (admittedly) somewhat madcap train rides around Britain, the scheme to link HS2 to Manchester and Leeds beyond Birmingham was unceremoniously dumped.

This political decision had been based on costs running beyond expectation, which was true, although not to such an extent that absolutely everyone was calling for the project to be scrapped. The move had, I will admit, cast a shadow over the journey to come. The dreams of high-speed trains from London to the north (to Manchester in 1 hour and 11 minutes, down from 2 hours and 6 minutes) were over, it appeared. That was it – gone.

The scenario felt deflating. With the bicentenary of the Stockton and Darlington Railway looming – a chance to commemorate the bold leaps forward the line represented – the country that invented trains had turned its back on the biggest plan to revamp the nation's railways in years.

How this had come to such a pass, it was hard precisely to determine. But that was what had happened.

As the journey progressed around Britain, I soon realized I was not alone in feeling down about the lack of joined-up thinking HS2's failure seemed to symbolize. Sarah Price, head of the Locomotion museum in Shildon, had talked about the need to maintain faith after "hiccups" to the project. It was not just about passengers getting about more easily. She believed a new line would have taken lorries off the motorways and "revolutionize[d] freight", introducing greater environmental sustainability.

Her colleague Clive Goult had agreed: "Sadly, Tom, we can't afford it. Or we think we can't afford it. It's the British problem. We don't look at the benefits against the direct costs." The long-term benefits would outweigh the immediate costs, he implied.

AFTERWORD

"It's tragic what's happened," the man I shared a compartment with on the Isle of Wight Steam Railway said, summarizing the general mood.

Those representing railways at a national level were of the same opinion.

Speaking after the National Audit Office announced it would cost £100 million to undo work already begun on HS2 between Birmingham and Manchester (on top of £592 million spent on buying property and land along the route), Darren Caplan, chief executive of the Railway Industry Association (RIA), said, "The West Coast Main Line transport corridor is clearly a vital artery for UK economic growth, carrying millions of rail passengers and tonnes of freight… The current position of no new significant capacity to ease congestion on this rail corridor is simply untenable. Ministers in the new Labour government now need to ensure it has all the powers and approvals required to facilitate rail growth north of Birmingham – without which Birmingham risks becoming a terminal, rather than the national hub it should be."

As things stood, the West Coast Main Line would be full by the mid-2030s. A report commissioned by the RIA had found that rail passenger numbers in Britain were likely to increase between 37 per cent and 97 per cent by 2050 as the UK population grew.

The High Speed Rail Group, supporters of HS2, as their name suggested, said dropping the plan would badly damage the economy: "What's needed is extra capacity, not new bottlenecks." Which was what was feared would develop at Birmingham. "Done properly, high-speed rail can stimulate growth in our regional economies."

The only problem was this was not happening.

Meanwhile, taking a perhaps cynical (but amusing) view of it all, the satirical magazine *Private Eye* ran a "news story" about those National Audit Office findings, quoting a spoof NAO spokesman: "We're now recommending that the remaining £10 billion to be spent on HS2 should instead be piled high and burned. We believe this will provide much greater value for money for the taxpayer."

Two hundred years on from the great strides forward made by Stephenson and Pease at the Stockton and Darlington Railway, sadness, frustration and gallows humour about the state of Britain's railways, once the envy of the world, had set in. A new government may have arrived, but all the momentum seemed to have been lost. The big moment over… or so it seemed.

Suggestions had emerged for a potential "HS2 light" railway, with slower trains on less costly tracks between Birmingham and Manchester, potentially linking up with better lines operated by the Northern Powerhouse Rail scheme (referred to by some as "HS3"), offering glimmers of hope for an improved national north–south rail network. Yet these seemed, at the time of writing, to be at the ideas rather than *definite action* stage.

Definite action carried out on time and within budget was in short supply and had been for a while. That said, it did appear likely that trains on HS2 from Birmingham would be routed to London Euston, after all, rather than to Old Oak Common out in Acton in the west of the capital.

Plenty of talk swirled about.

Who really knew, though, how it would all pan out?

Trying not to put too much of a dampener on things, British railways were not exactly thriving in other areas either.

It was clear the new Labour government faced a mountain of train problems. One of these was how to realize its ambitions to renationalize the country's twenty-plus main-line passenger railways. The plan was to let rail operator contracts expire, with the state stepping in to improve performances, curb fat-cat salaries and put an end to public money being turned into dividends for shareholders, all overseen by an "arm's length" body named Great British Railways that would act as a "directing mind", comprising "empowered rail industry experts and professionals tasked by the Secretary of State with improving the rail network". Politics and trains, as ever, were never far apart – just as

AFTERWORD

they had been during Labour's nationalization of the railways in 1948 under Clement Attlee.

Regarding this, one transport expert with impeccable Department for Transport contacts, who asked not to be named, said, "Well, that's not going to make much difference. The trains are effectively nationalized already. All the ticket revenue is sent directly to the Treasury and each train operator is paid a management fee for running their railway. Labour, when they begin to look under the hood of the railways, will find so many entrenched problems that renationalizing will prove to be one almighty task."

Already, again at the time of writing, seven of the rail operators were publicly owned, taken over after failing to meet minimum cancellation/delay targets: London North Eastern Railway (LNER), Northern, Transport for Wales, Southeastern, ScotRail, Caledonian Sleeper and TransPennine Express.

Then there was the matter of industrial action.

So far as strikes and government relations with unions were concerned, there was little cheerful to report there either. With eighteen strikes over two years, the Associated Society of Locomotive Engineers and Firemen (ASLEF) had been in the middle of the longest rail dispute in years when I went.

The initial good news was that the new Labour government – after I had returned – had brought disruption to an abrupt halt by proposing a 14 per cent pay increase. "LABOUR OFFERS TRAIN DRIVERS BUMPER PAY DEAL TO END STRIKES" ran the headline in the *Daily Mail*. This had been accepted and it seemed as though peace between Number Ten and the unions had finally descended.

Yet two days later the same paper was asking, "HAS LABOUR LOST CONTROL OF THE UNIONS ALREADY?" What had happened? The answer was that ASLEF said its members were happy with the pay offer but would be going on strike over a separate matter to do with "bullying by management and persistent breaking of agreements by the company" at LNER.

All hopes of progress seemed to have been dashed, although – in yet another twist – this industrial action was suddenly cancelled. Mick Whelan, the union's general secretary, said, "better working practices" had been negotiated and commented, "ASLEF will continue to campaign for a fully staffed railway that doesn't rely on excessive use of driver overtime… we look forward to normal working resuming."

All was well again. For a while, at least.

It seemed highly likely that a feisty time between the government and the unions lay ahead.

But this book was not meant to be a polemic about the (often dire) state of British trains. It was supposed to be a celebration of 200 years of them seen from a long, winding – admittedly completely and utterly self-indulgent – series of rail journeys. A great wallow in British trains. A train jamboree! A trainfest!

So what were the enjoyments of a long trip around the country, seeing things from so many trains – 143 in all (if I had that right) covering 4,088 miles (give or take a few, perhaps)?

Well, they were many and varied.

Firstly, you began to see Britain completely differently.

Not your opinion of it as a nation, how you *literally visualized it*. When considering the country's geography, I had reached a stage where I no longer simply pictured the outline of Britain, imagining where the cities, counties and borders with Wales and Scotland lay. How simplistic, how dull merely to do that. No, instead I had begun to think of the National Rail route diagram map, and which places you could practically visit by train and which you simply could not. For example, you could go to St Ives but not Padstow in Cornwall – so you no longer thought of Padstow at all, in train terms, and considered only ever going to St Ives. You could make it to Blaenau Ffestiniog but not Denbigh in Wales – so you booked a break to Blaenau Ffestiniog. Yes, to Thurso. Forget it, John o' Groats. Sorry.

AFTERWORD

This new vision of Britain had an added bonus in that you were more adept when considering journeys: how Leeds connected to Carlisle, Doncaster to Hull, Liverpool to Llandudno and so on. You recognized the great importance, railway-wise, of the likes of Crewe, Preston, Carlisle, Exeter, Peterborough, Inverness and Doncaster. You knew, almost instinctively, where termini lay, which dead ends to avoid if intending to travel through. You had, if you like, developed a nineteenth-century (post 1825) perspective: you could only go where the trains went.

All this was liberating, being able to switch on your "train map brain" and forget anything else was possible. You had, when I thought about it, created a new parallel way of thinking. Your perspective of Britain had, for better or worse, forever changed. You had developed a two-track mind.

Another subtle shift came in your historical appreciation of Britain. What Henry VIII did down on the south coast, the Romans along Hadrian's Wall or Queen Elizabeth at Tilbury – well, these and other such histories were still interesting enough in their own non-train ways. However, when did the station first open? What effect did that have on the place? What was it like before and after the arrival of the iron horses? How did George and Robert Stephenson fit in? What about brilliant Brunel? And that scoundrel Hudson? From Middlesbrough to Grange-over-Sands, to Penzance, Bognor Regis, Southend, Doncaster, Skegness, Grimsby and biggies like Manchester and Liverpool, too, if you took a historical look through "rail glasses", suddenly your understanding of places sharpened.

Another "brain" had sprung up: the *rail history background knowledge appreciation brain*, if you like. A three-track mind.

Of course, there was straightforward train-buff stuff. What class of train? Diesel or electric? What year? Hitachi or Siemens? All that kind of railway guff. I tried my hardest, but this had proven a step too far. I just could not quite crack it (not in a sustained way, even if I had tried back in Shoeburyness). Something deep within prevented me caring enough to swot up about the technical side. Apologies, George Stephenson and

Isambard Kingdom Brunel, up in the sky. It was a world beyond me, although there was a certain interest in understanding what type of "wheels" you were riding and there was no harm in spending a moment or two attempting to work out what you were on, like a passenger on a plane assessing if it is Airbus or Boeing. You could always ask a trainspotter, when in doubt, and I was extremely touched to be invited (in an email sent by Mike a few days after my visit) to be an "honorary junior member" of the Carlisle old boys Wednesday spotters club.

I may have gone "full Train Nut", but perhaps not "hardcore full Train Nut". I would never reach the heights of train knowledge of the Carlisle old boys, or railway-guru John back in Doncaster. But I had made strides in that direction.

When it came down to it, I just liked train travel a lot.

Which brought me to heritage lines. Britain had more than 170 heritage railways operating around 600 miles of tracks when I went, run by an army of volunteers. These were magnificent places to gain an insight into earlier train travel and to enjoy some extremely pleasurable clattering rides pulled by lovely old locomotives that spouted steam, hissed and hooted – marvellous throwbacks from another time. (I will not forget rattling by Corfe Castle shovelling coal into the furnace in a hurry.)

Nowhere else on the planet had such a high concentration of heritage lines and they appeared to be thriving. I liked Kerry Noble of the West Somerset Railway's take on their continuing popularity: "There's a general want for 'vintage' right now. Vintage clothing, vintage records." And vintage trains, too.

I got that. Surely there could be no better way to celebrate 200 years of British trains than by visiting one of them. And it was hugely impressive to witness the dedication of some of the more than 22,000 volunteers and 4,000 paid employees at Britain's heritage railways; those numbers were just the members of the official Heritage Railway Association (there were no doubt many more). Their shared driving passion? A love of the British invention of trains and their place in British history.

AFTERWORD

What other enjoyments did a long journey around the country offer?

Well, perhaps as much as anything previously mentioned, it was "glimpses" along the way. Glimpses of life, places and people seen through the carriage window and on arrival, or read about in the local newspapers, or experienced through encounters with fellow travellers such as with Sally on ScotRail (fiddler on the hoof). It was impossible to cover the whole of Britain comprehensively on a long train tour – see it all, report it all – but you could let serendipity deliver whatever came your way, as Philip Larkin, the newly statue-ized bard of Hull Paragon station, had understood so well in "The Whitsun Weddings".

Glimpses: aren't they all we ever get of anything, really?

More straightforwardly, you also had the freedom of the line.

Britain was blessed with 10,072 route miles of railways rolling into 2,593 stations during my rides in the run-up to the bicentenary of the Stockton and Darlington Railway. This compared with 26 route miles in 1825, 49 miles in 1839, 1,800 miles in 1843, 6,000 miles in 1854, 23,440 miles in 1914, 17,830 miles in 1963 and 12,098 miles in 1970. The figures highlighted both the rapid acceleration in railways once begun as well as how Dr Beeching's "reshaping" had affected distances in the 1960s. The numbers themselves told the story. But 10,072 miles was not bad, all things considered, and nothing was stopping you travelling along all of them as you wished (budget and ticket prices permitting). At the latest count, 1,385 million journeys were made annually on Britain's railways; trains, despite everything said earlier, continued to be an extremely popular way of getting about.

George Stephenson had definitely been on to something back in 1825 so far as that was concerned.

And what might have happened if the Chinese or the Russians, the Germans or the French had got there first? If the trains had not begun in Britain?

Things would certainly have been different in Victorian times. How might the world order, then and today, have panned out? How might

Britain's prosperity have fared? Who knew? But it was clear that what happened over the 26 miles of the Stockton and Darlington Railway in 1825 was a key part of what made the country what it was to become in so many corners in so many different ways, as I hope these rambling tales from the tracks convey (at least a little).

Would I recommend hopping on a train to visit Shildon to see for yourself?

Absolutely.

Locomotion No 1 is waiting down the line.

Trains still count for something in Britain… no matter what the politicians might say (and do).

London, October 2024

ACKNOWLEDGEMENTS

As ever, I am indebted to a great number of people who generously helped with this book, many of whom are mentioned in the text. The journey was as much about encounters as it was about trains and the history of railways, so I am extremely grateful to those who shared their time, fellow passengers and employees of Britain's railways, who do a usually great job under difficult circumstances and were (almost always) friendly and generous with their time and knowledge. Fellow passengers also brought this "train quest" to life; rail enthusiasts and trainspotters of the world unite! Luckily, meeting people on trains (and train platforms) often seems to come with the territory. Thanks for helping with some of the journey's logistics are due to Pam Porter, John Arthur, Andy Croxton, Alison Grange, Esme Bloomfield, Jill Read, Charlotte Kingston, Jane Harris, Kayleigh Bonner, Laura Delaney, Nina Sawetz, Chanel Goy, Caroline Calvert and Rae White. Special thanks also to Ben Clatworthy, Naomi Grimley, Danny Kelly, my brother Ed (despite not going to Sheerness-on-Sea), my sister Kate, my aunt Meg and my parents Robert and Christine Chesshyre, who (patiently) listened to quite a few tales from the tracks, often while down at The Ship in Mortlake. Special thanks also to my brilliant colleagues: Mark Palmer, Harriet Sime, Laura Sharman, Jessica Hamilton, Esther Marshall, Sarah Hartley and Ted Thornhill. The staff at Stanfords maps and travel bookshop in Covent Garden and the Open Book in Richmond have been incredibly supportive, as ever, for which I am extremely grateful. Thanks also to Simon Bradley, Hunter Davies, Simon Jenkins and Christian Wolmar for their excellent historical books about British railways. Extra special thanks to Claire Plimmer and Debbie Chapman, respectively editorial director and senior commissioning editor at Summersdale, for their vision regarding this book. Thanks also to Donna Hillyer for her insightful structural edit, Victoria O'Dowd for her sharp-eyed copy-edit, Jasmin Burkitt for her fantastic publicity pushes and Hamish Braid for the tricky maps.

TRAINS TAKEN

1. Darlington to Shildon – Northern, 18 minutes, 9 miles
2. Shildon to Darlington – Northern, 18 minutes, 9 miles
3. Darlington to Thornaby – Northern, 23 minutes, 12 miles
4. Thornaby to Stockton – Northern, 6 minutes, 2 miles
5. Stockton to Middlesbrough – Northern, 12 minutes, 4 miles
6. Middlesbrough to Grosmont – Northern, 1 hour 28 minutes, 27 miles
7. Grosmont to Pickering – North Yorkshire Moors Railway, 1 hour and 15 minutes, 16 miles
8. Pickering to Grosmont – North Yorkshire Moors Railway, 1 hour and 15 minutes, 16 miles
9. Grosmont to Middlesbrough – Northern, 1 hour 14 minutes, 27 miles
10. Middlesbrough to York – TransPennine Express, 57 minutes, 51 miles
11. York to Leeds – TransPennine Express, 36 minutes, 23 miles
12. Leeds to Keighley – Northern, 25 minutes, 18 miles
13. Ingrow West to Oxenhope – Keighley & Worth Valley Railway, 19 minutes, 5 miles
14. Oxenhope to Haworth – Keighley & Worth Valley Railway, 5 minutes, 2 miles
15. Haworth to Ingrow West – Keighley & Worth Valley Railway, 14 minutes, 3 miles
16. Keighley to Settle – Northern, 36 minutes, 24 miles
17. Settle to Ribblehead – Northern, 16 minutes, 12 miles
18. Ribblehead to Appleby – Northern, 39 minutes, 35 miles
19. Appleby to Carlisle – Northern, 42 minutes, 31 miles
20. Carlisle to Ravenglass – Northern, 1 hour 42 minutes, 52 miles
21. Ravenglass to Dalegarth – Ravenglass and Eskdale Railway, 40 minutes, 7 miles
22. Dalegarth to Ravenglass – Ravenglass and Eskdale Railway, 40 minutes, 7 miles
23. Ravenglass to Barrow-in-Furness – Northern, 50 minutes, 27 miles
24. Barrow-in-Furness to Grange-over-Sands – Northern, 34 minutes, 22 miles
25. Grange-over-Sands to Preston – Northern, 16 minutes, 46 miles
26. Preston to Liverpool Lime Street – Northern, 51 minutes, 30 miles
27. Liverpool Lime Street to Manchester Victoria – TransPennine Express, 36 minutes, 35 miles
28. Wharfside to Pomona – Manchester Metrolink, 2 minutes, 1 mile
29. Pomona to Manchester Piccadilly – Manchester Metrolink, 16 minutes, 3 miles
30. Manchester Piccadilly to Llandudno Junction – Transport for Wales, 2 hours and 4 minutes, 78 miles
31. Llandudno Junction to Blaenau Ffestiniog – Transport for Wales, 1 hour and 3 minutes, 27 miles

TRAINS TAKEN

32. Blaenau Ffestiniog to Porthmadog – Ffestiniog & Welsh Highland Railways, 1 hour and 10 minutes, 13½ miles
33. Porthmadog to Caernarfon – Ffestiniog & Welsh Highland Railways, 2 hours and 20 minutes, 25 miles
34. Porthmadog to Blaenau Ffestiniog – Ffestiniog & Welsh Highland Railways, 1 hour and 10 minutes, 13½ miles
35. Blaenau Ffestiniog to Llandudno Junction – Transport for Wales, 1 hour and 3 minutes, 27 miles
36. Llandudno Junction to Prestatyn – Transport for Wales, 25 minutes, 19 miles
37. Prestatyn to Crewe – Avanti West Coast, 50 minutes, 49 miles
38. Crewe to Craven Arms – Transport for Wales, 57 minutes, 54 miles
39. Craven Arms to Llanelli – Transport for Wales, 3 hours and 9 minutes, 89 miles
40. Llanelli to Swansea – Transport for Wales, 25 minutes, 11 miles
41. Swansea to Bristol Parkway – Great Western Railway, 1 hour and 26 minutes, 77 miles
42. Bristol Parkway to Plymouth – CrossCountry, 3 hours 9 minutes, 120 miles
43. Plymouth to Truro – Great Western Railway, 1 hour and 41 minutes, 47 miles
44. Truro to Penzance – Great Western Railway, 40 minutes, 25 miles
45. Penzance to St Erth – Great Western Railway, 7 minutes, 6 miles
46. St Erth to St Ives – Great Western Railway, 10 minutes, 5 miles
47. St Ives to St Erth – Great Western Railway, 10 minutes, 5 miles
48. St Erth to Newton Abbot – Great Western Railway, 2 hours and 33 minutes, 96 miles
49. Newton Abbot to Torquay – Great Western Railway, 12 minutes, 6 miles
50. Torquay to Exeter – Great Western Railway, 54 minutes, 23 miles
51. Exeter to Okehampton – Great Western Railway, 38 minutes, 15 miles
52. Okehampton to Exeter – Great Western Railway, 38 minutes, 15 miles
53. Exeter to Taunton – Great Western Railway, 26 minutes, 31 miles
54. Bishops Lydeard to Minehead – West Somerset Railway, 1 hour and 20 minutes, 23 miles
55. Minehead to Bishops Lydeard – West Somerset Railway, 1 hour and 20 minutes, 23 miles
56. Taunton to Castle Cary – Great Western Railway, 19 minutes, 29 miles
57. Castle Cary to Dorchester West – Great Western Railway, 49 minutes, 30 miles
58. Dorchester South to Poole – South Western Railway, 25 minutes, 23 miles
59. Norden to Swanage – Swanage Railway, 22 minutes, 6 miles
60. Swanage to Corfe Castle – Swanage Railway, 17 minutes, 5 miles
61. Wareham to Poole – South Western Railway, 11 minutes, 9 miles
62. Poole to Southampton Central – South Western Railway, 48 minutes, 35 miles
63. Southampton Central to Portsmouth Harbour – South Western Railway, 46 minutes, 18 miles
64. Ryde St Johns Road to Shanklin – Island Line, 21 minutes, 8 miles
65. Shanklin to Smallbrook Junction – Island Line, 17 minutes, 5 miles

66. Smallbrook Junction to Wootton – Isle of Wight Steam Railway, 11 minutes, 5 miles
67. Wootton to Havenstreet – Isle of Wight Steam Railway, 6 minutes, 2 miles
68. Havenstreet to Smallbrook Junction – Isle of Wight Steam Railway, 5 minutes, 3 miles
69. Smallbrook Junction to Ryde Pier Head – Island Line, 10 minutes, 3 miles
70. Portsmouth Harbour to Barnham – Southern, 47 minutes, 25 miles
71. Barnham to Bognor Regis – Southern, 7 minutes, 3 miles
72. Bognor Regis to Barnham – Southern, 7 minutes, 3 miles
73. Barnham to Brighton – Southern, 42 minutes, 25 miles
74. Brighton to Lewes – Southern, 13 minutes, 9 miles
75. Pevensey and Westham to Hastings – Southern, 21 minutes, 12 miles
76. Hastings to Rye – Southern, 22 minutes, 11 miles
77. New Romney to Dungeness – Romney, Hythe and Dymchurch Railway, 35 minutes, 6 miles
78. Dungeness to Hythe – Romney, Hythe and Dymchurch Railway, 1 hour and 10 minutes, 14 miles
79. Sandling to Dover Priory – Southeastern, 18 minutes, 13 miles
80. Deal to Ramsgate – Southeastern, 19 minutes, 12 miles
81. Ramsgate to Herne Bay – Southeastern, 28 minutes, 12 miles
82. Sittingbourne to Sheerness-on-Sea – Southeastern, 19 minutes, 9 miles
83. Sheerness-on-Sea to Sittingbourne – Southeastern, 19 minutes, 9 miles
84. Sittingbourne to London Victoria – Southeastern, 1 hour and 6 minutes, 45 miles
85. London Victoria to Upminster – London Underground District line, 58 minutes, 19 miles
86. Upminster to Shoeburyness – c2c, 44 minutes, 27 miles
87. Southend Pier to Southend Pier Head – Southend Pier Railway, 10 minutes, 1½ miles
88. Southend Pier Head to Southend – Southend Pier Railway, 10 minutes, 1½ miles
89. Southend Cliff Lift – 4 minutes, 80 metres
90. Southend Victoria to Shenfield – Greater Anglia, 35 minutes, 20 miles
91. Shenfield to Thorpe-le-Soken – Greater Anglia, 54 minutes, 46 miles
92. Thorpe-le-Soken to Walton-on-the-Naze – Greater Anglia, 12 minutes, 5 miles
93. Walton-on-the-Naze to Colchester – Greater Anglia, 54 minutes, 18 miles
94. Colchester to Norwich – Greater Anglia, 1 hour, 60 miles
95. Norwich to Sheringham – Greater Anglia, 58 minutes, 25 miles
96. Sheringham to Holt – North Norfolk Railway, 25 minutes, 5½ miles
97. Holt to Weybourne – North Norfolk Railway, 9 minutes, 3 miles
98. Weybourne to Sheringham – North Norfolk Railway, 10 minutes, 2½ miles
99. Sheringham to Norwich – Greater Anglia, 58 minutes, 25 miles
100. Norwich to Grantham – East Midlands Railway, 2 hours and 4 minutes, 92 miles

TRAINS TAKEN

101. Grantham to Skegness – East Midlands Railway, 1 hour and 24 minutes, 51 miles
102. Skegness to Sleaford – East Midlands Railway, 57 minutes, 39 miles
103. Sleaford to Lincoln – East Midlands Railway, 29 minutes, 18 miles
104. Lincoln to Grimsby – East Midlands Railway, 53 minutes, 34 miles
105. Grimsby to Barton-on-Humber – East Midlands Railway, 42 minutes, 21 miles
106. Barton-on-Humber to Habrough – East Midlands Railway, 25 minutes, 12 miles
107. Scunthorpe to Doncaster – TransPennine Express, 33 minutes, 24 miles
108. Doncaster to Goole – Northern, 26 minutes, 20 miles
109. Hull to Beverley – Northern, 13 minutes, 8 miles
110. Beverley to Cottingham – Northern, 6 minutes, 6 miles
111. Cottingham to Scarborough – Northern, 1 hour and 13 minutes, 40 miles
112. Peasholm to Scalby Mills – Scarborough North Bay Railway, 15 minutes, 1 mile
113. Scalby Mills to Peasholm – Scarborough North Bay Railway, 15 minutes, 1 mile
114. Central Tramway Company, Scarborough – 4 minutes, 152 metres
115. Scarborough to York – TransPennine Express, 49 minutes, 41 miles
116. York to Sheffield – CrossCountry, 48 minutes, 50 miles
117. Sheffield to Chinley – Northern, 41 minutes, 24 miles
118. Chinley to Stockport – Northern, 24 minutes, 12 miles
119. Stockport to Stafford – CrossCountry, 47 minutes, 47 miles
120. Stafford to Smethwick Galton Bridge – West Midlands Trains, 30 minutes, 24 miles
121. Smethwick Galton Bridge to Kidderminster – West Midlands Trains, 28 minutes, 15 miles
122. Kidderminster to Worcester Foregate Street – West Midlands Trains, 23 minutes, 15 miles
123. Evesham to Moreton-in-Marsh – Great Western Railway, 17 minutes, 15 miles
124. Kingham to Reading – Great Western Railway, 54 minutes, 48 miles
125. Reading to Staines – South Western Railway, 49 minutes, 24 miles
126. Staines to Barnes Bridge – South Western Railway, 29 minutes, 12 miles
127. Barnes Bridge to London Waterloo – South Western Railway, 24 minutes, 7 miles
128. London Waterloo to London Euston – London Underground Northern Line, 11 minutes, 2 miles
129. London Euston to Aberdeen – Caledonian Sleeper, 10 hours and 15 minutes, 496 miles
130. Aberdeen to Stonehaven – ScotRail, 20 minutes, 15 miles
131. Stonehaven to Aberdeen – ScotRail, 20 minutes, 15 miles
132. Aberdeen to Inverness – ScotRail, 2 hours and 12 minutes, 102 miles
133. Inverness to Thurso – ScotRail, 3 hours and 43 minutes, 107 miles
134. Thurso to Dingwall – ScotRail, 3 hours and 16 minutes, 98 miles

135. Dingwall to Kyle of Lochalsh – ScotRail, 2 hours and 5 minutes, 66 miles
136. Mallaig to Dumbarton Central – ScotRail, 4 hours and 49 minutes, 128 miles
137. Dumbarton Central to Glasgow Queen Street – ScotRail, 26 minutes, 15 miles
138. Glasgow Queen Street to Edinburgh Haymarket – ScotRail, 43 minutes, 46 miles
139. Edinburgh Haymarket to Dalmeny – ScotRail, 11 minutes, 11 miles
140. Dalmeny to Edinburgh Waverley – ScotRail, 17 minutes, 13 miles
141. Edinburgh Waverley to Darlington – London North Eastern Railway, 2 hours, 136 miles
142. Darlington to Shildon – Northern, 18 minutes, 9 miles
143. Locomotion museum, Shildon – *Rocket* replica, 10 minutes, 1 mile

Total distance: 4,088 miles

Total time spent on trains: 120 hours, or precisely five days

Please note: *Distances and times are approximate. Journeys were conducted between February and May 2024.*

INDEX

Aberdeen 45, 214, 271, 287, 290-1, 294-7
Adlestrop 276, 282-3,
Alnmouth 311
AML 120
Amos, Tony 231-2, 239
Armadale 301
Asylum seekers 267, 277
Appleby 82-3, 276
Aspatria 82, 89
Associated Society of Locomotive Engineers and Firemen 264, 319-20
Attlee, Clement 43, 319
Avanti West Coast 89, 91, 129-30, 132, 138, 140, 279

Balmoral 214, 294
Bank Holidays Act (1871) 209
Barking 230
Barnes Bridge 283
Barnham 207-8, 213-4
Barton-on-Humber 259-60
Barrow-on-Furness 95-6
Basildon 231
Beatles 49, 80, 139, 156, 206-7, 209
Becontree 230
Beeching, Dr 58-9, 63, 66, 72, 76, 92, 121, 130, 142, 167, 177-8, 182, 201, 229, 241, 244-5, 249, 283, 323
Beeston Regis 242
Berwick-upon-Tweed 295
Betjeman, Sir John 85, 174, 234, 244, 266
Beverley 269-70
Billingsgate Market 255
Biomass wagons 261
Birmingham 94, 113, 164, 177-9, 204, 277, 280, 316-8

Bishop Auckland 23, 30, 34, 314
Bishops Lydeard 188, 191, 196
Bittern Line 240, 246
Blaenau Ffestiniog 117, 119-20, 126, 132, 320
Blue Train 299
Blur 238, 290
Bognor Regis 207-13, 242, 246, 258, 321
Bookshops 50, 79, 83-4, 113, 120, 177, 197, 205-7, 250, 309
Bouch, Sir Thomas 293, 307
Bradley, Simon 325
Bridges 27, 38-9, 43, 115, 155, 159, 229, 259-60, 265, 292-3, 305-8, 311
Brigg 261
Brighton 208, 213-6, 229
British Rail/Railways 43, 55, 58, 76, 131, 136, 170, 189, 206, 231, 243, 282,
British Transport Police 239, 277
Bristol Parkway 151-3
Bromley South 229
Brontes 66, 69, 71-2, 75, 165, 272
Brunel, Isambard Kingdom 63-4, 154-6, 159, 166-7, 181, 191, 193-5, 204, 214, 308, 321-2
Brusselton Incline 312-3
Butlin, Billy 210-11, 242, 247, 273

c2c 231-3
Caledonian Sleeper 45, 162, 187, 271, 276, 287-96, 319
Caplan, Darren 317

Carbis Bay 167
Cardiff 135, 153
Carlisle 44, 75, 78-9, 82, 84-8
Catch Me Who Can 172
Caernarfon 121, 124-6, 135, 263
Chatham 229
Chelmsford 236
Chester 119
Chinley 276, 278-9
Christie, Agatha 175-6, 287
Churchill, Winston 94, 102, 150, 156, 236, 273
Clapham Junction 46, 130, 136
Class 37 138, 241
Class 66 261
Class 92 287
Class 150 168, 261
Class 180 261
Cleethorpes 255, 271
Colas Rail Freight 21-2, 47, 308, 311
Colchester 236, 238-9, 289-90
Compagnie Internationale des Wagons-Lits 32, 225
Conservative Party 43, 81, 136, 177-8, 228, 234
Corfe Castle 195, 197, 322
Cornishman, The 164
Cornish Riviera Express 167-8, 170-1
Corrour 303
Cotman, John Sell 243
Cottingham 269-70
Coventry 264, 270
Craven Arms 129, 138, 140-2, 145
Crewe 46, 68, 87, 128-38, 280

Crome, John 243
CrossCountry 154, 277
Crown Street Park, Liverpool 102-4
Cumbrian Coast Line 44, 86, 91

Daily Mail 94, 319
Daily Post 128
Dagenham East 230
Dalmeny 305-6, 308
Darlington 17, 21-40, 44-45, 48, 62, 260, 268, 270, 306-7, 310-16, 323-4
Davies, Hunter 325
Dawlish 157, 166, 178
Deal 225, 227
Delays 25, 130, 136, 153, 159-60, 219, 267, 280
Derby 154, 231, 243, 248, 277
Dent 81-2
Department for Transport 43, 239, 319
Dickens, Charles 75, 200-1, 223-4
Diesel trains 22, 32, 47, 54, 58, 71-2, 129, 131, 137, 160, 206, 218, 231, 234, 243, 271, 277, 321
Diesel Multiple Units 54, 71, 87, 168, 231
Dingwall 301
Disraeli, Benjamin 235
District line 229-30
Dobbin, John 28, 39
Doncaster 22, 46, 88, 130, 136, 250, 255, 259-64, 276, 280, 321-2
Dorchester 191
Doncaster Rovers 263
Dover 32, 224-6, 229
Duke of Sutherland 122, 295, 299
Dumbarton Central 46, 305
Dundee 293, 297
Dungeness 213, 217-9

Durrington-by-Sea 214

Earl of Scarborough 246, 248
Earl of Yarborough 255
Eastern Daily Press 240
East Midlands Railway 135, 243
Edinburgh 45, 53, 89, 245, 287, 292, 294-5, 300, 305, 308-9
Edinburgh Haymarket 305
Edinburgh Waverley 308-9
Elizabeth line 204, 230
European Union 211, 256
Evesham 282
Exeter 135, 154-155, 157, 173, 175-7, 179-81, 183, 187, 277

Farringdon 230
Fawlty Towers 173, 175, 273
Ferneyhough, Frank 27-8
Ffestiniog & Welsh Highland Railways 123-6
Fleche d'Or 225
Fletcher, Martin 239
Flying Scotsman 34-5, 263
Folkestone Central 224
Forth Bridge 292-3, 305-8, 311
Fort William 287-9, 295, 297, 301-2, 304
Frances, Leila 232
Freight 21-22, 24, 28, 33-34, 46-7, 86-8, 100, 116, 130, 150, 179, 194, 250, 261, 279, 280-1, 308, 311, 316-7
Frinton-on-Sea 236

Gainsborough 261
Gibb, Gemma 114-5
Gillingham FC 229
Glancey, Jonathan 85, 244-5
Glasgow Queen Street 305

Glenfinnan Viaduct 292, 302
Golden Arrow 225
Goring-by-Sea 214
Goult, Clive 34-7, 59, 316
Grange-over-Sands 95-8, 120, 210, 321
Grantham 136, 243, 245
Greater Anglia 235-6, 239, 243, 261, 280
Great British Railways 318
Great Eastern Main Line 236
Great Northern Railway 242, 263
Great Western Railway 43, 153-4, 170-1,
Gresley, Sir Nigel 35, 263
Grimsby 45, 249-59
Grimsby Fishing Heritage Centre 257
Grindleford 279
Grosmont 38, 53-4, 57-60

Habrough 250, 260
Hackworth, Timothy 32-3, 102
Harvey, Anne 283
Hassall, John 242, 247
Hastings 215-7
Haworth 66, 69-72
Heart of Wales Line 129, 141-5
Heighington 23, 311-2
Hepworth, Barbara 169
Heritage railways 54-60, 66-72, 91-5, 121-6, 188-91, 193-7, 203-7, 217-220, 233-5, 240-1, 271, 313-5
Heygate, William 234
Herne Bay 227
High Speed Rail Group 317
Hitachi 135, 263, 321
HMP Featherstone 281, 289
Hope 279
Hotham, Sir Richard 208-9

INDEX

Holidays With Pay Act (1938) 210, 217
Holt 240
Hopetown Darlington 38
Howey, Captain John Edwards Presgrave 217
HS2 33-4, 37, 44, 61, 94, 100, 113, 164, 178-9, 204-5, 240-1, 316-8
Hudson, George 295, 321
Hull 45, 69, 109, 113, 127-8, 264-71
Hull Paragon Interchange 265-70, 323
Hull Trains 264
Humber Bridge 259-60, 265
Hunslet Engine Company Ltd 123, 240
Huskisson, William 36-7, 101-2, 105, 110, 116, 133, 314
Hythe 220, 223

Inverness 287, 295-6, 298, 300, 304, 321
Island Line 199, 202
Isle of Sheppey 225, 227, 231, 233
Isle of Skye 292, 301
Isle of Wight 45, 187, 198-207

Johnson, Boris 177, 249
Jolly Fisherman 242, 246-7, 259

Keadby Power Stations 260
Keegan, Kevin 262-3
Keighley 66-8, 71-2
Keighley and Worth Valley Railway 66-72
Kidderminster 129, 281
Killingworth Colliery 315
Kingham 283
Kyle of Lochalsh 45, 291, 295, 301

Labour Party 93, 177-8

Laindon 231
Larkin, Philip 126-8, 177, 266-7, 269-71, 282, 323
Lane, Allen 176
Leeds 34, 49, 58, 61, 64-6, 69-71, 80, 82, 113, 123, 136, 204, 240, 267, 277-8, 316, 321
Lewes 214-5
Lime and soda 82, 120, 278
Lincoln 250
Lincoln Castle Explorer 243
Liverpool Lime Street 97, 102, 104, 108-10, 113
Liverpool and Manchester Railway 28, 32, 36, 44, 64, 69, 97, 105-6, 113, 116-7, 133, 316
Llandudno Junction 118-9, 121, 126, 132
Llanelli 129, 141, 145-151
Locomotion museum 31-7, 59, 85, 100, 131, 225, 313, 316
Locomotion No 1 27-33, 39, 156, 173, 180, 231, 292, 306, 312, 314, 324
Locomotive Services Ltd 60
London, Brighton and South Coast Railway 229
London, Chatham and Dover Railway 229
London North Eastern Railway 43, 62, 135, 245, 263-4, 319
London Euston 45, 63, 99, 27, 276-7, 283, 287
London Kings Cross 242, 263-4
London Paddington 88, 162, 165, 167-8, 214, 230, 287
London Transport Museum 299
London Underground 230, 247

London Victoria 225, 229
London Waterloo 196, 200-1, 283

Major, John 43, 136, 245
Mallard 64, 245, 263
Mail, The 98
Mallaig 292, 295, 301-6
Manchester 28-9, 32, 34, 36, 44, 61, 64, 69-70, 77-8, 87, 94-7, 99, 102-107, 110, 113-8, 124, 130, 136, 156, 164, 178-9, 204, 276, 279, 299, 314, 316-8, 321
Manchester Metrolink 118
Manchester Piccadilly 118
Marazion 161, 164-5
Market Rasen 250
Martin, Sir Tim 263
Masons Arms, Shildon 312-4
McBey, James 295
McGonagall, William 293
Metropolitan line 230
Middlesbrough 28, 38, 52-4, 60, 62, 65, 96, 120, 178, 232, 260, 268,
Minehead 188, 190-1, 210
Moreton-in-Marsh 282

National Audit Office 317
National Express 231
National Rail 43-6, 126, 141, 236, 238, 276, 291-2, 320
National Railway Museum, York 62-4
Navvies 75, 77, 80
Network Rail 21, 43, 62, 157, 276
Newcastle 31, 52, 177, 295, 311, 315
New Romney 213, 218-9
Night Riviera 162, 287, 299
Noble, Kerry 189-90, 193, 322

Northern 23, 26, 48, 52-3, 61-2, 65, 72, 79, 83, 89, 91, 95, 97, 232, 261, 269-70, 278, 292, 314, 319
Northern Powerhouse 113, 318
North London Railway 33
North Norfolk Railway 239-41
North Yorkshire Moors Railway 35, 37-8, 47, 54-60
Norwich 236, 240, 242-4
Norwich School of Painters 243-4

Old Oak Common 318
Okehampton 173, 176-81
Orkney Islands 300, 304
Orwell, George 238

Pease, Edward 315, 318
Penlee House Gallery & Museum 161, 165-7, 169
Penzance 45, 126, 152, 154, 158-68, 172, 182, 247, 263, 287, 291, 299, 321
Pevensey and Westham 215-6
Pickering 35, 38, 54, 57-60
Piers 198, 210-11, 233-5, 236-8, 269, 306-7, 308
Plymouth 152, 154, 157-9, 177, 180, 277
Poacher Line 246
Polegate 215
Poole 45, 192-3, 197
Poppy Line 239, 241
Porthmadog 120-1, 123, 125
Portillo, Michael 81-2, 84, 90, 234, 268
Portsmouth Harbour 197, 207
Port Talbot 153, 190
Prestatyn 119, 126-8

Preston 97, 99, 321
Private Eye 317
Promontory Summit, Utah 29
Price, Sarah 33-4, 100, 316
Pubs 38, 51, 76-9, 80, 82, 85, 97, 102, 120-1, 125, 149, 160-1, 164-5, 179, 202, 220, 225-6, 228-9, 245-6, 251, 255-6, 258-9, 260, 262-3, 269, 278-9, 306-7
Puffing Devil 172-3
Pullman, George Mortimer 137

Quintinshill 245

Rail enthusiasts 71, 80, 92, 121, 129, 136, 182, 205-6, 241, 277, 303, 312
Railway Industry Association 317
Railwaypeople.com 232
Railway vinyl records 205-6
Rail replacement buses 213, 215, 225, 227, 260-1, 264-5, 282
Ramsgate 225, 227
Ravenglass 91-2,
Ravenglass and Eskdale Railway 91-5, 217
Reading 230, 283
Revenue Protection officers 281, 278, 289
Ribblehead Viaduct 75, 77, 80-1
Rochester 223, 229
Rocket 28, 32, 37, 64, 101-3, 105, 116, 133, 156, 173, 313-4
Roger Hosking 137
Romney, Hythe and Dymchurch Railway 187, 213, 217-20, 223
Royal Albert Bridge 155, 159
Royal Scotsman 303, 305

Ryde 198-201, 206-7
Rye 216-7

Sandling 223-4
Sandwich 227
Sans Pareil 32, 102
Scarborough 45, 187, 269-76
Scarborough North Bay Railway 271
Science and Industry Museum, Manchester 97, 214-7
ScotRail 91, 296, 298-300, 306, 319, 323
Scrabster 300
Scunthorpe 90, 250, 255, 260-1, 263
Seago, Edward 243
Settle 72, 75-9
Settle and Carlisle Railway 75, 78-84
Severn Valley Railway 129, 131, 281
Shanghai 29, 84
Shanklin 200-2
Sheerness-on-Sea 225, 227-9
Sheerness Times Guardian 228
Sheffield 130, 276-9
Shenfield 230, 235-6
Sheringham 238-42
Shrewsbury 138, 140
Shildon 22, 25-7, 29-38, 88, 101, 131, 225, 263, 292, 307, 311-5, 316, 324
Shoeburyness 230-3
Sittingbourne 225, 227, 229
Skegness 242, 245-9
Skerne Bridge 27, 39, 260, 306, 311
Sleeper trains 32, 45, 162, 187, 225, 240, 271, 276, 287-94, 296, 319
Slough 88, 214
Smallbrook Junction 200-3, 205

INDEX

Smethwick Galton Bridge 281, 289
Society for Lincolnshire History and Archaeology 250
Southampton Central 197
Southeastern 224, 229, 319
Southend Cliff Lift 235
Southend-on-Sea 233-5
Southend Pier Railway 233-5
Southern 21, 32, 43, 206, 212
South Humber Bank Power Station 251
South Western Railway 192, 196, 206
South Queensferry 305-7, 309
Squires, Stuart E. 250
St Erth 167-8, 171
St Ives 165, 167-71
Sy Ives Bay Line 167
St Helens 100-1
St Michael's Mount 161, 164-5, 175
Stafford 261, 276, 280-1, 289
Staplehurst 224
Statesman Rail 137
Station cafés 21, 67-8, 119, 126, 150-1, 191, 198, 212, 234, 311
Stephenson, George 27, 29, 39, 59, 91, 97, 106, 115, 133, 156, 172, 204, 312, 314-5, 321, 323
Stephenson, Robert 31, 33, 40, 102, 314, 321
Stevenson, Robert Louis 306
Stockport 279
Stockton 17, 27-9, 38, 49-52
Stockton and Darlington Railway 28-29, 31-2, 34, 36-7, 40, 50, 69-70, 83, 94, 97, 100, 103,
106, 114, 116, 154, 172, 208, 214, 224, 230, 245, 312-6, 318, 323-4
Stoke-on-Trent 280, 297
Stonehaven 296, 309
Strikes 25, 136, 150-1, 165, 167, 262, 264-5, 319,
Sunak, Rishi 164
Sunday Times, The 273
Sunshine Coast Line 236, 246
Swanage Railway 187, 193-7
Swansea 151-3

Taunton 154-5, 187-8, 191
Tay Bridge 293
Thatcher, Margaret 43, 136, 187, 245
The Jacobite 301-2
Thomas, Edward 276, 282-3
Thorpe-le-Soken 236
Thurso 291, 295, 298-300
Ticket prices 25, 31, 151, 323
Times, The 98, 122-3, 239
Torness Nuclear Power Station 310
Torquay 173-5
Totnes 277
Trainspotters 22, 86-9, 97, 129, 134-8, 163, 182, 205-6, 241, 261, 276-7, 280, 311, 313, 322
TransPennine Express 61-2, 65, 260, 277, 319
Transport for Wales 118-9, 130, 136, 141, 319
Trenitalia 231
Trevithick, Richard 172, 315,
Trump, Donald 288
Truro 159-60, 167

Upminster 229-30,
106, 114, 116, 154,
Victoria, Queen 26, 88, 200, 214, 268, 272, 294

Wabtec 263
Walton-on-the-Naze 236-8
West Highland Line 301
West Midlands Trains 282
Westmorland Gazette, The 98
West Somerset Railway 187-91
West Worthing 214
Wetherspoons 30, 32, 85, 123, 125, 161-2, 228, 246, 251, 255-6, 262-3
Whitstable 227
Wigan Athletic FC 138
Wilson, Harold 245
Winchelsea 217
Wolmar, Christian 106, 117, 294
Worcester Foregate 282
Workington 89-90, 258

York 60-65, 69, 132, 178, 260, 268, 276-7, 299
Yorkshire Post, The 273, 277

Zborowski, Count Louis 217

Have you enjoyed this book?

If so, why not write a review on your favourite website?

If you're interested in finding out more about our books, find us on Facebook at **Summersdale Publishers**, on Twitter/X at **@Summersdale** and on Instagram and TikTok at **@summersdalebooks** and get in touch. We'd love to hear from you!

Thanks very much for buying this Summersdale book.

www.summersdale.com